MALACHY McCOURT

A MONK SWIMMING

HarperCollins*Publishers*

Pages 127-128, lyrics from *Sean South of Garryowen*,
by Sean Costelloe, © Mary Costelloe and Warner-Tamerlane
Publishing Corp. All Rights Reserved. Used by Permission.
Warner Bros. Publications U.S. Inc., Miami, FL 33014.

HarperCollins*Publishers*
77–85 Fulham Palace Road,
Hammersmith, London W6 8JB

Published by HarperCollins*Publishers* 1999
9

First published in the USA by
Hyperion 1998

A catalogue record for this book
is available from the British Library

ISBN 0 00 653115 6

Printed and bound in Great Britain by
Clays Ltd, St Ives plc

For my beloved brilliant beautiful
Diana
Who gives the resounding yes to life, to love,
and to the song of the morning.
I cherish you.

ACKNOWLEDGMENTS

With much gratitude to the brothers Frank—for opening the golden door and leading the way—and to Mike and Alphie with my love and thanks.

To my children—Siobhan, Malachy, Nina, Conor, and Cormac— for raising me to maturity.

To my grandchildren—Fiona, Mark, and Adrianna—for the joy.

To Bernice and John for bringing Diana into the world.

To Charlie DeFanti for walking me through the golden door and to John Weber for saying welcome. To David Chalfant, my intrepid agent, no stranger to Midas.

To Helena Carroll and the late Dermot McNamara for the first acting job. To the late Tom O'Malley for catapulting me onto *The Tonight Show*. To Marge Greene, who was and is always there. To Richard Harris for the riotous times. To Ed Burns for leading the cheers.

To John and Tinka Finn for the house that spoke to me. To Terry Moran and the mysterious First Friday Club. To my editor, Maureen O'Brien, for her joyful trust in this, my first book. To Howard Mittelmark, who took chaos and put it in order.

To the Costelloes of Limerick for the wit and the song. To Robert Hayden Jones for he knows what. To Adrian Flannelly for the friendship and the microphone. To Paul O'Dwyer, hero, for his joy in standing for principle.

To Bob Cranny—a friend indeed! To Angela and Malachy, who know not what they wrought. To Bill W. and all his friends.

To the English for stuffing their language down our throats so that we could regurgitate it in glorious colors.

To New York, I love you!

CONTENTS

A MONK SWIMMING

THERE WAS ALWAYS THE STORY IN ANY GATHERING IN LIMerick. Be it boys, girls, the men, the women, bald facts were considered cold and inhuman; therefore all storied events had to be wrapped in words. Warm words, serried words, glittering, poetic, harsh, and even blasphemous words.

So the cold evenings were made warm with myths and tales of dirty doings and derring-do, and horrific yarns of the tortures of hell awaiting the evildoer. We the children sat in darkness, shivering in horrored delight, having been told we had two ears and unready tongue.

My father, Malachy, and his chums, Mr. Meehan, Mr. Looney, and Mr. Moran, spun out the silver-gold yarns and, by sheer eloquence, made our miserable surroundings disappear. And my father would sing his patriotic odes to Ireland, like the one about Roddy McCorley going to die on the bridge of Toome. My mother sang droopy love songs like, "We Are in Love with You, My Heart and I."

Death brought a silence to our house. First Baby Margaret Mary

1

and then the twins—Eugene at four, and Oliver, four-and-a-half. Poverty killed them. My father left, to go on a lifelong drinking binge, never to come back, and I hated him for depriving me of him. It was many years before my mother sang another droopy love song, because she sank into a deep depression and love fled into the damp, grey Limerick sky, never to return.

The poor will always be with us, it sez in the Bible, and having had the strange privilege of being born into a not poor, but poverty-stricken, family, it became my passionate intention to be always with someone, but, by the living Jesus Christ, I would not be poor or poverty stricken.

I did not like being damp all the time. I did not like being cold and wet in the winter. I did not like looking in windows of shops filled with meats sweets biscuits breads, and my eyes bulging, the mouth aching for the chance to chew on something substantial. I did not like being eaten by fleas, gorging themselves on my bitter blood. I did not like having lice and nits in my hair my arse my armpits my eyebrows and every seam of the trousers and gansey I wore. I didn't like the boils and pimples on my small epidermis, not to mention the shame of scabies and ringworm. I didn't like having badly patched clothes and broken boots that Van Gogh would have sneered at. I didn't like having caked shit in my trousers because they couldn't be washed for the want of a replacement to wear while they were drying. I didn't like being made fun of and sneered at by the upper classes, who had tea and buns in the afternoon and electric light in every room.

I have never liked the smell of the newly made, newly varnished coffins that were brought in to take away our dead forever.

I was a smiley little fella with a raging heart and murderous instincts. One day I would show THEM—yes, you rotten fucking arsehole counter-jumping stuck-up jumped-up whore's-melts nose-holding tuppence-ha'penny-looking-down-on-tuppence snobs. I'll go back to America where I was born and I'll fart in yer faces.

And I did.

ONE

TO THE MANOR BORNE

There is a story in our family that one day my mother was strolling along with my brother Frank and myself, and pushing our twins in a pram. A huge black motorcar stopped at the kerb, and out hopped a smartly dressed chauffeur, who opened the rear door for a bejeweled, befurred grande-dame type of woman who, putting the well-shod feet on the ground, commanded the mother to stop, which she did promptly. Then the grande dame waxed lyrical on the subject of myself—how she had never seen a more beautiful little boy: the blonde hair, the gleaming teeth, the gorgeous skin, and the smile—and how she would pay any amount of money to the mother to allow her to adopt me.

The mother, as the story is told, thought, and thought, and thought, and said it was an attractive proposition, but she couldn't think of a way to explain my disappearance to my father, who had not yet disappeared himself, so she reluctantly declined the offer.

In later years, 'twas often thrown in my face by the mother and the brothers that a great mistake had been made by my retention in the family circle. Privately, I was always of the opinion that a grande dame had gotten herself in the family way outside of wedlock and had paid my mother to take me. How else can it be explained, my easy and effortless assimilation into the good life, life in America?

The brother Frank had somehow got to the U.S.A. in 1949, at the age of nineteen, and then saved up enough money to send for me in 1952, when I was twenty. Two hundred dollars paid my passage on the good ship America. Talk about the good life: clean beds, clean sheets, pillow, light to read by, and the food! As many meals and as much as you wanted, and you could have sandwiches in the middle of the night if you wanted. And there was a swimming pool. It was still embarrassing to have patched clothes and mended shoes, and all of it too heavy for the summer climate toward which we sped.

What was I going to do in the U.S. of A., they asked me, and how in God's name was I to tell them that I'd left school at thirteen and had no certificates to prove I'd been to school at all, as I had failed the primary exams twice and was considered a dunce, doomed, doomed to mendicancy, criminality or, worse, manual labor to the end of my natural days, that's what they'd said.

But the Americans were kind, so I'd tell them I was going to be a doctor an engineer a surgeon a pilot a navigator—anything to bring a smile to the lips of these kindly folks. Truth is, I knew I couldn't do anything at all but tell stories and lies.

When I got here to the U.S., Frank was gone in the army to Germany and a family named McManus met me and guided me around. I had to register for the draft too, and found myself in the service for a couple of years, and out I came discharged, still not knowing what to do at the age of twenty-three.

———

I WENT TO THE DOCKS and, as I swore I wasn't a Communist or a member of organized crime, I was allowed to register for work. In England, you were called a "docker," but here in the U.S. you were a "longshoreman," a romantic-sounding name for a laborer unloading the ships. There was a comforting monotony to the job, especially if you were fit, strong, and not too high in the I.Q. department.

New York was still a thriving port, the terminal point for a greater variety of cargoes than the brother Frank and myself. Hell's Kitchen, a hard and ragged neighborhood on the West Side of Manhattan, next to the Hudson River, was dominated by the Irish, and it was said there used to be signs on the piers there that read NO WOPS; in Brooklyn the Italians were in charge, and they put up signs on the piers there that said NO MICKS.

I'd wander from pier to pier, to the Jersey City, Bayonne, and Hoboken hiring halls, echoey, smelly places, with green walls, dirty floors, and the usual flickering fluorescent lights. We'd shape up early in the morning, freezing in the winter, us garbed in the longshoreman's uniform: heavy boots, heavy trousers, sweater, pea jacket, woolen cap, work gloves, and the cargo hook unsteady from last night's excesses. If there were a lot of ships, the greenhorns like me worked; if not, it was another arse-scratching day.

This was in 1955, the days of the Waterfront Commission, established to clean up unions. Any time a union endeavored to clean up the horrendous, dangerous conditions under which workers were mutilated and killed, the bosses set in motion the propaganda machine to break the union under the guise of stamping out corruption.

Elia Kazan, who squealed on his friends to the House Un-American Activities Committee, got the job of directing the movie *On the Waterfront* as a reward for his treachery. Between Hollywood, the government, and the Church, they managed to practically destroy the International Longshoreman's Association by kicking out the great seekers for justice.

There was one dedicated little fellow with glasses who felt the union should do better. He ran for office time and time again. They'd shoot at him, beat him up, sabotage his car, and yet he lived to fight another day. The heart's a wonder, as Synge said.

I stayed out of the union doings, as I was not too keen on getting beaten up and, being a fresh-faced young immigrant, I was still reasonably ignorant of the issues in dispute.

Was there thievery on the docks? Hell, yes! We helped ourselves to fine Italian shoes, and there were days we dropped our trousers and wound yards of suit fabric around the torso, so that at quitting time, you'd observe scores of portly males waddling off the pier. When there was a shipment of alcohol of any sort, it was a day of accidents involving fork lifts being drunkenly driven over the side of the pier, men falling into holds, fisticuffs, arguments, and much simple rejoicing.

There was a day I was working on a Brooklyn pier, and a cargo of artificial flowers arrived, which were duly tithed among the toilers. A thoroughly useless item it was, and I asked the other Irishman working there that day, an older fellow named McCabe, why they were stealing such a thing.

"Ah," sez he, "if they shipped shit over here in one-pound boxes, they'd steal all of it."

"They," of course, were the Italians, who stole everything, as distinct from the Irish, who only stole on principle—that according to my elder.

My favorite cargo was rubber: huge, five-hundred-pound bales of the stuff, imported from Malaysia. Sometimes the crane man would let a bale fall out of the net from a great height, and the huge projectile would come bounding and bouncing erratically along the pier, sending even the most arthritic nonagenarian leaping for safety with gay abandon.

Along with shifting cargo on my handcart, I was keeping fit by playing with the New York Rugby Football Club. This was a polyglot of expatriates from the U.K., New Zealand, Australia, and South Africa, plus a sprinkling of anglophilic Yanks, some of whom hoped they would be mistaken for English. For a while, I was the only Irisher on the team, outside of a fellow named Brad Brady from Cork, who was so Brit-oriented he could hardly speak.

Many of those Brits lamented the coarseness of the Yanks, their lack of sportsmanship. "They actually care more about winning than playing the game, old boy." Perhaps one day they would see the error of their ways, return to the Empire, learn good manners, and become good subjects.

There was a lot of swilling of beer, chug-a-lug contests, and the like. At our annual dinner, toasts were proposed to the President and the Queen. When I proposed a toast to the President of Ireland, I was ruled out of order, so I proposed we eliminate the Queen's toast. Though I followed Robert's Rules, this counterproposal received little support.

We played games against colleges, wherever we could get 'em, from Princeton to Boston to Dartmouth. One of my first games was against Harvard, and it was a rough one with a lot of dirty play and fisticuffs. Several players were ordered off the field by the ref, including one Boston boy named Kennedy, known to we lads as Ted.

I couldn't get over being accepted into what is called "civilized, middle-class society." Jesus, here I was, a manual laborer, hob-nobbing with college-educated folk, doctors, engineers, and stock-brokers. There was the occasional feeling that one day they would find me out—that I was uneducated, a guttersnipe from the lanes of Limerick, an upstart. My weapon, my defense, to ensure my acceptance, was to drink more and drink faster than anyone on the team, to sing more songs, to be the larger-than-life of the party. I knew they would not have had anything to do with me in another clime, but here we were all exiles with no choice but to play the game, drink the drink, sing the song, and hide whatever need be hidden.

These rugby piss-ups were almost always totally male get-togethers. We men of the world would descend on a college, and all the undergraduates would be impressed at our savoir faire. At times, there'd be the leggy Aryan coed attached to an American Hero type. I'd look, lust, and leave, knowing I could never have one of them for myself.

Women fascinated me: their aromas, budding, blooming, busting-out breasts, the bottoms, the lips, the legs, the softness and round-ness of all the parts, the dulcetness of speech, and that mysterious place guarded by thighs and downy hair. But what, in God's name, was I to say to them?

Cursed with shyness, I continued letting it all out on the field of battle, and during the off-season, continued the practice of shaking hands with the unemployed. Wanking, the Irish called it, that is, spilling the seed onto the ground, or anywhere else the trajectory sped it.

Mother Church had had strong views on sins of the flesh, and I never got over the feeling of being a sinner, of being unworthy, an excrescence in the eyes of God. I thought about the biblical injunc-tion to Onan: Better to spill your seed in the belly of a whore than waste it on the ground.

Why, I would like to ask at this late date, is it less of a sin to stick the winkie into a paid lady than to wank? Theologians, please note.

Anyway, these rugby affairs were sexless, except for one preten-tious Brit with a game leg, who babbled in that plummy way they have. Some of these Brits who are very class conscious speak as if they are about to expire, and each breath is their very last. This fellow, who was corpulent, to say the least, had a little boyfriend named Johnny. He was the sort of lightweight lad who'd be nervous using a feather duster, lest it fatally wound someone, and our man Harold, whose playing days were long done, would insist on Johnny playing the game.

Sheer terror guided Johnny on the field. He behaved like a gazelle who knows there are hungry lions waiting for him in the veldt, and he ran as if he had a ripe strawberry stuck 'tween the cheeks of his arse, which he had been instructed not to crush.

Eventually, Johnny got weary of being one with the turf and fled with a clothing designer to California, leaving Harold with a broken heart, from which he died.

W ITH A FEW QUID IN MY POCKET FROM MY LABORS ON the docks, a proper place to lay the head was in order, and I found one on West Eighty-first Street, in an apartment overlooking the Museum of Natural History, which, being so close, I never set foot in. The roommate who bid me share his bode was a tall, gaunt fellow, a construction engineer by profession, and totally around the bend. He staggered under the name of George Giles Green. George had been a pilot in the Korean War, and whilst absent from home during that forgotten conflict, fighting for America's honor, didn't his spouse dump him? She strolled off with another lad, who happened to be of the Hebraic persuasion, which led George to feel a very strong empathy with the late A. Hitler. The Jews, said he, were behind everything, including the voting machine. When he was exercising his citizen's right to vote, I was thoroughly and repeatedly informed, they manipulated the controls so that George voted for Jewish candidates against his will.

An ardent craw-thumping follower of Gucci-shoed popes was old

G.G.G., who cast a cold orb upon me when I'd share with him my inflated tales of fleshly pursuits, until I decided I'd show him, and kept them to myself.

On the table in our living room there stood in eternal vigilance a stone bird, beak up, wings folded, greenish grey—an ornithologist's dilemma. George warned me to be careful what I said, as our friend the boid had the habit of flying around to the other apartments in the building after we went to bed and relating to all the Jews living there every word we had spoken. And there was much to be reported, as our chats, such as they were, would by then have been quite brief were it not for the latest doings of the Jews (G.G.G.) and the weather (me).

The end of this apartment share came after only a few months, the night G.G.G. and myself were sitting digesting the evening's repast and, having been filled in by my roommate on the daily doings of Moses' henchmen, I was reading quietly. Suddenly my attention was drawn to the floor. Eichmann's admirer was crawling toward me, eyes ablaze, flecks of ye olde foam at the corners of the mouth. "Get down," he urged. "Get down on the floor. Quick! Quick!"

George was a veteran of the latest police action in Korea and, although a pilot, knew ground warfare too. As my knowledge of warfare partook of neither the sky nor the battlefield, but extended only to the occasional barroom set-to, I deferred to his greater experience and assumed we were under attack, even though we were on the seventh floor. Fear accelerated my dive to the carpet, where I found myself stretched out on the belly, face-to-face with my foaming friend.

Having taken all possible precautions against being blown away by sniper fire from the Museum of Natural History, I ventured a query to George.

"What is going on, George?" sez I.

"Can't you hear them!"

"Who?" sez I.

"The Jew cab drivers."

I tried to look thoughtful, and indeed I was, thinking how a distinction could be made between the words "Jew" and "Jewish."

"What about them, George?"

"As if you don't know! They've been told to honk their horns when they pass this building!"

"I see. And what are we doing on the floor?"

"They can see our shadows on the ceiling!"

It's embarrassing to realize you've been conned into entering the province of a first-class, ocean-going lunatic, so up on the pins with me, announcing, "You're talking through your arsehole!"

Thereupon, the slavering George said that I was a brainwashed Jew-lover, no better than the Judas bird, and there was no place for me in a decent Christian society, much less his apartment, so I'd better get out. I left the following morning, after an alert and sleepless night.

I didn't see old G.G.G. for some years, until I spotted him on Third Avenue pacing up and down across the street from Malachy's I, a saloon I owned at that time. With a bit of trepidation, I approached the man. He seemed glad to see me, and when I invited him to step across the boulevard to the saloon, he demurred, and instead invited me to dine with him the following week at the New York Athletic Club.

I was relieved to see the man had apparently achieved normalcy, so I accepted. The New York Athletic Club at that time was a bastion of Franco-loving, Mussolini-mourning, God-fearing Hitlereans, but, not being too discriminating in those days, I hied myself over there and presented myself for the free dinner. Got a warmish greeting from George and, after a beaker of Irish whiskey (N.B.: No other whiskey is entitled to be spelled with an "e"), he invited me to inspect the new wrestling mats in the gym.

Myrmidonish sort of laddie that I was, I assented, and off we strolled to the gym to view said mats. On the way there, George said that he was living here now, as it was a very safe place from Jews. Jesus, here we go again. But I hadn't had the dinner yet. Or seen the new mats.

We stepped into the gym, which was bereft of human beings, and George said, "There they are!" with a wave toward the pile of mats.

I said something brilliant, like, "Very nice." A glance then at good old George showed me that the face of the madman had emerged again—the blazing eyes, the foam, etc.—and a choked voice told me that I had fucked a Jew whore and told her I was George Giles Green and now she was pregnant and demanding money from him. I, of course, said I hadn't, a weak statement, I'll admit, but the best I could muster at the mo'. George paid no attention to the denial, which, I suppose, should not have come as a surprise.

Though not in the best of physical form, he was capable of moving with celerity, in this case unleashing an uppercut that would have pleased Mr. M. Ali of fisticuffs fame, had he dispatched it. It landed a couple of degrees west of the chin, on the jawline. I found myself inspecting the new wrestling mat more closely than I had intended when George extended the invite to view them.

When the head cleared, I was alone, face down, Georgeless once more. George had fled the premi. I departed the N.Y.A.C., dinnerless and with a very sore jaw. The last I heard of George, he was in a safe place, attended by white-garbed folk. He was most agreeable in their company, as he thought they were off-duty members of the K.K.K.

The lesson learned then, and revisited over the years, was that all anti-Semites, and bigots as a general class, are either sick or stupid. Ah, I thought, as this obvious bit of sociology dawned on me, aren't I the clever little immigrant to have figured that out?

AMONGST MY RUGBY-PLAYING PALS WAS A FELLOW NAMED Bob Lichenstein, and amongst the uncertainties of his life was the fact of his New Jersey origins. He eventually married a daughter of Big Jim Folsom, the governor of Alabama, and the teammates were subjected to a barrage of Big Jim this and Big Jim that forevermore. A more unabashed social climber was never encountered, and he could see that I was one too.

There was a hostelry named Michael II in the East Seventies, where, Bob told me, the scions of wealthy American families forgathered to gossip and tear each other apart. He also informed me that there was so much inbreeding among them that the males were rendered impotent, incapable of keeping a stiff upper anything, and thus there were a myriad, give or take a thou, of upper-class maidens panting to expose the inner thighs and hand over the honor to virile, rugby-playing, balding New Jerseyans and newly arrived Irish immigrants.

I was still quite deficient in the social-grace department at the age of twenty-three, but a couple of stiff drams of the waters of life, 86 proof, allowed me to feel comfortable in the company of the aforesaid scions and to maintain the reputation of the Irish as the golden-tongued charmers of the English-speaking world. Some said I spoke bullshit, others said blarney, but the young women said I was cute, and that was good enough for me.

When it came to dipping the wick, I ran across an acute shortage of maidenheads to penetrate. If, as in earlier times, these young things had had fans, they would have all sniggered behind them at my attempts at seduction. All, with the exception of Anita Whitney.

Ah, Anita! Was she one of those Whitneys? Who doth know, and who doth give a fiddler's fart, for she had the trim figure, the lively leg, the long, graceful neck. And the face, the countenance, guaranteed to launch a fleet of nuclear submarines. The wide, almond eyes, dark and changing and laughing. The exquisite nose, and the full-lipped mouth engorged with sensuality, glowing so ruby red that I thought, "If ever I get to put my lips to hers, I shall not remove them 'til I die."

Came the day when the New York Rugby Football Club British secretary announced that Her Majesty QE2, and her bedmate, Prince Phil, were arriving in New York and would be receiving loyal subjects at the Sixty-sixth Street Armory. The club had a limited number of tickets, and for a lark I took a couple of the ducats, with the idea of inviting the subject of my dreams, Anita Whitney, to be my date. She assented, and came the night, we arrived at the armory— she, nervous, because it was the royal yahoos; me, aquiver, because it was Anita on my arm. We moved easily through the not-so-strict security of those years, and into the great hall of the Armory.

For some reason, I thought it was going to be a reasonable number of bods shaking the hand and kissing the royal arses. But no, there were about six thousand hysterical Brits and assorted Anglophiles behaving like Margaret Thatcher soccer hooligans; respectable-looking old colonials and dames, pushing to get the best view and screaming—yes, screaming—"The Queeeeen, Gawd Bless 'er!"

The heat, the glare, the sweat, and the odor of thousands of unwashed Britons was too much for my beautiful Anita, who suddenly got the vapors. We had to whack our way through a savage horde to get out of the mess.

Hallelujah! There at the corner of the hall was a very large, oak door, and guarding it was a cop I knew, named Jimmy Snow. I appealed for help and he let us through.

It was one of those wood-paneled anterooms, cool and free of babbling Brits, and there in the corner I spied a bar and a white-coated, bowtied barman. 'Twas the work of a mo' to secure two large cognacs from this human St. Bernard and recovery was set in motion for Anita, fair and faint. An offer to pay for the drinks was declined by our rescuer, and so several more were ordered, which followed the first down easily.

Then the doors opened wide, and in trooped Elizabeth II with Governor Nelson Rockefeller, followed by Philip, the Duke of Edinburgh, Mayor Robert Wagner, and assorted bods in very colorful military uniforms. One of these generals came over to where Anita and self were ensconced behind the cognacs and told us Her Majesty was ready for the formal receiving line. He asked our names and requested we stand in line. About ten of us fell into formation, whereupon the major general presented all to Liz and Phil as they walked down the line, shaking the hand and offering the greeting: the Governor Rockefeller, the Mayor Wagner, Mrs. Rock, Mrs. Wag, Mr. this and that, Miss Anita Whitney, Mr. Malachy McCourt. When the presentation was done, Phil of Edinburgh headed in my direction and struck up the small talk.

"What do you do in New York?

"I work on the docks as a longshoreman. That's a 'docker' to you."

'You're Irish, are you not?"

"That I am."

"There was a demonstration against us at the pier yesterday. You weren't there, were you?"

"No. The need to work was pressing, the rent being due."

"I see. How do you like America?"

"I love it here. George was foolish to let it go."

"We all make mistakes."

Our chat was interrupted when the tiny queen toddled over to join us, and asked what I did in New York. My new pal Phil said, "Don't question him too closely, my dear."

"Ah, shall we be going then?"

Phil said, "Indeed," shook my hand, and off they went. Phil turned back to tell me that should I ever get to London, I should look him up.

Of course.

I did have the chance, on this occasion, to resolve a long-standing issue of interest to subjects both loyal and not: what the queen does with her old clothes.

She wears them.

During this Peasant–Royalty dialogue, Anita was standing with her gorgeous mouth agape at my temerity and chattiness. I explained to her I was just getting used to dealing with my inferiors. We departed the armory and took a small pub crawl, and not one soul believed our brush with the House of Hanover that night.

A S THE WINTER OF 1955 ASSERTED ITSELF, THE BROTHER Frank secured living quarters on Downing Street in Da Village. It was for some reason called a "cold water flat," though the aqua was quite hot. The bathtub was in the kitchen, and the toilet was down the tiled hallway on the left. Because I now needed a new place to lay the head and, I was hoping, the odd bird, the brudder allowed me to share these sumptuous accommodations, with their staggering rent of twenty-five dollars per month. Frank wasn't there much, for he was going to New York University, working on the docks, and doing a bit of night labor at some bank, as well as trying to spend time with his wife-to-be, a female of uncertain temper, hereinafter known as The War Department. So, generally speaking, I had the premi to myself. Con Edison kept sending a bill for electricity, which was fair enough, but I objected to the gas bill, as there was a noticeable absence of a gas stove or anything else that might use gas in this habitation.

There were other annoying bills, too, for services rendered, which I was not as a rule in a position to pay, due to the pressing need to pay for alcohol. A bright idea, and a swift trip to the local stationery shop, brought a temporary cessation of the dunning mail. A small investment of three dollars or so secured for me a rubber stamp, which, when inked and pressed to the exterior of an envelope containing a bill, proclaimed for anyone to plainly see: DECEASED.

Con Edison promptly disconnected the electricity, leaving me with no light but that from the blinking sign outside the window, advertising the bar on the ground floor. Fortunately, I found that by coordinating my own blinking with that of the sign, I was able to read well enough.

Most evenings, though, found me absent from the premi, doing my blinking in various nightspots. Clavin's, on East Fifty-eighth Street, had become an alternative to Michael II with the lockjawed set, with the occasional side trip to P.J. Clarke's, not far away on Third Avenue, and I remained in their orbit, the large, loud, lad from Limerick.

Behind the stick (that's the bar, for you latecomers to New York jargon) at Clavin's reigned one Hugh Magill, a trim, six-foot, brisk sort of lad, who had been expelled from various prep schools and colleges and who on occasion guested at some of the more prestigious loony bins on the East Coast. An extraordinarily well-read man was he, with E. Hemingway leading the literary list. To my utter delight and surprise, he belonged to that society of unregistered maniacs devoted to the works of P.G. Wodehouse, so it was with glad cries we fell on each other's necks, quoting the Gospel According to Jeeves and the mewlings of Bertie Wooster.

It was there and then my drinking identity was established. The denizens of Clavin's were famous for being the tax deductions of successful burghers, and to give myself distinction amongst this assortment of trust-fund recipients, I decided to drink only Powers

Irish Whiskey, for which I rarely paid and, when I did, it was with a line from P.G. Wodehouse.

My reputation as a trencherman in the booze department was solidified with the help of Clavin's son, Stewart, the evening he was born. "Drinks on the house!" bellowed the blocky fellow. Half in jest, I ordered a bottle of Powers, expecting a laugh and a drink, but, no, Clavin said, "Give it to the man!"

Expecting the bottle to be removed presently, I set to work to lower the level as rapidly as possible. In the midst of the revelry, I was tapped on the noggin by a thin, dark-visaged hanger-on-the-fringe-type laddie, who informed me that I had consumed a bottle of whiskey in forty-five minutes and he was of the opinion that I couldn't do it again. He was, in fact, willing to wager a hundred dollars to make the point. "Bring me another bottle," sez I to Magill, and it was then I learned the difference between convivial quaffing and forcing the amber liquid past the tonsils.

Wagers issued forth galore, and the atmosphere turned from rowdy celebration to the deathly silence of a chess tournament. With no great story to divert me, and forty-five minutes disallowing the singing of songs, there was nothing to do but pour the whiskey (no ice), drink, swallow, and think, "Oh, God! The bottle is three-quarters full yet."

Most of the body was yielding to the importunings of the whiskey: "Yield, yield, close your eyes." But above the neck, life persisted: eyes on the hundred, lips on the drink, and still swallowing. 'Twas will-power alone that kept that acrid river from reversing direction and defying gravity, rising up and spewing forth onto the betting crowd.

At last, about four ounces left, paralysis invading the head, lips, and brain, I downed it, and somewhere away in an echo chamber there arose a cheer. In slow motion, people shook the hand and slapped me on the back. It looked to me like a scene in one of those boxing movies where the champ has been floored and is trying to clear the head.

'Twas there I handled a hundred dollars for the first time in my life, 'twas there I got applauded for a stupid act of dare-deviltry that has often been fatal, and 'twas there I earned the glowing approval of a large number of people, most of whom are supine now under the sod from failed livers and brains.

ONE OF THE RESIDENT LUNATICS AT CLAVIN'S WAS ED Wilcox, a sometime gossip columnist. One night, the irrepressible Wilcox was listening intently to a chap who was yawing about the wipeout of the family fortunes in the crash of '29, and how his grandfather had done the leap out the high window to his death. Wilcox spoke up to say that his family had suffered a similar fate. Murmurs of sympathy went round the table at first, as Wilcox explained that his grandfather was on Wall Street, too. He had a pushcart from which he sold hot dogs and didn't some fucking, high-diving, ruined broker come falling out of the sky and land on the pushcart, totally destroying it and leaving the Wilcoxes destitute. Some of the lockjawed were amused, while others tut-tutted.

One night at P.J. Clarke's, Wilcox spotted the football players Kyle Rote and Frank Gifford heading back toward the pub's lavatory. Without a moment's hesitation, he shouted out for all to hear, "See what the backs in the boys' room will have!"

There was another night at Clavin's, during a period when the beautiful Anita Whitney had been keeping company with a masochistic chap named Bill Gray, who had more scars and bone fractures than your average pro football team. He was a nasty lad when in his cups, and given to heavy sarcasm, which is what brought about the ongoing damage. Taunted beyond endurance by Bill that night, Anita picked up a beer bottle and smote him across the kisser, opening a goodish wound, stitchable across his left cheekbone. As the blood pumped forth, Wilcox shouted, "Put that beer on my tab!"

In the end, the gods played a practical joke on Wilcox. Ed, a man of the riposte, the quip, the speedy retort, a man of wondrous and glorious malice, feared by the hypocrite, the arsehole, the bore, was stricken by throat cancer, leaving him without the tools of his trade. Ah, yes, he would try to keep up by croaking and writing fast notes, but 'twasn't the same. They said it was cancer did him in, but I believe it was the verbal coitus interruptus. He attempted to launch the thousands of barbed words out of his mouth, but they hit the NO GO cancer zone, and fell back, decomposing, poisoning their creator. Ed never spoke ill of anyone except members of the human race, and if he is now in the warmer part of creation, I know the devil is beseeching his mercy.

NIGHT AFTER NIGHT, THE SAME PEOPLE GATHERED IN THIS hole in the wall, fearful of missing something, or of being gossiped about *in absentia*. Same drunks, same talk, same place at the bar, the alcohol convincing us all that we were active, vital people, living life to the fullest degree. And while that conclusion might be questioned, we did keep each other amused.

There was the fellow who insisted, in a desperate effort to belong to the exalted crowd, that he was an Italian prince, although he was of Bronx working-class origins, which are hard to conceal.

There was Ching Lung, a sometime Columbia student, who drove a Mercedes and generally parked it on the sidewalk. His father, a general with Chiang Kai-shek, resided in Taiwan. His uncle was on the opposite side, a general with Mao Tse-tung. A divided family, you might say. He was deported after being turned in by someone who would have a fair impact on my life, not long after.

Brigid Berlin, daughter of Richard Berlin of Hearst Publications, was a chunky sweet-faced girl with a generous nature. One night, using Daddy's credit card, she took ten or so of the Clavin's inmates on a flying jaunt to Puerto Rico. Upon her return, it was said that she spent an enforced period of time at rest and recuperation as a result of that little caper.

There were underage drinkers, too. One particularly lissome virgin was in love with one of the older denizens. He did everything he could think of to bed her down, without success, until he proposed and convinced her to elope with him. He organized one of his friends to pose as a clergyman in a New Jersey church for a fake ceremony. He quickly got her to a motel, where the defloration took place. She was a bit upset when he informed her of the deception but continued to see him nonetheless, demonstrating something about human nature, which now, as then, eludes me.

George Hamilton, even then white-toothed and tanned. Douglas Fairbanks Jr., not averse to the bit of younger flesh. Walter Winchell Jr., a violent young man, who would get teary-eyed with nostalgic memories of Adolf Hitler. These were other strange saloon fellows of those mad nights. Odd Wot!

I had many impromptu parties at the Downing Street digs, and frequent overnight guests. One chap from Clavin's—Gordon Patterson was his name—begged asylum, as his family had given him the boot.

There was a bed in what we laughingly called the "living room," positioned quite close to the window; our Man Gordon, having the habit of going to bed with his shoes on, kicked out one of the windowpanes. A piece of cardboard thereafter deflected most of the incoming elements, and whilst not exactly "comfy, cozy, and toasty," as the club ladies would say, it was better than an igloo.

One wintry night of high wind and driving snow, I fell asleep, glad of a blanket or two and the ceiling over my head, and my seemingly permanent guest, Mr. G. Patterson, snuggled in t'other bed. Blissful slumber was interrupted by a wave of acrid smoke, which came uninvited into the room and penetrated the lungs. I bounded outa the bed to seek ye olde source of smoke, and, lo and behold, there was bould Gordon, completely fluthered, snoring away, with the mattress smoldering right next to his arse. The cardboard covering for the window had been kicked out, and the foot of the bed was covered with snow: a man of extremes, Gordon was, with his feet snowbound and his arse afire.

Hastily, I transferred the snow to the burning part of the mattress and extinguished it, I thought, but an hour or so after I went back to sleep, the smoke revisited me. Bounding out of the bed again, I went for a jug of water and sloshed it all over the spifflicated Patterson. The man hardly stirred, but my mission was complete: Fire Out! and back to bed.

Sometime later I was awakened abruptly and rudely by a rough hand shaking and thumping me. When I opened my eyes to see who it was that had the temerity to behave thusly, I almost had the cardiac seizure. I saw a head crowned with spikes of ice, icily protruding eyebrows and eyelashes, icicles dripping from the nose. In a very high, indignant voice, the arctic apparition informed me that he was nearly frozen to death. Never in his life had he been subjected to such a horrible place, and he was leaving, and there was no point in trying to stop him.

Closer examination revealed that the specter was Gordon P. He didn't mention the broken window, the burnt mattress, or anything about throwing in a dollar or two to assist with the rent. No sir, he dwelt on the deficiencies with nary a word of gratitude for unstinted shelter. "Bye, bye," sez I, and he was gone, taking with him some of Frank's good shirts and his only tie.

At a later date, I was approached by a sometime girlfriend of Gordon's, who holds the record for silencing me. She said, "I don't know how you can live the way you do! Gordon is not used to it!"

Forty years it is since those words were flung at me, with all the passion of Émile Zola fighting for Dreyfus, and as good as I am with the quick retort, never have I come close to a response. Perhaps on my deathbed I will murmur something pithy and germane, and that will be the answer, but for now I bear the heavy burden of defeat, and Frank the loss of his shirts forever.

Another of my guests stole Frank's raincoat, and another stole his umbrella. When Frank remarked—he was never a complainer— that it was odd my guests stole only his stuff, I told him they would consider it bad form to steal from me, as they knew me and didn't know him.

Frank said, "I see," which he probably didn't, but he was too polite to persist.

JOSH REYNOLDS (R.J. III, OF TOBACCO FAME) WAS A FREquent popper-in at Downing Street. This was in 1956, and he and Bill Galetly, his guru and personal philosopher, were the first people I had encountered expanding the menu of intoxicants from mere alcohol to the more exotic. They were doing considerable amounts of research, it seems, on the effects of various chemicals on an abstract region of the brain. It was not unusual for me to come home to find the two of them bent over a basin, heads covered by a towel, inhaling vapors rising to the nostrils. By the time they took their leave after one of their research expeditions, fumes, smoke, aromas, powders, pills, and weeds of all descriptions filled the otherwise barren habitation, but the lads didn't seem to notice.

Galetly, a completely honest man who eschewed clothing indoors, had the gaunt look of Jesus after a few bad days with the Romans. He was in constant fear of the telephone, as it represented the outside world. Due to his principled probity, though, when there was a call for him, we couldn't say he wasn't there until he had stepped into the hallway—naked—to say he didn't reside at our address. I had trouble comprehending why he continued to give out my number as a place to reach him.

The Italian couple across the hall were outraged at the sight of this naked bone heap lurking in the hallways of a respectable tenement. The constabulary would be summoned, and just try to explain that Galetly was in the hall because he was doing G. Washington one better: He could not tell, nor even cause to be told, a lie. To the New York cop, lying is normal, but nudity indicates a person of perversion.

Galetly had also taken a vow of celibacy, and ate not the flesh of the beast. Reynolds, on the other hand, had no such compunctions. He smoked, drank screwdrivers for the vitamins, ingested drugs, and had sexual relations, but only with the call girl. He was following his father's dictum, "Pay now and you won't have to pay later."

Josh later invited me to North Carolina with him to visit the mother and the brothers, John, Zack, and Will. At Winston-Salem Airport, I took a taxi to the "house," as Josh called it: a great, big, bloody mansion it was, staffed with platoons of lovely folk who tended to the every need. The general of this army was a large black lady, who carried an upside-down watch attached to her monumental bosom. Everything was geared to the time on that timepiece. She ruled that place with all the benevolence of Margaret Thatcher. There wasn't a member of the household, be they family, friend, or employee, who wasn't terrified of her, including Josh Reynolds' mother, "Blitz," as she was called, an indication of her temperament.

Josh hadn't told Blitz that he had invited me for a week or so until the last minute, and she had dispatched a telegram informing me that she could not entertain me at this time. The telegram and I had apparently crossed paths whilst in transit. Josh was unwilling to tell me of the mother's pissed-offedness, so I was a bit surprised at the frostiness of the welcome at the Reynolds' manse. But, the family being very southern, and hospitality being a watchword, nothing was said of the telegram. Indeed, I didn't find out about it 'til I returned to New York and received it. After a day or so, though, I had managed to overcome the wariness of the mother, and actually charmed her, so the visit was quite pleasant.

Those born to wealth are quite conspicuous in their consumption, in that they treat luxuries as necessities. The Reynoldses had three habitations in the general area: the Winston-Salem house; what Josh called "the farm," a mere thirty thousand acres about forty miles distant; and what is called a "lodge" up in the mountains, a little estate of a hundred or so acres.

Up in the mountain retreat, rustic externals, like log walls, flagstone floors, hewn beams, and bearskins scattered casually about concealed the luxury and plenitude of the well-stocked kitchen, the unlimited alcoholic beverages, the quiet air-conditioning, and the discreet servants: a life one could get used to.

Raised in poverty, in a place where there was no work, the brothers and self consequently had nothing to do as we were growing up, and there I was in a position to do nothing, proving that there is no difference between the rich and the poor, except poverty.

Distinctive among the farm's holdings was a veritable arsenal: handguns, rifles, carbines, and even some kind of machine gun. One day, as Josh and self were wending our way down the driveway in the jeep, I remarked on the little spurts of dust that erupted at intervals in front of us. Josh informed me that it was probably his brother John shooting at us from the roof, but not to worry, he was a poor marksman who was lucky enough to hit the driveway.

I tried to repel the image of a bullet entering the top portion of my cranium, but, try as I might, the feeling persisted. I urged Josh to speed up, but he only laughed that grating, garbley, evil-sounding laugh of his, whilst thoroughly enjoying my discomfiture. And lived to tell the tale.

They were a strange, tragic family. Brother Zack was named after the uncle who was found shot to death one New Year's Eve. His new wife, Libby Holman, a—what else?—sultry nightclub singer, was supposedly in the general vicinity. She went into seclusion and came out a year or so later, it is said, carrying an infant, whom she introduced as Zack's son and, of course, new heir to the Reynolds' fortune. The boy, Chris, was killed at the age of eighteen in a mountain-climbing fall. Two of Josh's brothers died young, one a suicide, the other in a hunting accident. As for Josh, the product that made the Reynoldses rich, Camels, killed him in 1995.

IN NEW YORK, THE SUMMER OF 1956 WAS APPROACHING with little bursts of sunshine nurturing the brave clumps of weeds 'twixt the cracks in the sidewalk. Those were the good old days people talk about now, when the subways were safe, but you had to be careful when approaching the news, as you might be assaulted by a new inanity from Eisenhower and his bewildering syntax. Nixon was still learning to tuck his upper lip into his gum, in what he mistook for a smile. Rockefeller hi fella'd all over town, and Mayor Robert Wagner, with a face like an abandoned animal shelter, made his deals with Mike Quill, the most missed labor leader in history.

Women still hung out in the kitchen then, and blacks were invisible. Chinatown was an exotic venue for the tourists, with just a whiff of danger. Greenwich Village was a draw for the wide-eyed, with its bohemians and Beats and the queers who shamelessly kissed and held hands out in the open.

Hoover had promised a chicken in every pot, but now Joe

McCarthy guaranteed a Communist under every bed. The Church was ruled by a pudgy little grocer's son, Frankie Cardinal Spellman, a dubious celibate with a penchant for fresh-faced seminarians. 'Twas said at a later date, when the bold little man went to bless the guns with which the U.S. slaughtered the Vietnamese, that there was an assassination attempt in Saigon: They sent him a poisoned altar boy.

The House Un-American Activities Committee was still in hot pursuit of the Commies. Out in Hollywood, glad to lend a hand, John Wayne, Adolphe Menjou, Ward Bond, and other assorted ya-hoos, who had never donned the uniform of their country, drove good people into exile, suicide, and abject poverty.

Did I know all this then? Not on your nellie. Politically naive, I was, at the age of twenty-four. To me, all things American were still noble and decent and good, and we never dropped bombs or killed people unless they deserved it.

———

ONE OF THE RUGBY CROWD, Jerry Lyons, an M.I.T. engineer and recently discharged navy lieutenant, told me about a place called Fire Island. It could only be reached by ferry from Long Island, I was informed, and, during the summer, it was overflowing with beautiful girls whose main purpose in life was to fuck all the men they could fit. Essentially, he said, all you had to do was get off the boat, pick any of the birds on the pier, and you were set for the weekend in the flesh department.

I set about getting a house and roommates.

It was a ramshackle affair on the beach, with old discolored spoons, old discolored sheets, and doors that didn't close—in every respect, pretty awful, with all the charms of an Alabama sharecrop-per's shack. In my sales presentation to prospective roomies, however, it was only slightly less grand than Hearst's San Simeon. Three lads bought the sales pitch. Tom McLaughlin, who was still in the navy. Bob Plasto, a British banker with red hair and fair skin, who had at the time two goals in life, neither of which were reached: He never got a tan and he never felt the thighs of a Vassar girl clasped tight around his waist. The third roommate was Walter Marais, a tall, lean South African, from whom no reflecting surface was safe, be it a mirror, the sea, or a fraction of an old paint can. The women adored him, because unlike most men, they'd tell you, he paid attention to what they said. So they might have believed, but he was just trying to catch a glimpse of himself in their eyes.

Six hundred dollars for the summer; a huge sum, but my sales presentation did it. When the other three arrived to discover that the hacienda was only an increment above squalor, there were displays of dudgeon. Indignation was in the air, charges of deception were flung at me, fraud and lies, too. McLaughlin, the navy officer, muttered that he shouldn't be surprised if he couldn't make a charge of high treason stick.

They stayed for the one weekend, and that was it for them. I was left with this run-down manse for the summer. A friend, Steve Epstein, had lent me a white convertible Cadillac, so I was able to breeze into New York for my fix of carbon monoxide and other doings. It was inconvenient to work on the docks in that hot weather, but a living had to be made, so I answered an ad in a Long Island paper for a salesman who, with hardly any work, would make vast fortunes. The product was the Bible—leatherbound, with gold-edged pages for forty dollars—the King James version for the Prods, the Douai version for the Papists, and the Old Testament for the mohel's men.

The bossman, who had all the spirituality of Legs Diamond, told us he'd been made a Knight of Malta by the Pope for his good work. He then told us to get out there, ring bells, tell 'em you're conducting a survey in the parish, and get in the door. If the targets were elderly, talk to the woman and imply that the man is mortal, and after he is gone she'd have this lovely book with its soft leather skin and gilt pages to comfort her in bed.

I didn't do well in the Word of God arena. Doors were not opened to me, and soon I was a defeated man whose sales pitch was reduced to a negative proposition—"I don't suppose you'd want to buy a Bible, would you?" In every case, this supposition was correct.

Wandering about Bayshore by day and ferrying back to Fire Island at night became tedious, and the ferry cost a few dollars, so it was expensive as well. I hit on the solution of selling the Four Gospels to the decadents of Ocean Beach and Ocean Bay Park, adjoining communities on Fire Island.

So there I would be, Saturdays and Sundays, on the beach, in the bathing suit, vodka and grapefruit juice in one fist, a Bible in the other. I'd stroll from group to group, who'd never let me want for the cooling beverage. I'd exhort them to buy the book to save their souls and my skin. 'Twas there I read Revelations and Genesis with all the stuff about a time to live and a time to die and a time to work and a time to go on the dole and all that grand stuff. I found the juicy bits in the Song of Solomon and read them aloud, and convulsed the crowd with all the carnality, but I think it only aroused them for further fleshly pursuits, as no sales ensued.

Someone mentioned the term "unemployment insurance" to me. "Wha' dat?" sez I, and it was explained to me. I quickly hied my way to the local office, applied, and was awarded the princely sum of thirty dollars per week.

Many of the generous folk on the Island had given me keys to their houses and invited me to finish hams, roast beef, capons, chickens, eggs, and all kinds of grub, as well as to drink whatever was around. There being quite a number of young wives and girlfriends present on the Island during the week, I, the only male not fulfilling the American dream in the city, was frequently invited to share a repast with a lonely young thing. Some of them confided how scary it was to be alone in a strange house, with its creakings and sounds of scurrying animals in the walls and ceilings. I never turned down a plea for my overnight company and the physical comfort I could give to a scared girl, to keep her safe from the darkness and all the things that woosh in the seaside night.

It was a heavenly, blissful time in life, with no shortage of the morning egg, the glass of whiskey or the cup of tea, or the welcoming limbs and breasts of a reasonable number of undemanding yet passionate women. There was only one cloud on the rim of the earth, a small one, but a cloud nevertheless, and that was the matter of the unsold Bible.

The Pope's pal, Knight of Malt, came hunting for me one early morning, and discovered me about to plunge into God's most sought-after orifice, me on top, she on her back. Poised, trembling, the limbs tensed in pure agonized ecstasy, lips full, eyes gleaming, thighs wide apart, the blood pounding, the ears shutting out all earthly sounds, but the blast-off was aborted by a voice saying insistently, "Hey! I wanna talk to you."

My bedmate shrieked and somehow managed to hide her entire body under a pillow. I got to my feet and told the Knight of Small Talk to get the fuck out of my bedroom before I sent him to his reward. I got into some garb and went out to confront this peeping Pope's friend. He said he wanted to either get back the sample Bible or give me one more chance. I said, "I quit!"

"Why?" sez he.

"Because you can't sell a product you don't believe in!"

———

EARLIER THAT SUMMER, WHEN I first arrived on Fire Island, I'd secured a nice, silken ascot and hit on a rather useful function for it. I told all the bods in the immediate vicinity that when I wore said ascot, it meant I was available for the evening and that the girls should be aware that if they spent any time talking to me, I'd take it to mean they were interested in sharing my bed. Wearing the ascot meant, "The flag is up!"

I spent many of those available evenings in Flynn's Bar and made the acquaintance of some wonderful folk, to be friends for life. Jim Brady of *Women's Wear Daily*, and later *Vogue* and *Parade*, made sure I was never short of a meal or a drink. And Tom Stern, even then, at the age of twenty, a brilliant fellow, who talked incessantly yet intelligently. He'd read widely and remembered it all, even page numbers. Staggering home down the beach one night from Flynn's, I literally ran into Tom, who was staggering toward Flynn's. Fortunately, the terrain was sandy and soft, so we remained on the ground, where we both had fallen, until daybreak. Another scion, you might say. His father was the publisher of the the *Philadelphia Daily News*, and his grandfather was publisher of the *New York Post* when it was a decent, liberal paper, long before its descent into today's slime, with *Mein Kampf* required editorial reading under its present Führer.

Another lifelong friend I made that summer was Pat McCormick, one of the funniest men in the world. In forty years, never has he failed to make me laugh. He and Tom O'Malley would team up to do comedy routines on the beach. Pat being six feet eight inches, and Tom being five feet six inches, they looked like Goliath and his walking stick.

Pat wrote for Johnny Carson, Jack Paar, Dick Cavett, Merv Griffin, Danny Kaye, Red Skelton, and Lucille Ball. Bobby Kennedy, with serious work to do, needed to get more humor into his speeches, and Pat was the one who supplied it.

Tom O'Malley, a writer for *TV Guide*, exposed the scandalous little fact that one Dorothy Kilgallen of *What's My Line?* could see through her mask and thus had no difficulty in identifying the "mystery" guests. He went on to become a talent booker for Jack Paar and Carson, and, with Marge Green and Jimmy Desmond, made *Candid Camera* in its prime the funniest show on television.

When that summer ended, I was a sad fellow. For the first time in my life, I had been free: free of clothes, free of church, free of strictures and neighborly judgments. I could eat, drink, make love, swim, run, laugh, and talk at will. Hedonistic, you say? Well, having been the victim of other people's idea of sin, original and otherwise, from the time of birth, "Indulgence is mine," henceforth saith the Malachy.

For the first and only time in my life, I got a tan, and there'd be times on the beach, in the midst of the color, the energy, the bodies, the volleyball, the shouted, uproarious inanities, I'd put the head down, close the eyes, and hark back to the fetid slum in Limerick, with its stink and glowering darkness and the allover hopelessness. Taunting myself with remembered misery, I'd remain in my dark reverie, knowing full well all I had to do was lift my head, open my eyes, and I was forward in time to the Heaven of America again.

For the hundreds gathered there on Saturdays and Sundays, it was merely a weekend in the sun; for me, it was the height of ecstasy. It was license, liberty, freedom all rolled into one, and at times I'd go running on the sand, leaping, jumping, punching the air, loosing great shouts of joy at a tolerant, smiling sun, and then dive into the salt waters of the Atlantic and out again to resume my capers, not caring if the other folk there thought I was a raving lunatic.

Ah, yes, that was the summer of my content. There was a summer paper published on the island, the *Fire Island Press*, as I recall. One of the columns, covering the lighter Island antics, generally included one or the other of my doings, and on that last day, in the last edition, the last lines of the column were, "The flag is down. Good night, Malachy, wherever you are."

TWO

MALACHY ASCENDING

The mother loved love songs, romantic novels, and the movies—in Limerick, we called them the fillums, or the pictures. She could recount in exquisite detail what had gone on in a fillum she had just sat through, and she'd sigh and laugh as she did the reenactment for us that night at home.

The brothers and the friends and myself all loved gangster fillums and cowboy fillums, and we went whenever we could. And Jasus, didn't Tarzan have the best of everything, with yer wan there, Jane, with scarcely as much clothes on her as would stuff a crutch. The priests warned us away from Tarzan, for wasn't he living in sin with that temptress, Jane? You'd never see them going to Communion—and they couldn't, could they, in their unwed state—and Boy, not even baptized, was headed straight for Limbo.

I stayed at the pictures for four showings of Tarzan once, because I thought that eventually Jane's little bit of clothing would ride up on her thigh and I'd get to see the holey land.

The father, on the other hand, thought that only patriotic songs should *be sung, only histories of Ireland's struggles should be read, and if we wanted to see pictures, he'd tell us, we could look at the holy pictures on the wall.*

———

BACK TO NEW YORK CITY, then, it was: the honk, the blare, the decibels, the endemic hostility, all designed to keep people from sitting on their arses and obstructing progress. There are a number of things American that are never seen in New York City, front porches with rocking chairs being two.

By day, I'd head out from Downing Street and trudge to the docks, shape up, get hired or not hired, but, either way, it worked out, as I wasn't afraid of either work or the looming day.

Once in a while, I'd sneak off and go to the theater, without telling anyone, of course, for fear of being laughed at for being, as the Brits say, a "poof." At that time, you could set fire to a succession of crowded theaters, wiping out entire audiences, and win enormous sums of money by wagering there would be no Irish lost, so I knew I was safe from the dangers of mickery in the fifth row of any theater in New York City.

One Friday, having gotten ye olde pay packet for a pretty good week, almost a hundred dollars, I hied myself to the theater to see three one-act plays by John Millington Synge at the Theatre East on East Sixtieth Street. Never was I more entranced by language than I was that night. The glorious flow, a silvery torrent of words, yet human, yet humorous, yet tragic, the language of a people who took a dull tongue, English, and made it roar. I left the theater, giddy with the intoxicating effect of the speech, so that I was floating rather than walking.

Reaching the end of the block, the blinding thought drilled its way into my brain: Wouldn't it be grand to be an actor? Jesus! Ah, Jesus, yes! Go back and talk to them.

"All right, now. Don't push me," I sez to myself, and before the argument could escalate, it was back to the lobby.

"Excuse me, sir, could I speak to the boss?"

"Do you mean the producer?"

"Whoever."

"That's me," sez he.

"Good. I saw the plays tonight, and I've decided I'd like to join your group as an actor."

"What experience do you have?"

"None. Shure, I wouldn't need any fer the things ye are doing there."

"Do you have any pictures?"

"A passport picture. Would that do?"

"Would you come on Sunday to read for us?"

I told him I could read and would prove it on the spot if he wished, but he explained himself, so I assented.

"See you on Sunday," sez he, "at 1:30 P.M."

Fortified with a couple of beakers of the Marys Bloodied, I arrived, read, and carried the day. Hired! An actor in an off-Broadway show. I didn't give a fiddler's fart that the weekly stipend was only thirty-five dollars per, that I would have to forego the docks and my somewhat higher standard of living, and that rehearsals began at once, as the actor I was replacing was leaving in a week.

The producers, Dermot McNamara and Helena Carroll, were quite tolerant of my cockiness, knowing full well that the demanding nature of acting brings the most arrogant of neophytes to heel. The distaff director took me in hand, literally and metaphorically. I'd a quick and good memory, she would give me the moves, and many was the day we'd finish ahead of schedule. There being a bed on the stage, she had no problem getting a rise out of me, and she would take me in hand, mouth, and the place where all young men desire to enter. Despite the lack of applause, our rehearsals always ended with a moving climax. What an introduction to the theater!

Once I opened, there were applause and hugs both, and my mentors told me they were getting laughs where there had been none before. It was a good job, and I had to stop wearing a hat then, as the head kept expanding. Accolades poured in, the press treated us well, and more and more people came to see the plays.

As it happened, Clavin's bar was only two blocks away. There I'd repair with assorted audiences afterwards for the revelry. One eve, Clavin said, "If you are going to bring all these fookin' people in here, you had better get behind the bar and serve them."

That was fine with Magill, as he didn't like to be hurried at any time, he being a scion, and all of that. So began the bar career. What a position of power has the man behind the bar! Equal to the C.E.O. behind the big desk, the professor behind the podium, the judge on the bench, the actor on the stage—but perhaps most equivalent to the priest at the altar. The barman, like the priest, deals with wine and water; he mutters incantations: $1.10 plus $1.10 = $2.20 + tax = $2.30; his congregation are supplicants for grace, which he dispenses upon proper and ample contributions. He hears confessions of wrongdoing and absolves the sinner, and at the end of the night, gives the old cry, *Ita Missa Est*—Go, Ye are Dismissed—and closes up, going to his bed satisfied at having ministered well to his congregation.

Within ten days, my life took a sharp flight from the ordinary into a path that has been ever since hilarious and mad and sad. At the theater, people had to watch me onstage, or else the show was a money waster, and at Clavin's, they watched me to ensure my attention to their drink needs. A cynosure was what I was: I was *In*.

To the rear of the enlarged shoebox that was Clavin's was a piano bar, at which various habitués took turns. Sam Anderson, the regular man, played the regulation cocktail stuff, Cole Porter, Irving Berlin, and the popular, singable tunes from Broadway.

Alternating with Sam were Fulton (Buddy) Lewis III, whose father, Fulton Lewis Jr., was a well-known right-wing commentator on radio, bosom buddy of Senator Joseph McCarthy and that other yahoo, Roy Cohn. Buddy attracted many young blonde things. He played rather badly, but overcame that by looking deeply into their eyes.

We weren't too careful about checking the ages at the bar, so it's likely that when Buddy bedded his pretty young things, he also had to help them with their homework.

Another of the alternates was Peter Duchin, he of orchestra fame. An orphan, he was being raised by the Harriman family. A good lad, and a grand musician.

There was a young, aspiring actor named Warren Beatty, whose sister, Shirley MacLaine, was in a Broadway show at the time, thus opening the door for Warren into the acting world. Shirley and myself have aged, but Warren, not a bit.

Lewis took a group of us to a public meeting of the Communist Party one night. He was spotted as his father's son by the boss man, Gus Hall, who ridiculed him from the podium until he got up and left. He asked us to take notes on the goings-on in his absence, but all I was interested in were the people. They might have been Communists, but they looked and sounded perfectly American to me.

Later on that night, we caught up with good ole Buddy, who launched into a violent tirade about the Commie Jew conspiracy, with their plans to take away all private property and institute a society devoted to promiscuity. This, mind you, from a lad who was inserting the sausage into a different lubricious casing every night of the week. Furthermore, if he had his way, by Christ, he would put all the Jews in the middle of the Sahara and drop an atomic bomb on them.

Being relatively new to this society, and unsure of the protocol—and if I'd asked, Lewis would probably have referred me to *The Protocols of the Elders of Zion*—I found myself wondering why I was sitting and listening to this chump slavering on about killing people in the millions, so I intimated to him that if he didn't shut the flow of fucking excrescence, I'd perforce have to ram my fist down his gob and flatten his fucking tonsils. He moved on to other subjects.

THE IRISH PLAYERS, THE COMPANY BY WHOM I WAS EM-
ployed as a thespian, had a couple of good p.r. men, John
Bruder and Howard Attlee, and they were getting me around in great
style. One of the p.r. activities was an appearance on Dumont's
Channel 5, on a show called *Nightbeat*. In the course of the interview,
the host got me onto the subject of Clavin's and its roster of out-
patients, gadflies, and semifamous pianists. Mine host asked if Fulton, the Turd, Lewis shared the view of his father, Fulton, the genius.
I said I presumed he did, and told about the plan to hecatomb the
entire Hebraic population.

It was live television, so nothing could be edited. Damage control
swept in, but too late. This is not my opinion, the station's opinion,
the sponsor's opinion, the receptionist's opinion, etc. The elder
Lewis—bosom buddy of Joe McCarthy and Roy Cohn, the gay
homophobe who died of AIDS—lost several sponsors from his
blighted radio show and sued for a million American dollars. He
sued me, the station, the sponsors, the host, and the receptionist.

I had never been so flattered in all my living days. If they could only see me now in the slums of Limerick, a big shot, sued for a million. Bejesus, isn't America a great and wonderful country, when a young guttersnipe, half a hooligan, hardly in the country for ten minutes, is sued for a million? *That* is rising to the top.

Endless conferences and meetings were held on the matter, as Lewis Sr. said he would drop the suit if I apologized. "Not on your Nellie," sez I. "The son said what I said he said, and I'm not going to apologize for telling the truth."

The whole affair, which got very boring after the first flush of importance, was finally settled by me saying I was sorry for the inconveniences and losses suffered by the Lewis family as a result of my remarks, truthful though they were. I was sorry I'd caused the station the loss of sponsors, and the receptionists such difficulties. They were innocent bystanders when I launched my verbal broadside. Thus ended my first million-dollar lawsuit.

ANOTHER NOISY NIGHT AT CLAVIN'S, THE PHONE RANG—it was for Malachy. The voice at the other end identified itself as one Tom O'Malley. He'd met me on Fire Island whilst I was purveying the Word of God on the beach and had heard me say that I always sent back bills with the word "DECEASED" stamped on them. He was now the talent coordinator of the *Tonight* show, which was hosted by a lad named Jack Paar, and would I be interested in appearing and telling some of my yarns and they would pay me three hundred dollars.

Jesus! They're all mad in America; they sue you for talking, and then they pay you for talking, but it was better than in Ireland, where they were always telling me to shut up without pay.

The day set for this momentous event was the first day of 1958, New Year's Day. It being Hogmanay, the most important holiday for the Scots, involving the open door and the welcome stranger, and it being of total inconsequence to me, I borrowed some kilts and a sporran and a *sciandhu* dagger and paraded all over the East Side in same, going from party to party.

Everywhere in N.Y.C. the steady motion of elbow-bending held sway, bringing to the lips bedazzling varieties of beverages: eggnogs made from ostrich eggs, yak milk, and the juice of fermented maggots, imported from the rain forest. Whiskey, whisky, wine, sherry, port, mixed drinks, unmixed drinks, Irish coffee, non-Irish coffee with whisky, rums, and there was even beer. What they call "open houses" were ubiquitous, with no shortages of anything, and for a lad like myself, with the sharp memory historical and otherwise, and just a hundred years from the last famine in Ireland, this was the ticket.

I couldn't get over the plenitude and the extravagance, and how out-of-reach luxuries in Ireland were commonplace, almost necessities, here, and it wasn't just at Christmas or at death there was whiskey in the house, but all year long, and if the supply got depleted, they just rang what they call a "liquor store" and restocked. The folks didn't measure out the drink or watch you drink it, but with a careless wave of the hand, they'd tell you, "Help yourself!" Chicago may be "The City of the Big Shoulders," as Sandburg called it, but New York was the city of "The Big and Giving Hand."

After sampling the festivities in numerous apartments, I ended up at Tom O'Malley's place in the East Fifties. The doings there on that day were normal for him, but would be insane in any other home. Pat McCormick, wearing a sheet in the form of a diaper, holding forth as the Baby New Year and demanding they lower the legal drinking age to one; Mona McCormick, Pat's sister, a young woman who could infect a whole room with her laughter, egging Pat on. Jonathan Winters popped in at one point, as did Dick Cavett. The air was thick with quips, the ripostes, the sallies, the jibes, the puns, like showers of arrows at the Battle of Little Big Horn, and as always in the company of witty people, never was there a joke attempted or told.

But then, work intervened, and 'twas time for O'Malley to get me to the *Tonight Show*, which was televised from the Hudson Theater on West Forty-fourth Street, and, believe me, it *was* live and spontaneous. Paar was the kind of man who didn't want to clutter his mind with what would become debris anyway: He had Hugh Downs, one of the truly grand minds of television to pong in the intelligent inquiry to a guest. Thus, the show was driven by the intelligence and deliberate ignorance of one man, Jack Paar, and the intelligence and knowledge of another, Hugh Downs.

We arrived at about 10:30 P.M. at the greenroom, where the guests waited. There was a great rushing about to get coffee into my system, people still thinking coffee sobers the drunk. But the old dictum applied, then as always: Before coffee, you've got a drunk; after coffee, you've got a wide-awake drunk.

I drank the coffee and was introduced to the other guests. Elsa Maxwell was both a society gossip columnist and a decision-maker regarding who was to be considered society. Handy, that.

For a fee, if you were an Anglophilic, nouveau riche arse-licker, she would arrange for the Duke and Duchess of Windsor to attend your function. I believe the fees were as follows:

$5,000 to come to your cocktail party;

$10,000 to come to lunch;

$20,000 for cocktails and dinner.

Elsa M. played the piano as a young girl at one of the big hotels in San Francisco, the same one Enrico Caruso was staying in when the big earthquake of 1906 hit. The only thing Caruso grabbed was a photograph of himself. Elsa grabbed Caruso, and off they ran for the hills.

She was a seventyish, stoutish lump of a lady, with more than her share of chins. She had somewhere acquired a British diction, and when she moved she looked like a Spanish galleon. I imagine her gowns were more likely the work of a sailmaker than a seamstress. Oh, how they fawned on her, the self-appointed arbiter of society, fashion, and personality.

Moral of the story: If you are fat, unattractive, and frumpish, cultivate a British accent, study the Spanish Armada, sail into the boudoir of social climbers, listen to their drivel, and you will have arrived.

Jack Paar, the somewhat neurotic host, loved outsider-starting-from-the-bottom types, and he loved eccentrics like Alexander King, a heroin addict before it was stylish or even acceptable. King had contempt for everything popular and fashionable, and he would sit with Paar and let loose a voluble flow of rich, contrary, cranky intellectual diatribes against fools, brokers, academics, and theologians, not to mention the military. The more he insulted America's mores, the more they loved him. He was another guest that night of my debut, but I'm afraid Johann Barleycorn has dimmed recollection of any others appearing, if indeed any others did.

When it was time for my entrance into fame, I was guided from the greenroom to a very dark backstage area and told to wait. Then, I heard Paar doing the introduction, the curtain was pulled back, and I was pushed onto the stage. The orchestra was playing some Irish reel, the audience was applauding wildly, and the lights were not conducive to seeing anything at all, they were so bright. Paar, in a very unusual move, I was told, moved two chairs to the front of the desk where the interview, such as it was, was to take place.

Not a vestige of recorded material remains of what went on that night, as there was no video yet, and the film is missing, but there were continuous bursts of laughter from the audience, and Paar and Downs seemed very amused, though I have no recollection of what I said. Paar invited me to come back again, and off I went to continue the imbibing on another whirl around the town.

MY OLD, SHIRT-FILCHING HOUSE GUEST, G. PATTERSON, decided, as a result of my newfound fame, to speak to me again. He was going out with a young thing whose pater had been an officer in Tsar Nick's Russian army, and he was well in with this down-at-the-heel mob of abandoned aristocrats, collectively known as White Russians. There were counts, countesses, barons, princes, and princesses working as doormen, seamstresses, housekeeps, and nannies, but every so often, they would have a get-together in a Park Avenue apartment (the owner being absent) to celebrate the death of Stalin, or the ousting of Khrushchev, or Russian Easter, or something. Gordon P. arranged to have me invited to the next.

One of their mob worked at a printer's, so he would use the facilities to print the most elaborate gold-embossed invitations I ever saw. Under the seal of the Tsar, it said, "Prince and Princess Karisovsky and the Count and Countess Petrouchka request the presence of Malachy McCourt to honor Princess Nicorder, who has just secured a position at Bloomingdale's." Then, this royal invite commanded, at the bottom on the left, "B.Y.O.B.," and bottom right it said, "Black Tie."

Of course, I went. Was I going to lose the opportunity to rub shoulders with royal yahoos? I secured a small bottle of Powers Irish Whiskey, about the size of an airline nip, and off with me to my first Park Avenue hooley!

Here it should be mentioned that a swift trip a couple of years prior to the Salvation Army had secured me a decent dinner jacket, complete with shirt studs, winged collar, and black tie, so that I was always prepared to take my place among the penguins of the world. I had discovered that New York always made way for the man garbed in the tuxedo. When I needed a good dinner in bad times, a quick perusal of the daily papers would tell me what conventions were in town, and many is the time I made my way to the Waldorf-Astoria and charmed my way into somebody's dinner. I'd attended steel manufacturers' dinners, hardware dinners, fashion dinners, newspaper publishers' dinners, and on one memorable occasion, a shipping-line owner's dinner.

After getting past the checklist people, to whom you say, "I just stepped out for a second," you find a table not fully occupied and ask if you can join them for a while, as your friend has not yet arrived. This one eve, on the menu was South African Rock Lobster, and I announced authoritatively that this denizen of the lower depths could not be consumed and digested unless properly accompanied by chilled Heinekens. Most men are afraid to disagree with emphatic assertions of this nature lest they be wrong, so they all nodded their noggins to show that they, too, were in possession of this obvious fact of epicurean propriety.

An inquiry to the waiter re securing the chilled amber beverage elicited the reply that he was only authorized to serve wine. Slight indignation flowed around the table like a mild current. A great anticipatory thirst for the beer had parched all throats, and a rebellion was in the offing unless it was forthcoming.

I offered to go and seek out the proper authority to make sure our drought would be ended. I was so delegated. I mentioned that some dollars might be needed, as I'd left my wallet at home, and some fives and singles were tendered.

Across this crowded banquet hall, I wended my way to where swinging doors were discharging waiters at a steady clip. Standing there, in a seeming reverie, was a stumpy man with all the haughtiness of a headwaiter. I produced two of the singles and waved them in front of him. I just barely refrained from saying, "My good man," but I did trot out the yarn about Heinekens and South African Rock Lobster.

His gaze shifted from the dollar bills to my face, and he asked me who I was.

"My name is Malachy McCourt," I said.

"Who are you with?"

"Table 47."

"I mean, what shipping line are you with?"

"Farrell Shipping Line."

"How long?

"Five years, four-and-a-half months." (That sort of precise answer always lends veracity to a tale.)

"Let me inform you of something, whoever you are. The host of this dinner is Farrell Shipping Lines. My name is John Farrell, chairman of Farrell Shipping, and if you don't get your lying ass outa here pronto, I'll have it kicked out."

I left, but I still had my tuxedo, if not my dignity, as well as the fourteen dollars from the collection at the table, which bought me a fine dinner elsewhere.

But back to the White Russian carrion, who have been waiting on Park Ave. At the door, there was a saturnine chap, togged out in some very colorful livery, including the buckled shoes, who asked my name, and then, pounding the floor with a heavy, ornate staff, he announced, "Mr. Malachy McCourt." Since I had no title, they paid no attention to me.

Another liveried footman directed me to the bar, where I handed over my precious two-ounce bottle of Irish. With a great flourish, the bartender wrote my name on a label, which was much bigger than my bottle, and another Tsarist general told me there was a five-dollar corkage fee, which was much more than I'd paid for the Powers. I forked over the five and requested a drink from my bottle, which was duly poured into a crystal glass, and off with me to circulate among the bemedaled men and bejeweled women with the tin tiaras perched on top.

There was a good deal of bowing and curtsying, your royal highness-ing, your excellency-ing, hand-kissing, and the odd bit of heel-clicking. My shirt-filching friend, Gordon P., was there with his popsy, smiling, exchanging drivel with all these off-duty doormen and seamstresses.

I went back to the bar to get some more of my labeled drink, and the barman told me that that was the end of it. I made the accusation that Tsarist types stole everything in Russia, and now they were stealing my whiskey. Just to quiet me, they let me have a drink from somebody else's bottle.

I joined another group, where one pigeon-chested chap was holding forth on how the world would have been a better place had the U.S. and Britain formed an alliance with Hitler to defeat Stalin. I said I thought Lenin had done a good job when he got rid of the Tsar and all the other parasites who infested that benighted land, a land of fops and dandies and painted women, where they had to have a lot of Royal Balls because the men didn't have any. When I'd pleasantly delivered myself of this little peroration, there was a sort of silence and then gasps and grunts, and then it seemed the whole costume-jeweled gang was fighting to get at me.

I backed up, fending off fists, fans, slippers, and other weapons, managed to grab the staff from the fellow at the door, and a few swings of that kept the irate mob from advancing.

I didn't wait for the elevator and, in a shortish time, I was dashing through the lobby at a fast rate of knottage, past some astonished doormen, and out into the safety of the streets of my beloved New York, where I have never been attacked by anybody. They are a dangerous crowd, these Tsarists, and very touchy. It is my considered opinion that an angry mob of geriatric, pseudo-royalists can do more harm to a democracy than all the Maos and Stalins put together. The authorities should keep an eye on them. They bear watching.

Just in case you're wondering, I thrust the staff into the hands of one of the astonished doormen as I fled my royal assailants. "It's no wonder the Bolshies gave 'em the heave-ho with their glittering uniforms and gowns," muttered I to self, as I trudged toward a friendly hostelry. "Flaunting their wealth, flogging peasants, eating and drinking too much, trying to be French. If they had only read their own prophetic writers, Tolstoy, Dostoyevsky, and good old Nicky Gogol, they might have mended their ways and shared the wealth, and then they wouldn't have wound up sneaking parties in other people's apartments and violating the free-speech rights of a truthful Irishman like myself."

They never asked me back. As far as I'm concerned, they can go and Farouk themselves.

MAGILL OF CLAVIN'S, BETWEEN VISITS TO EXCLUSIVE ASYlums and time spent behind the bar, had bought a car that was causing him great annoyance and inconvenience with parking and the general responsibility for a large, helpless, inanimate object, totally dependent on him for care, maintenance, fuel, registration, and all that stuff. I offered to look after it for him so long as, outside of petrol, I'd have no financial outlay. I had learned how to operate a car from a southern lunatic named Robinson Carleton Jones, when we were both concrete inspectors on the Jersey Turnpike. So when Magill offered me the use of his car, it was like another bit of the American Dream unveiled. I thought the whole population of this New York metropolis was looking at me driving this white Chevrolet with the tailfins, and saying, "Hasn't that Malachy McCourt come a long way since he left the lanes of Limerick! Look at him, actually driving a motorcar around the streets of New York!"

If only they could see me in Limerick now, they would be sorry for all the things they did to me when I was younger! I, like every resentful urchin, had visions of dying and lying in a coffin, with hordes of stupid big people who had abused me queuing up to weep and cry out their remorse, and, somehow or other, I would, though dead, communicate to them that it was too feckin' late (I'd say "feckin'" because you can't fuck in Heaven), and they would leave my coffinside to live out their lives weeping and unforgiven and vowing never to do it again to other urchins of the lane. But it was better than that to be driving a motorcar through the romantic street.

After five months of this useless possession of a car, Magill sent word that the repossess lads were on the prowl, as he had overlooked a small matter of monthly payments. He was going to spirit the thing out of New York City to avoid seizure. Our rendezvous was some pretentious little orifice in a wall on the East Side in the Fifties at around 9:30 P.M. A series of visits to other joints in advance put me in a jovial mood.

It was a wintry night with temperatures low, old snow on the ground, and the stars frozen in place. I breezily entered the premi and proceeded to the altar and, being a man of business, promptly ordered the double Irish sans ice, with a fraction of aqua on the side in case of sudden dehydration or any other aquatic emergency. The presiding prelate did not return my warm greeting with any enthusiasm, nor did he make any move toward the orderly array of bottles behind him to fulfill my liquid request. "You have to check your overcoat," sez he. "Why is dat?" sez I.

"Because we have a dress code here, and dat's the rule."

I'd heard of the Morse code, secret codes, military codes, codes of honor, codes of ethics, but the term "dress code" had to enter the ear hole slowly, as it was a stranger in my lexicon. Flippantly, I told the Keeper of the Dress Code that I was not wearing a dress. Like the dumpy dowager, Victoria, the chap was not amused. So, buckling down to the urgent matter at hand (i.e., securing the drink), I explained to this dour curate that I was meeting a friend, did not intend to stay the night in these inhospitable environs, and a drink of whiskey was needed to keep me in good spirits.

I knew all was lost when the glum one informed me that they didn't stock Irish Whiskey, and no matter how long I was staying, the outer garment must hang on a hook in a little cubbyhole rather than grace my back, or, as he expressed it more succinctly, "Ya gotta check ya coat!"

At the time, I was still of a mind that the U.S.A. was a place where reason, decency, and open intelligence were the normal modes of thought and action. For God's sake, 'twas barely a decade since Il Duce and the Führer had been hung up and put down, respectively, and were we going to behave like fucking fascists over overcoats? A Socratic flow bubbled from my lips.

"My good fellow, since it is my overcoat, and I'm not of a mind to give it into the custody of strangers, and it doth not do harm to your furniture or equipment, aesthetically it is not displeasing, since its texture is of the vale of Kashmir, and its hue doth not clash with your somewhat hideous decor (which, coincidentally, ought to be checked somewhere, preferably in a slurry pit on a pig farm, but I digress), and furthermore," and, this being the unanswerable, triumphant finale of my dialogue, I loudly and emphatically trumpeted, "are you in the business of selling whiskey for dollars or checking coats for quarters?"

I searched the vast bovine face of the niggling, obstructionist, stick-to-the-rules arsehole facsimile of an American for dawning understanding of my argument for coats at bars. His response: "I tol' ya, ya gotta check ya coat!"

Dudgeon of a high nature lifted me off the stool and out into the night, muttering, swearing, and loosing profanities about first-class, ocean-going arseholes. Plunking myself in the Magill hot rod, I reviewed the events of the preceding fifteen minutes and cogitated on how life can turn from being cheerful, warm, and cozy to negative in a sec, and all it takes is us handing the power of happiness over to another human being. And here I had forked it over to a complete stranger of dubious intellect, lacking in ability to comprehend simple facts, and with all the sensitivities of an ass and/or a Republican. "Action must be taken," sez I to myself, there being no other biped in my immediate vicinity to address.

It is not easy to doff the garments in the front seat of a motor car, but doff them I did. First the overcoat, then off came the shoes, the odd socks of the bohemian, the trousers, the shorts of the jockey (a.k.a. ball carriers), the short coat, the shirt, and the singlet. I replaced the shoes and bohemian socks, donned the overcoat *arís* (that's Irish for "again") and 'twas the work of a mo' to put the feet on terra firma, stand up, and head back into the pretentious orifice, with its exclusionary practices, for all its posture as a public restaurant.

I proceeded to the bar amidst the hub and the bub of satisfied diners, who were happily inhaling the fumes of the cognac and the satisfying smoke of the coffin nails. Others were eagerly awaiting the slab of decomposing meat or the body of the deceased and battered denizen of the sea, whose odoriferous fumes were doused by the judicious employment of sherry, shallots, and garlic. All said diners without overcoats, of course, bullied into shedding them by the imposition of a Dress Code. By God, sir, I'd show them a dress code—or its opposite!

With as breezy a manner as I could muster, and behaving as if I'd never set a trotter in the place afore, I cheerily addressed the granite head with pebbles for brains still presiding over the bottles. "Would you," sez I to him, "in the name of Jesus, Mary, and the Holy St. Joseph, in the name of all the saints in Heaven and of Cardinal Spellman, the man who loves to play leapfrog with acolytes, lift the giving hand and pour out two measures of the double-distilled fruits of the Emerald Isle so that my parched tonsils won't think I have abandoned them and run off with a woman?"

The brainless one gazed at me and spake, informing me that he didn't know what I was talking about, that there were no fruits in this house, they didn't allow any kind of queer in the house, that he tol' me before he wadn't goin' to serve me unless I checked my coat, and that he didn't want no trouble from me or nobody else. As my overcoat was buttoned up to the neck and he couldn't see the bare legs protruding from the hem, I felt safe in assuring him I was willing to now check this troublesome overcoat on condition that the coat-check attendant be summoned to fetch same.

A diminutive, wrinkled-faced, heavily made-up female named Myrtle reluctantly trudged toward me with ticket in hand and "Check your coat" on her lips. I turned my back to allow her to slide the coat off my nude bod. (Nude is when you choose to be seen in the buff; naked is when you are caught by the irate cuckold *en-flagrante*. Textbooks please take note, as there is a good deal of confusion on this issue.)

As the coat slid off the bod and I turned to give the masticating congregation a full frontal view of the complete epidermis—chest, belly button, the fur of the pube, a reasonable-sized dangler leaning to the right (God forgive me!), a somewhat shriveled ball bearer (due to the slight chill) thighs, knees, shins, odd socks, and footwear—a silence descended upon the room, much the same, I imagine, as when Jesus bade farewell to his Apostles and left the upper room forever at the Last Supper.

People formed sitting tableaux, caught in the mundane actions of dining. Some were caught with the fork halfway to the food hole, others had fork in the hole, some were examining the bill for the usual fraud, which is no doubt the standard at an establishment requiring the checking of coats. There were nose scratchers, ear-pullers, leaning-on-handers, about-to-leavers, half-stander-uppers, all caught as though the bomb had hit and they had been petrified in place. All were different in act and deed except for the focus of the peepers. Had I been arrested and put in a criminal lineup, not one soul there could have identified my face; but had I dropped the trousers and exhibited the three-piece set, fingering me would have been no trouble. In the Western World, men possess a fierce curiosity about each other's wee-wees.

The McCourt family motto is "Fierce When Roused," which appears under a pseudo coat-of-arms with nary a penis in the artwork. But the dangler was far from being roused this eve; indeed, had it shrunk any further, it would have become a hemorrhoid.

Much fear enriched the lives of the munchers the night of my nude lark. One moment there was a hushed silence, all breathing and respiratory activity suspended, motion stopped, and then there was a communal inhalation, followed by bellows, shrieks, and imprecations.

"Goddam!"

"Son-of-a-bitch."

"Dirty pervert!"

"Flasher!"

One distinguished English voice bleated, "Mopery, mopery!" and a politically aware lad bellowed, "Commie! Commie!"

The hatcheck woman, Myrtle, was still standing transfixed, holding the coat as if it were the garment just taken off the bod of Jesus at Calvary. The nitwit behind the bar had now bounded over the mahogany, but was nonplussed by never having handled a naked man before. Out of the kitchen poured a phalanx of white-clad defenders of America's purity. A high-hatted chef, a small-hatted chef, assorted assistants, and some damp Hispanic dishwashers, some bearing pots, others frying pans, and some with very sharp-looking cutting instruments. I had a passing thought that it was my uncircumcised state was the cause of the consternation, and I prayed that there be no opportunistic mohel among my assailants, but the thought soon passed as more troops joined in the assault on my person, bringing larger concerns.

All the male diners, egged on by shrieking females, leapt into the fray. Waiters pummeled me, kitchen help bonged my head with resounding pots. Fortunately for me, so many hands were intent on doing me damage that they managed to whack each other as well. A whirling, swirling mass of bods went typhooning toward the door, knocking over tables, bar stools, hysterical women, dinners, pictures on the walls, and all else in its path.

There wasn't a swinging door to that entrance, but it seemed as if there were when this teeming mass exited onto the sidewalks of New York. Suddenly, I was on the street, naked and alone, for all my attackers, having done God's work and plunged me into Outer Darkness, had now returned to the interior to congratulate each other and to relive each one's heroic moment in the battle against Communistic Mopery.

Outside, I was bedeviled by a new and unforeseen problem. Having locked the car and put the keys in the overcoat, there was aught I could do but retrieve the bloody thing, and how was I going to do that? Whilst cogitating this problem, still reasonably flushed and warm from the blood sport just finished, there were native New Yorkers making little detours around this large, naked, red-bearded man standing in the middle of the sidewalk, who seemed lost in thought on a frosty wintry eve. You could almost hear them saying, "Oh, look, there's another naked, bearded man lost in thought in the middle of winter on the sidewalks of New York."

Now my dilemma was, should I beseech and beg them for the return of the outer garment, or should I get belligerent and threaten resumption of hostilities? I was beginning to freeze and hadn't time for the former, so hostilities seemed to be the course. 'Twas the work of a mo' to open the door, duck the head in, and yell that if my coat wasn't forthcoming, I would come in and wave my wee-wee in their wives' faces. As it so happened, Myrtle was just inside the door, still holding the coat, apparently reliving the horror of seeing a nude man and losing a tip. When I reappeared, she sank slowly to the floor with a low moan; I nipped in and tried to liberate the coat, but by the living Jesus, it appeared as if rigor mortis had set in, her claws were clasped so tightly on the cloth. Pry and pray as I might, she wasn't letting go, so I lifted her and the coat and backed out into the street again. It now appearing as if a hostage situation had developed, the assorted mob that had assembled for a rapid deployment adopted a placatory demeanor.

"Don't hurt her! She's an innocent woman!" they called to me, as if I were holding a gun to her noggin. All I wanted was my coat, and fate, being kind, gave it back to me. The cold blast of air revived Myrtle, who let go and, not wanting to be seen in public with a man clad only in skin, fled back into the orifice in the wall posing as a restaurant. I got the keys out, walked to car, opened door, locked same, started car, and drove through and scattered the newly revived lynch mob, off to the safety of the cold-water flat in the village.

It should be known that in ancient times, the itinerant, warring, mercenary Celts always went into battle sans hides, armor, or any kind of covering, the theory being that the enemy would be totally confused by thousands of swaying peni and balls, there being nothing more invulnerable on the field of battle than a naked madman.

> The great Gaels of Ireland
> Are men that God made mad,
> For all their wars are merry,
> And all their songs are sad.

Some inquires re the absence of Magill on that night elicited the news that he'd had another encounter with the little black demons that gnaw at the soul of some of our more brilliant friends and cause the electrical-emotional-spiritual short that extinguishes all light for a time, and sometimes life itself, forever. So he was, if you will excuse the expression, in straitened circumstances in some upper-class loony bin, hence his being amongst those not present at my coming-out party. I held onto the hot rod until its registration expired; not being the owner, I couldn't renew it, so I returned the vehicle to the family.

There were quiet days occasionally, when I wouldn't quaff a lot. The bit of celebrity that had descended on my shoulders was most pleasant, but not a bit edible, nor could it be bartered for shoes, rent, or toilet paper. Therefore, I still had to appear at the theater and turn up at Clavin's for the money that was in it. As our old chum Buddha remarked, as he was downing a pint of stout, "Before enlightenment, ye will hew wood and carry water. And after enlightenment, ye will hew wood and carry water," a not-too-cheery prospect for one in search of constant excitement. But then, I didn't have to get into hard labor again, so I shouldn't complain.

I was fit, healthy, and young, with a vast panorama of life and lust ahead. Still, there were days when I was stuck with my own company, and all the interior demons seized the opportunity to remind me I was a loser, an idiot, lacking in decency and intelligence, and one day "they," the ubiquitous "they," would find out that I was from the slums of Limerick, that I'd failed everything except reading and writing in our school, Leamy's National School, known to us as the Leamy College of

Surgeons because the masters cut us up so much. In reality, the school was operating as a holding pen for potential convicts.

I failed the most basic examination, which was called the "Primary Certificate." People who were borderline retarded passed this one, but not I. Despite my omnivorous and avaricious reading of anything I could get my hands on, this testing of my capabilities resulted in my failing, and the resultant thumping I got from the master only caused more brain damage.

Diminishing returns was school for me: The more I returned, the more diminished I became. Yes, I was learning something, but no matter where you go, there you are, and you are always learning. If you, for example, drop your nether garments and hoist both cheeks of your arse into a sitting position on the top of a red-hot wood-burning stove, you will, I guarantee, become an instant expert on the subject of seared, scorched arses.

So it was for me at Leamy's. I learned about fear, terror, and foreboding. I learned what a useless lump of lard I was and how I would never amount to anything. "This is a vale of tears, you Kaffir, and you are here to suffer the consequences of the dirty doings of Adam and Eve, before you either head for Purgatory to suffer again, or, more likely, to the eternal suffering of Hell, where ye will be poked and jabbed with pitchforks, with your bollocks burning in an eternal, agonizing flame, these bollocks being the organs causing all the sin, and if any of ye think that the suffering Jesus would have the likes of ye in Heaven, put it out of yeer stupid noggins, for Christ would only have to remember his time on the Cross to know that looking at yeer dirty faces for a minute would be like an eternity on Calvary."

These are the ruminations I was subject to between the stage, the bar, and the bit of television. I have since found out that I was suffering from what is known in the psychobabble circle as "Low Self-esteem." Jesus! If only I'da known that at the time, I'da put a jack under it and raised it up.

THERE CAME A NIGHT WHEN a couple of chaps, Roland Martinez and Hal Kemp Jr.—another scion of sorts, whose pater had been a band leader in the thirties and forties—asked if I would meet them, as they had a business proposition to discuss with me. My watchword being "Sí!" to everything, of course, I agreed.

Roland was an extremely nervous man, constantly on the move, with tics and spasmodic gestures animating his entire corpus. Later, he took to chomping on toothpicks, and the devastation wrought on the rain forests by his consumption of wood cannot be measured.

Hal was a balding, chubby chap, concerned mainly with the chub, the thinning hair, and dipping his wick. In all the time I knew him, he searched for a remedy for the excess avoirdupois festooning his frame. A very gentle, good-humored fellow was Hal, and much loved by the ladies of all ages. "Ooooh," they would begin, as they hugged the lad. "You are sooo cuddly." Hal would agree, and he was fairly successful in persuading them that cuddling *sans culottes* was great fun, too.

Women are always wary of the lounge lizard Lothario, he of teeth and tan, but a roundish, pink, bespectacled chap could pose no danger.

His other quest was for the restoration of the hair to the head, and he rubbed everything into the scalp, from the urine of the pregnant woman to the saliva of the black bear, but still the hair fell, and more scalp showed, and no one loved him any the less because he had too much flesh and too little hair.

Their business proposition was as follows: They wanted to open a saloon on the East Side, and they wanted me to be a partner. They would name it "Malachy's," my having become a bit of a celebrity, and the money would flow in. For the huge sum of fifteen hundred dollars invested on my part, I would own a twenty-five percent share. Of course, I didn't have fifteen hundred dollars, nor a hope of accumulating it, either. Hal Jr. said that would not present any problem, as he would lend it to me, sans interest.

"Good enough," sez I, so the search for a suitable premi began, as did the tedious process of securing clearances for the license. The two hurdles in the way of uncorking a bottle and vending its spirituous contents were the A.B.C. and the S.L.A. These were not organizations devoted to education and terrorism, they were the Alcoholic Beverage Commission and the State Liquor Authority. These were the folk who demanded proof that you were of good character, an upstanding citizen, and that your money source was clean and free from any organized-crime patina. One sign of good citizenship was the flutter of crisp lettuce in the form of one-hundred-dollar bills slipped 'twixt the pages of applications attesting to our honesty and fierce devotion to God and country, and to our promises never to sell a vodka to a dying Communist, even if he promised to convert to capitalism, should he recover.

Those offices were run by hacks, hypocrites, and whores who, whilst accepting bribes to do what they were being paid to do, opening up their arseholes for the biggest pricks in the Mafia, deigned to pass judgment on innocent idiots like Martinez, Kemp, and myself.

It seemed the cleaner you were, the more trouble these agencies gave you. All over the city, you'd see these little *boites* springing up: black Formica bar, leather bar stools, spangled walls, fluorescent lights, and men-only staff—barmen and waiters togged out in white shirt, black bow tie, red form-fitting bellboy jackets, black hair, and lots of teeth. These were places patronized by elderly men of sallow complexion, in dark suits and wide-brimmed hats, with the flashy pinky ring, accompanied by sequined young blondes, who shrieked their laughter at every utterance, to show they were having a "wunnerful" time.

The exigencies of being a crime-free citizen has not yet been dealt with in literature. At that time—the fifties and sixties—you had to serve food and prove you had a kitchen. You had to have a table for every two feet of bar, or something like that. You could open twenty hours a day, 8 A.M. 'til 4 A.M. the next morning, except early Sunday morning, when you had to close at 3 A.M. and not reopen until 1 P.M., to allow people to attend church.

Surely.

You had to have soap in the lavatories, under penalty of law, and any law enforcer could snaffle your soap and issue a ticket for same, for which you actually had to go to court. Picture that. A portion of the criminal justice system had to be given over to the Case of the Missing Soap!

The lighting had to be of sufficient brightness to allow the reading of newspaper print. Indeed, I once answered a summons relating to this matter. In court I said I thought the light in the bar was sufficient, as I often transacted my business paperwork there. The surprisingly enlightened judge then called the cop, that paragon of literacy, to the stand, and asked him the name of the newspaper he had tried to read in the bar. The *Daily Mirror* was his reply. The judge said (1) he disapproved of the choice of reading material, and (2), if the man wanted to read, try the public library. Case dismissed.

Acquire enough of these violations, though they were nearly always dismissed, and the S.L.A. would request your presence at a hearing to determine your suitability as a licensee, operating on the theory that, where there is smoke, there is a little glowing conflagration lurking somewhere. Meanwhile, in the wide-open Mafia Formica fiefdoms, people were shot, garroted, poisoned, and stabbed, not to mention assaulted and robbed by the open-thighed ladies who rented their various orifi for a living. Yes, sir, soap missing from a lavatory in which you cannot read the *Mirror* is a serious criminal matter.

Nonetheless, having crossed various palms with silver, we did indeed secure a license to operate a premise between Sixty-third and Sixty-fourth Streets on Third Avenue, previously known as

"O'Rourke's." It had been a traditional New York Irish saloon, dark and old, the walls mortared with depression and despond. A bit of cream paint, a bit of red carpet on the floor, a bit of housecleaning, and we were ready for biz.

Hal Kemp installed a brightly lit fish tank, which added a nice touch to the place. On the floor waiting tables, in the kitchen cooking burgers, was Earl Walker, a jack-of-all-doings, who came with a pedigree as a hash slinger in a hamburger joint called "Rikers." I liked his briskness and his easy way with all kinds of people, so he became an important fixture at Malachy's.

I had neglected to mention to my then-current employer, Frank Clavin, that I was opening a competing premises five blocks away. I needed the continuing income and was a bit scared of the little man, as well, for he had what is known as an uncertain temper. So, there I was, caught between publicizing my new saloon to the congregation each night, and trying to keep it secret from El Toro Clavin and his largish Missus, Marylyn. The matter was resolved the day my partners hoisted a canopy outside the new saloon proclaiming to the world that this was to be Malachy's. It was seen and remarked on by various bods, and when I arrived for the evening duties at Clavin's, I was greeted with torrents of words, including "treachery," "robbery," "Judas," "Benedict and all the Arnolds," and something about being stabbed in the back.

Now, I'd made a somewhat cursory study of various economic systems, my reading encompassing John Locke, Adam Smith, and *Das Kapital* by K. Marx, and all of that stuff had given me an idea of what constitutes capitalism, a system that seems to operate in the U.S.A. I endeavored to explain to the Clavins that, operating on the theory that competition is essential to economic progress and good for it, I was doing them a favor by opening up next door. My point was not well taken and I was told to shut the fuck up and get the fuck out and forget about the fucking wages, as I couldn't ever hope to make up what I'd cost them.

I would miss the camaraderie of Clavin's, and my conscience was bothered by the deceitful way I'd behaved—I'd had a free hand there, with no restrictions on what I ate or drank, and Frank Clavin was far from stingy with the money—but ambition must be served, and Malachy's must be opened. As the soothsayers say, it came to pass that on the 12th day of May in the Year of our Lord 1958, the maidenhead of the first singles bar in the world was penetrated by the vanguard of the horny hordes trooping in so that they could say, "I was there in the beginning."

There may be some who will contradict me when I say that Malachy's was the first singles bar in the United States of America, if not in the world, but it was. It was a happy accident of luck and location, abetted by the Irish historical memory of the Law of Hospitality. Before St. Patrick came and ruined a perfectly decent society, Ireland was governed by traditional laws, called the "Brehon Laws," which covered everything: property, education, medicine, death, succession, inheritance, crime. These included the law of hospitality: not tradition, not rule, but *law* of hospitality. You would disgrace yourself, your family, and your tribe if perchance a stranger were strolling in your part of the country and he were allowed to pass your portals without being offered sustenance for the journey. And not just leavings of the table, but the best of what you had.

So, when the doors of Malachy's opened, it was incumbent on me to put up the Cead Mile Failté, pronounced "Kade Meela Fall-chee,"—"a hundred thousand welcomes to all."

And I meant to all. At that time, by tradition and by fear, females were not allowed at the bar proper. In Ireland, they had little cubicles known as "snugs," for ladies with a taste for the stuff, and in the famous Alvino's in London, a hangout for the Fleet Street crowd, women had to sit six feet from the bar. On Third Avenue in the Fifties, any seat would do as long as it was not a bar stool. That was tradition, and the fear part was that a titted person at a bar was there for one reason—to entice the poor, gullible males. This view of bar life was held by police, priests, and politicians, and it was so widespread that there was a general impression that it was the law of the land. Not so. I looked into the matter and found that man or woman, of legal age and sober, and in possession of legal currency, could plank the arse on the stool and order the refreshing nectar.

As it happened, around the corner at Lexington and Sixty-first Street was the Barbizon Hotel for Women, a large building throbbing with post-pubescent sexuality. We used to fantasize about being let loose in there for a week, and it was proposed and seconded and passed that every man among us would be willing to die at the end of the week if the wish were granted. Second best, and as was the case, the lovely young things learned that at Malachy's, the cute, new place around the corner, there were lots of cute guys and you could go there without a date or escort.

Among those guys were several young actors from Blighty who found the plenitude of pulchritude very much to their liking. Peter O'Toole, Richard Burton, and Alan Bates would stop by, as would Richard Harris, who had grown up in Limerick, not that we associated much there.

Dickie was from the part of Limerick where the gentry lived in the big houses with lawns, trees, shrubbery, and private lavatories within the house. The Harrises were well-to-do; they trooped off to private schools, were well shod, went en masse to the seaside for the yearly holiday season. They played tennis in gleaming whites, and the boys were always togged out nicely for the rugby game.

I only played one game against R.H. in Limerick. It was an Under Twenty final, the rule being that all players had to be under twenty years old at the beginning of the season. Harris and several members of his team were over twenty when we played—as a matter of fact, he was twenty-one on the very day of the game, October First, 1951. A Jesuit-trained team it was, so you'd expect diligence and honor from these laddies.

When I ran into Harris again, he told me he remembered every-

one on my team except me. As a Limerick laner—that's slum kid
to you—I was used to people not remembering me, especially Limerick aristocracy.

But now he, along with everyone else, would perform the only
civilized act they knew in a pub, which was to offer to buy me a
drink, and I, in turn, would reciprocate the civility by accepting.
There were times when I'd have a dozen whiskies lined up for attention. All of a sudden, I was King of the Castle, with all kinds of
guys punching me lightly on the shoulder, saying, "How ya doin',"
and the dainty young things telling me I was cute and had a cute
Irish brogue. I misunderstood that "cute" business for a while, as in
Ireland "cute" retains its original meaning of sly, cunning, tricky,
slippery, but the light soon dawned, and that only helped swell the
head a little more.

One of the liveliest of those dainty young things was named
Grace Kelly, and well named she was. The only problem was that
she was generally accompanied by ugly, thuggish, beetle-browed
types. This was cause for wonder, and rumors grew that she had a
fondness for men sharing a certain overstated attribute, not immediately apparent in a public place. And one wondered where Prince
Rainier was hanging his hat those nights.

A young would-be singer and actress named Barbra Streisand
would pop in, and Gig Young, a very talented light-comedy actor
of the day, with a huge capacity for alcohol, had a favorite table.
Like a lot of bods who do comedy for a living, there was a dark
side to Gig, but still, he was delightful company.

I was surrounded by the charming and the delightful. Michael
Thomas, a bright, friendly young chap, would discourse on anything
from the benefits of sea salt to the architecture of the Seagram
Building. He was married to Brooke Hayward, the scioness of Leland
Hayward and that extraordinary actress, Margaret Sullavan; he would
go on to be a financier, novelist, and columnist.

Willie Louglin, an heir to the Mellon millions, became a regular, as he made his nightly rounds: '21,' the Stork Club, Clarke's, Clavin's, and now Malachy's. I shared with him a story about the patriarch of his clan. When Thomas Mellon made his vast fortune, he returned to Ireland for a visit, bringing with him some of the grandchildren. After a tour and a look at the old ruined cottage from which he sprang, they repaired to a pub for a bit of lunch. At the bar was an old man, William Toner, who greeted Mellon warmly, saying they had been schoolmates. Mellon, teasing him for the amusement of his brood, said, "I remember you very well! Indeed, I remember your first pair of new boots."

"Indeed," sez Toner. "I remember you asking what they were."

Willie Louglin was the most prodigious reader I'd ever met. He brought in Lewis Lapham, now the editor of *Harper's*, then the first published author I had ever met. In a novel he had written, he had a fellow say to a girl, "I'll meet you at Malachy's." I was immortalized! That had me treading softly on the clouds with exhilaration. It didn't take much in those days.

History was made at a corner table where a talented young writer-composer-rugby player named David Hess wrote the songs "Speedy Gonzalez" and "All Shook Up." He wrote under the pen name of David Hill.

THERE WAS LITTLE THEN TO DISTURB MY EQUANIMITY. NO matter what I did, it was a thousand-league leg-up from Limerick, and wasn't I a grand fellow altogether, the object of attention, approval, praise, and love: a winner for once in my life and loving it.

Tom O'Malley booked me again several times for *The Tonight Show*, and again my modus operandi was to get fluthered on the sauce and let the stream of consciousness take over. I never answered Jack Paar's questions, just rambled on about anything that was in the head.

A peculiar incident occurred during one of my appearances. I was sitting on the couch, going on as per, when Jack Paar said, "There is a very famous actor in town to direct a play here, and he very much wants to meet you and offer you a part. Would you like to meet him?"

I gulped and nodded.

Paar's intro of the famous actor was eloquent, even effusive, and ended with, "Would you welcome an actor who has never given a bad performance: Burgess Meredith."

Meredith said he'd been in every saloon in New York searching for me and finally found out at P.J. Clarke's that I was on the show. He was directing a stage adaptation of Joyce's *Ulysses*, called *Ulysses in Nighttown*, and would I consider the part of stately, plump Buck Mulligan. The production was to star Zero Mostel and feature a big cast of the most illustrious theater names in the city. "Here's the script, and let me know what you think."

What did I think? Flattened I was by the flattery of being offered a part by a movie star, without a reading or an audition, but I had already agreed to appear in another production. I thanked him, and told him later of my previous engagement, as I didn't want to spoil the moment.

————

THE IRISH PLAYERS COMPANY, IN the persons of Helena Carroll and Dermot McNamara, had decided to revive that great play by John Millington Synge, *The Playboy of the Western World*. (If there are some who think it was Hugh Hefner coined the word, may God burn your bottom and send you back to school.) A lovely cast was assembled, with Dermot as the playboy, Helena as Pegeen Mike, a terrific English actress named Elspeth March as the Widow Quin, and Ronnie Bishop, an enormous man with a preference for same (men, that is) as Old Mahon. Liam Lenihan, an unyielding Marxist who'd been blacklisted in his profession of newspaperman, would play Michael James, and myself, the Sean Keogh of Kilakeen. A brilliant director named Joe Gisterak pulled the whole thing together despite my know-it-all arrogance and several artistic disputes and differences mediated by Ned Faye, our energetic stage manager, a man of wit, erudition, and savage humor.

There was a month or so of rehearsal at the Seven Arts Theater on Madison Avenue at Thirtieth Street, which later became the American Academy of Dramatic Arts. Upstairs, rehearsing another play, called *The Making of Moo*, was Carroll O'Connor, who was seething over the fact that Burgess Meredith had offered me a part on national T.V. that Carroll had already been cast in, and in which he did in fact appear. I gathered he blamed me for the affront.

Days of rehearsal and nights of bartending at Malachy's. Home to bed at about 6 in the morning, up again at 10:30 A.M., snoozing in the theater and listening to the glorious words of Synge as spoken by Dermot and Helena. Day after day, those soaring phrases were repeated, worked on, shouted, whispered, thrown, caressed, mangled, elevated, and never, never could damage be done, for the play is actorproof.

Christy

Let you wait to hear me talking 'til we are astray in Erris when Good Friday is by. Drinking a sup from a well and making mighty kisses with our wetted mouths or gaming in a gap of sunshine with yourself stretched back unto your necklace in the flowers of the earth.

Pegeen

I'd be nice, so is it?

Christy

If the mitred bishops seen you that time, they'd be the likes of the holy prophets. I'm thinking do be straining the bars of Paradise to lay eyes on the Lady Helen of Troy and she abroad, packing back and forth with a nosegay in her golden shawl.

Then came the big night, the opening, with the nerves, the trembling, the overwhelming terror, as poised at the entrance to the stage you say to yourself that you could have gotten yourself a nice cushy job cleaning out the men's room, but here you are, terrorized, and knowing that this audience has been imported specially for their capacity to hate you. A swift return to the Faith of our Fathers ensues, a desperate prayer flung Heavenward: "O, Lord, fill my empty head with the lines of John Millington Synge and I will sin no more, going or coming."

God, too busy having a pedicure, does not reply. Helena, Pegeen Mike, is onstage first, reading a list of what she will wear on the day she is to marry my character, Seaneen Keogh, a man she despises, and so he is sneered at all during the play. Ned, the stage manager, taps me on the shoulder and whispers, "Get set!" Thanks be to Jesus, the entrance calls for me to be trembling and terrified, as Seaneen has just heard a man moaning and it's possible there's a murderer loose. You get the first lines out even though you are blinded by the stage lights, and confidence returns, and you tell God, "It's O.K., I don't need your help, I can do it myself." One after another, the actors come on, in ones and clumps, and the play builds to a great crescendo, with Pegeen Mike at the door lamenting, "I've lost him, surely I've lost the only Playboy of the Western World!"

Lights out, silence, then tentative applause, then more applause. We come out for our curtain calls, cheers, whistles, bow after bow after bow, and then the curtain comes down, and we hug each other, all differences gone, all angers diffused, and we go upstairs for the opening-night party and wait for the reviews. Back then, the critics came and wrote their reviews on opening night, and the papers came out at 11:00, so the tension was fierce and the waiting almost heart-stopping.

Not to worry: the *Times*, the *Herald Tribune*, the *Post*, the *Mirror*, the *News*, the *Journal American*, and the *World Telegram* gave us the rave, and we were set for a long run. Our diligent, perfectionist director wasn't altogether pleased with the performance though, no matter what "the fucking reviews" said. There were loose ends to be woven back into the tapestry of the play, so we were going to rehearse again tomorrow. So much for theatrical triumphs. Rehearse we did.

One review in a tiny little Irish paper, the *Irish World*, which was owned by the O'Connor family, was by none other than the bould Carroll O'Connor, late of A. Bunker fame. C.O'C. blasted the production, the acting, the accents, the lighting, the ushers, and anything that needed to be blasted, with one exception. There is an Irish word for home-brewed spirits, *poitín*, which is pronounced "po'cheen," or "pot cheen," depending on which part of the Emerald Isle you are from. Carroll, being an expert on all things Celtic, took us to task because none of us knew, he said, how to pronounce this word, with the exception of a voice offstage, which belonged to a scholar named Peadar Noonan, who got effusive praise from C.O'C. for saying, sight unseen, this *poitín* word correctly. It did smack of the rancid grape, that review.

The pressures eased then after the opening, and all I had to do was go to the theater at around 7:30, do the performance, and cab it back to Malachy's, bringing in tow as many audience as would come, have some grub and grog, and start performing again, this time behind the bar.

Close up at four, at least lock the doors, huddle in the rear of the premi, drinking in the dark, and then off for a huge breakfast of fried eggs, bacon, home fries, muffins Anglaises slathered with butter, and we all liked apple pie à la ye olde mode, and off to the bed with that heavy load resting gently on a liquid foundation of whiskey and other still and distilled waters.

T HE DAYS BEING FREE, I NOW HAD TIME TO SLEEP, READ, and have the late lunch with other ne'er-do-wells. One day, talking with R.J. III, I mentioned the thought of moving out of the brother Frank's Village digs to midtown, whereupon Josh suggested sharing an apartment. A splendid idea, me thought, so a search for suitable quarters began, and a studio apartment on East Fifty-third Street was secured. Josh's father and mother supplied the furniture; beds, chairs, and a table, two teaspoons, the odd fork here and there, and a huge color television set, which, this being 1958, awed me no end. A cranky thing it was, as the colors kept slipping, but still a thing of wonder.

I had arrived as the East Side of Manhattan was beginning to pulsate with new life. The airlines now quartered their stewardesses there, the publishing houses had their share of prestigious-jobbed galley slaves, and aspiring actors thronged the acting schools. Real estate developers were slavering at the face hole at the thoughts of the money to be made from the thousands of young things pouring into the city, and other entrepreneurs saw the commercial prospects of singles bars, which began to proliferate. The East Side was the place to be. The ocean liners all left from the piers of the West Side, and the silly old joke, "The only time I go to the West Side is on my way to Europe" was repeated and guffawed at ad nauseam.

So, the East Side became an enlargement of the Barbizon Hotel for Women, and all rules and home behaviors were abandoned. Eisenhower was still in office, and Nixon was still hunting the Commies, so on the surface, America was still "respectable." If only the parents, who dwelt in suburban safety, knew what their daughters were up to—or down to—in the sinful city of Gotham, the streets would have been clogged with station wagons leaving town, filled with said daughters and their belongings, to save them from perdition.

————

ONE OF THE THINGS I read during my leisurely afternoons was a book of Josh's, *The Doors of Perception* by Aldous Huxley, containing a lot of stuff about spiritual travels under the influence of mushrooms, peyote, mescaline, and L.S.D. (which in the British Isles meant pounds, shillings, and pence, a coincidence causing no end of confusion to doddering old Brit judges who had been on the bench so long they would have disintegrated had they been moved). A chat with Joshua elicited the fact that he had ventured on one of these journeys, aye, several of them. I expressed an interest and, a week later, Josh produced some mescaline, a synthetic substance that had all the properties of peyote, he said.

"Lay it on me," sez I.

It was Monday, my night off from the theater, so I had plenty of time to go on a journey and return, or so I thought. After ingesting the powder and washing it down with the good water of New York, I lay back and closed the eyes. The first effect of this stuff was to sharpen all the senses to the point of the strangely absurd. We lived on the fourth floor of our building, yet I could hear every person walking on the street. The sound of the automobiles was almost unbearably loud, especially if the drivers were hitting the horn. I heard the ticking of a small wall clock in the kitchen, which was a goodish bit from my bed, and I smelt the bread in the bread box in the kitchen.

I was hugely enjoying all the sensations, which were not assaultive, but revelatory. I'd a certain sense of power, that I was in charge of the whole world, and could bend all to my will. The same way Hitler felt, without the stuff, I gather.

Josh said, "You look settled, so I'll leave you for now, but I'll be back to check on you." I bade him go, as if I were some high priest in a temple in Burma, seeing off some junior monk on an important mission.

Alone now, and retreating into the inner self, I had a look at my heart, the lungs, the kidneys, and the remains of the Chinese dinner in the stomach. Turned inward, I explored for a while, then opened the peepers and saw the room with all things familiar. Then, my attention was drawn to something that seemed to scuttle into the apartment from under the front door. Whatever it was, it skittered into the large closet, of which one of the sliding doors was open slightly. I was vaguely uneasy about this little intrusion, as I thought it might be a rat, but I concluded a rat couldn't possibly fit under a door, and attempted to forget about it.

Easier said than done. My attention kept going back to that slightly open closet door and to what might be in there. A tremor of fear took root, and then it began, subtly, almost imperceptibly: a pellucid tendril of greenish, slimy hue reached out and explored a sliver of floor, began to undulate, then withdrew into the closet. It came forth again with more tendrils, inhabited a fraction more of the floor with the undulation, and withdrew again. There accompanied it a vague miasma, which seemed to infect all it touched, and got bolder the more it infected. I do not know what it was, but it was between me and the door and there was no other way out, no escape.

I was being driven mad by the terror of it. The only other exit was a four-story drop from the window, there being no fire escape, and I wasn't so far gone as to attempt that.

In a short time, one half of the apartment had been touched and befouled by this evil, miasmatic demon. Immobilized on the bed with my arms around my knees, whimpering, I knew this was the devil and as I had abandoned my old Catholic God for the fleshpots, I didn't have anyone to pray to for help. The undulating thing reached the foot of my bed and I knew I was fodder, indeed the main course in this banquet; it was only a matter of time ere I was covered with slime and then ingested.

My ears picked up the sound of a key in the door, and in walked Josh. I wanted to scream at him to get out before he was consumed, but all I could manage was a grunt. He was unaware of the danger, it seemed; indeed, he was quite cheery. I'd been going through my hell for eight or so hours, and I couldn't understand how it was that he was sitting there in the armchair, unslimed, with no pellucid tendrils around his neck, chatting as if all were well with the world.

I finally blurted out what had happened, what was happening; that he was in the middle of a hell, and its keeper was getting ready to swallow him like a boa constrictor. He didn't believe me, for some reason.

Josh then set about helping me get over the terror, by giving me salted water to make me puke, and after a time I was convinced that we were not in immediate danger of fates worse than death, but aspects of that terrifying experience stayed with me for days. I could taste every ingredient in my food, perceiving whether it had been salted, peppered, or spiced by a chef or a cook. I could taste the bit of earth that might be clinging to a carrot or potato. The ears were sensitive to all the sounds of the earth, be they human, animal, or mechanical.

And the eyes, oh, yes, the eyes. Gradations of color, of light, of movement. Little creatures seemed to be doing little disappearing acts in my peripheral vision. I'd pretend not to see them and then swiftly turn the head to look, and they'd be gone—poof!

I returned to the play after taking an extra night off, using the pretext of a contaminated clam. (I don't particularly like clams, and if there's anything I can do to malign the character of this malignant mollusk, then 'tis done.) Onstage, the bright lights were as fascinating to me as the mobile suspended over a wee baby's crib. Instead of speaking my lines, I wanted to point out to my fellow actors the wonderful colorful patterns beaming forth.

Our producer thought I was suddenly and severely infected with that strange actorial syndrome known as The Method, which is manifested in actors by much staring, the deliberate slow scratching of the bollocks and the armpits, prefacing every utterance with the words, "Um, y'know," and then taking an agonizingly long time to get out the line.

I told my producer that I hadn't fallen victim to The Method but that ptomaine from the clam had the same effect on actors, hence my somnambulistic delivery. He told me to snap out of it and get on with the performance.

———

AFTER THE MATINEE AND EVENING performances on Sundays, 'twas our wont to repair to P.J. Clarke's for the repast between shows. It is possible that none of the sustenance we sought was in solid form, though on occasion a hamburger would appear and disappear. As the folks employed there, Charlie Clarke, Jim Ennis, and Frankie Ribondo, all knew we were engaged in entertaining the public, an eye was kept on us so that we didn't stay too late for half hour, which is the official time the actor must be at the theater in advance of curtain call. The stage manager announces "half hour," then "fifteen minutes," "five minutes," and "places," then "lights" and onstage you go.

There were times when we were all just a trifle too tiddly to give the sharp performance of the professional, not an honorable way to behave. People work a bit to acquire their share of the coin of the realm, and when they want to be entertained or engaged by the theatrical doings of the playwright and the actor, they ought to be given the best of what we entertainers can offer. Everyone has laughed at the exploits of Errol Flynn, John Barrymore, Brendan Behan, Dylan Thomas, Peter O'Toole, Richard Harris, and Richard Burton under the influence of J. Barleycorn, Esq., and it all seems to be glamorous and great fun. But, with the exceptions of Peter O'Toole and Richard Harris, all the above capped their exploits with interesting and delightful obituaries.

Anyway, we did our gargling on Sundays 'tween shows, and whilst we may have amused ourselves mightily, 'tis unsure the effect on an innocent and unsuspecting audience.

ONE EVENING, AT MALACHY'S, A STRANGELY ENERGETIC fellow approached me, stating he wished to speak with me. He had the hard, glittering eyes of that stranger to blinking, the professional lunatic.

"Prattle on!" I told him.

"Not here. Outside," he sez.

"What's wrong with here?"

"Too dangerous."

I told Earl the factotum that I was going outside for a mo' and should return shortly. Rule of thumb: Always, no matter what, get glittering-eyed folks out of the saloon as quickly as possible and without the use of force, which doesn't work, as they're usually impregnable to pain.

He stepped outside, motioning for me to move further down the street. A glance skyward elicited the presence of a full moon, and a silent "aha" from me.

My man, the unblinker, halted in the middle of the sidewalk and said, "Stop," which I did; then he dropped to his knees and took a piece of chalk out of his pocket and drew a circle around the size twelves that shod my feet. Upon resuming the vertical, he put his hands on my shoulders, grasped them firmly, fixed me with his gleaming orbs, and told me I was in grave danger. I was not to (a) stir out of the circle he had drawn, nor (b) reenter Malachy's under any circumstances, and off he strolled downtown.

New York City is a place of constant action and movement, so, with the exception of street dwellers, who sleep close to buildings, or leaflet hander-outers, no aimless loitering takes place in the middle of city sidewalks. I was struggling with two disparate feelings here, one being the fear that something was going to happen to me, the other that I was a complete ass for having listened to the madman who had just vacated the sidewalk.

A few people came by, so I bent down to tie a shoelace that didn't exist on my loafers. A couple of times, I took my longshore-man's union card out and studied it very carefully.

After about twenty minutes of dithering, I stepped out of the chalk circle and headed to Sixty-second Street, where there was a public phone. I rang the saloon, got Earl, and asked him to look around to see if there was a package or briefcase lurking in the vicinity of the bar, as I'd come up with the idea that the unblinker might have advertently left some kind of bomb. Earl did a swift reconnoiter of the premi and reported that the place was bereft of the unaccompanied package or briefcase.

The discreet man did not inquire the reason for my stepping outside and then calling in from the street, and I returned safely, limbs and toes intact.

Another jolly fellow, whose name was Ted, brought in a very beautiful young thing one night when I had the occasion to tend the bar and wait on tables. As does happen, a male does the peacock act when greeted by name by the owner of the establishment, and this case was no exception.

The lad then informed me, in a private mo', that he was very interested in bedding down this young thing, so would I do him a favor by secretly adding a shot of vodka to her Southern Comfort and ginger ale, and to give him a very light vodka and grapefruit juice, as he needed his wits about him for the seduction.

I agreed, of course, but in theory alone. I put no vodka in her drink—and very little Southern Comfort—and doubled the vodka up for Ted, and as soon as I saw he was taste-bud dead, I tripled it. In a few hours, Ted's head was falling to his chest, and his eyes were closing, while the beautiful young thing chattered away to me, finding my company congenial.

Ted went to sleep, and I put the B.Y.T. in a taxicab and sent her to her home. I let Ted sleep the Sleep of the Lust until closing time. Then I awakened him with the coffee, presented him with a huge bill, and told him that the B.Y.T. had drunk everything in sight and then left with a newspaper-seller. Fit was he to be shackled with chains, but feeling too guilty to question the inflated bill as I bundled him off into the night.

I was more successful than Ted with a few of the fem denizens of Malachy's, but they were brief encounters until one night a slim, pretty, vivacious young model type said "Hi," to me, then made an odd request: She shampooed her hair with beer to help thicken it, and could I give her a bottle for this purpose. If I had known the consequences of acceding to that request, I would have a different outlook on life's plain today. But, as I eventually found out, all my troubles invariably involved alcohol, whether it's beer lathered into the hair, or whiskey sucked into the system.

"I'll get an empty bottle for you from the kitchen," sez I, intending to fill it from the tap at the bar, and off into that place I went. I secured said bot, and turned to exit the kitchen. There she stood, smiling at me.

"Come here to me," sez I, putting the bottle on the cutting table, wrapping the tentacles about her slim bod, and pulling her to me. It was about as swift a coming-together of two bodies as ever I'd experienced, and was I enjoying it: all systems go, juices awakened, and ready to flow!

An annoyed "Excuse me" came from the general direction of the door, so we turned the orbs to observe a festering young man glaring at us. She coolly said to me, "Oh, this is my date, Tony. Or Teddy. Or something." Without looking his way, she added, "This is Malachy."

Wow! She knew my name. He wanted to know what was going on, and she said, "Nothing, really," except that he was free to leave, as *I* was going to see her home.

The seeing-home biz was news to me, but I seconded the motion, and off her date went, leaving us to resume the explorations. We went back to the bar and filled up the beer bottle, finally, at no charge. We chatted about that and about this; she told me her name was Linda Claire and that she had just moved into the neighborhood. She really liked Malachy's, and came here a lot. She was a fashion model, but lacked the necessary inches to be "high fashion."

"This is the first time I've understood you have to be tall to be high," sez I.

She seemed to think that silly remark was quite funny, and laughed a trifle too heartily.

Another few gargles, and I said, "Time to drop you off at your apartment." At her door, I asked if I could come up, she said O.K., so I stayed until the morning.

The place was sparsely furnished, and we slept on a mattress securely flattened on the floor. It was pleasant, in the morn. Fall it was, and the odd bird could be heard chirping as we sipped the caffeined draught of life, she puffing on the Pall Mall as we got to know less and less about each other, and chatted inanely about buggerall.

Here were two people who, just a few hours previous, were performing the old biblical cleaving act, flesh to flesh, and here we were now, fencing nervously in fear of getting to know each other.

But we got dressed and perambulated out into the September

sunshine, and indeed, God was in His Heaven, and all was right with the world.

Other days were like that, as were the nights. She told me she had made enough money to live on for now, and, in any case, her parents would always help her out. Inquiries about the parents were turned away. "I don't get along too well with them, and I don't particularly like them, so I don't want to talk about them."

It's a relatively free society in the right-of-association department, so that was fine with me.

I, on the other hand, harboring a full vat of shame, on account of the poverty and the low class of family I came from, generally concealed my background. With Linda, I was still not too forthcoming. I just let out the odd hint of well-to-do-ness and of learning that ran in the family. I wasn't about to let on about the retarded uncle on my mother's side who sold newspapers for a living, or divulge that the only job my mother had ever had was as a scullery maid in various locations, or that my father shagged off and left us to the height we grew.

I seized on some minor accomplishments of the members of the paternal side, though they lived far away from Limerick in the North of Ireland and barely knew my family except for the certainty that my mother was low-class.

My father's brother was in government service: I told her that but kept to myself that he was a bus driver and that, as a Catholic in that reformation-ridden part of Hibernia, he was damned lucky to have a job at all. One of the aunts had a small hotel, a B & B really, and two more of them were teachers, so I thought this might impress her.

Another aunt was a nun, and not only a nun, but a Mother Superior, Mother Mary Comgall of the Sisters of Mercy. Linda, not being of the Romish persuasion, did not seem impressed, and said, "That's nice."

We didn't dwell on the backgrounds, as the foreground needed attending.

ALL AROUND THE WORLD, THE BARDS AND THE POETS HERald the coming of spring. They wax rhapsodic about birds building nests and readying their little orifices for cock and all the robins. They yammer about lambs gamboling in the green swards, the crocus bullying its way through the snow, the buds popping out on the branches of bushes and trees, young lovers skipping hand-in-hand beside the babbling brook, just freed from the icy grip of winter, and a whole lot of old rubbish like that.

On the other hand, the New York poet has the muse of autumn. 'Tis then the city comes to life: The princes of commerce return to enliven the restaurants again, taxi drivers no longer have to murder each other for the fare, and the social season begins for the well-to-do: symphonies to be seen at, incomprehensible operas to yawn at, fashion shows to attend, hats to be bought, museums and exhibits to yelp over.

Then there is the United Nations, the opening of which fills

New York City with every class of people from all over this globe. You see robes that dazzle you, topped by turbans, burneese (plural of *burnoose*), kepis, sombreros, tams, fezzes, and so many other exotic head coverings that you wonder why we were given hair on the top of our heads at all.

The streets are clogged with kings, queens, ministers (prime and otherwise), jumped-up dictators, papal observers, and presidents, all on their way to somewhere, or coming from somewhere, but always getting in the natives' way.

Still, it's energetic and vital, and that year, 1958, was the year that the Irish Ambassador to the U.N. was elected president of the General Assembly. How proud were we Irish at this event! The exalted one was Freddie Boland, a genial and diplomatic man, with a great sense of humor and of the absurd. Ireland, this tiny nation, one-tenth the size of Texas, with one-sixth the population of California, was now the arbiter of disputes amongst first-, second-, and third-world countries.

Indeed, it was not that long ago that Ireland held the most humble third-world status, with the stinking arse of the British Lion sitting on her head. Ireland was the first oppressed nation to tweak the lion's tail and boot its eructating arse out, thereby leading the way for India, Africa, Palestine, and all the Arab nations to arise and rid themselves of the plague of chinless wonders who were sent out from England to make a bollocks of running their countries.

During the day, the Irish delegation were much sought after for conferences and consultations, but at night they came to Malachy's to play, and play they did. This playful crowd—comprised of Conor Cruise O'Brien, Eamon Kennedy, Maire McEntee (future wife of Conor Cruise O'B., back then an item not-too-public, as O'B. was then espoused to another lady, and how MM and O'B. did it, I do not know), Bob McDonagh, Sean Ronan, and Robin Fogarty—were the unstuffiest bunch you could ever hope to meet. They knew songs, epic poems, and bawdy stories, and weren't a bit shy of performing.

I took up with them, and was at U.N. headquarters so often that the security crowd thought I belonged to the delegation.

Nikita Khrushchev had then ascended to power in the Soviet Union, and, rambunctious man that he was, caused great tidal waves by denouncing his predecessor, José Stalin, for brutality and repression. There was a wave of hope that the Commies had seen the error of their ways and were about to present the national collective anus to Messrs. Nixon, McCarthy, and the self-loathing Roy Cohn, for a capitalist fucking. Not on your nellie! Good old Nicky K. thought the Commie system was workable, and all that was needed was the kindly, encouraging tap on the shoulder, rather than the unfriendly squeeze of the garrote.

On one occasion—which to this day I regret having missed but which I received a full accounting of later that night at Malachy's—during someone's speech, Nikita K. interrupted and Freddie Boland promptly informed him that he was Out of Order. "What do you mean, 'Out of Order'?" sez Nicky K. "Like a stuffed commode," sez Freddie the B. "I know not 'Out of Order,'" sez Nicky, getting a bit repetitious.

"According to Robert's Rules, the speaker who has the floor and the mike is the man of the mo'."

Nicky the Krush then averred that this Roberts fellow was a Running Dog of Capitalism and that his rules stemmed from a secret directive promulgated at hidden rendezvous in the Swiss Alps by a cabal of fat-lipped, cigar-smoking oppressors of the Workers of the World.

"Quite so," sez Freddie the Bo, "but you are still out of order," and gave the carved teak gavel, used to call together the assembled throngs of thugs, thieves, and other heads of state, a resounding whack, to emphasize the point.

Nikita wished with all his heart for that historic Russian point-emphasizer, the knout of the Cossack, but there being no knouts about, he removed one of his shoes (the left one, of course), and rapped smartly on the top of the escritoire in front of him, in rhythmic response to Freddie the B.'s challenge.

Freddie rat-tat-tatted with the gavel, and Nikita, at a slight disadvantage in trying to match the decibel level with the rubber heel on the shoe, acquitted himself quite well. Musical interludes of this nature are rare at U.N. sessions, especially drumming that utilizes everyday furnishings of the workplace. Freddie tapped, and Nikita whacked, and pretty soon the two disparate modes of drumming merged into a hypnotic rhythm that had the whole General Assembly swaying back and forth, shoulder to shoulder, at the point of clapping and giving thanks to God, Allah, Buddha, and Madalyn Murray O'Hair.

But lo and behold, in a tremendous, overwhelming victory for Atheistic Communism, Freddie's gavel broke, thereby ceding control of the rhythm to Nicky the K. and the Soviet Union. Seeing that he had triumphed, Nicky gave his trusty escritoire a few more hearty whacks, waved the victorious *in locum* sabot at the cheering masses, and put it back on his foot (left, that is). Freddie waved the splintered handle of the dead gavel, bowed to Nicky, and asked the mouth-agape speaker (who had been interrupted) to proceed with the speech on making the sands of the sea frugiferous.

Questions were asked why a Capitalist-made gavel gave out before a silly old, factory-made Commie shoe, but the results of the commission's investigation have never been published. Another Capitalist Conspiracy cover-up.

(Nicky K., having unearthed his previously unsuspected tympanic talents, later put them to use in a funereal dirge with lyrics in memoriam to the West, when he proclaimed, "We will bury you.")

That night we had a grand time at Malachy's in celebration of Nikita's shoe-in. All the usual Irish crew were there, getting boisterously fluthered. Linda was there at the bar, looking on, and a friend of mine, Sam Jaffe, a reporter for CBS, brought over the U.N. TASS Agency correspondent, an ebullient Muscovite by the name of Vladimir Bogachev, about as Irish a Russian as ever did the chochski. Fond of the neutral-grain spirits, Vladimir was also fond of the song, the story, and the freestyle, primitive dance, and we had more than our share of all.

Kenneth Tynan once said that the only people who can do Russian drama, outside of the Russians themselves, are the Irish. I presume that's because we are somewhat manic in the mood department. It's no bother to soar from the darkest depths to the mountaintop of delight, with the heart borne by all of that which is alive and singing. It's even less bother to swan-dive into the pits of despair and total hopelessness, with the realization, as Daniel Patrick Moynihan once sagely observed, that it's no use being Irish unless you know the world is eventually going to break your heart. Maybe it's the same with the citizens of the Steppes.

That night in the saloon, Irish and Russian spirits merged as they were consumed, in honor of the duel of the shoe and gavel.

WHAT HAD BEEN A REGULAR SEEING OF LINDA HAD NOW developed into a steady kind of thing that was rapidly approaching involvement. The current was taking me along, although, of course, I could have abandoned ship and swum for shore, but I was very scared of hurting her feelings, so I pretended I was enjoying this hurtling toward the falls.

I had planned to go to Ireland for Christmas to see the mother and the younger brother Alphie, and to renew acquaintance with all the old pals and do a little boasting and showing-off of my new-found fame and bit of affluence after six years in America.

A mention of this proposed familial venture to the current object of my fleshly desires caused an eruption of Vesuvian proportions, to wit:

"You're WHAT?"

"Um, going to Ireland."

"At Christmas, leaving me here by myself, with nothing to do, and nowhere to go? You are a selfish, inconsiderate bastard, with no thought for anyone but yourself at any time or any place."

I tried to interject that I was being considerate by going to see the mother and the bro, and she being of the Hebraic persuasion, I didn't think the celebration of Jesus' anniversary on this plane was of great, or indeed any, interest to her.

But the flow of verbal lava was too hot and too heavy for me to stem the tide of, so I let it flow 'til there was an exhausted stoppage. I then expounded on the strict moral climate then suffocating the Emerald Isle: how, if we went to the mother's house, it would be separate rooms and thin walls; how we would be watched for any attempt at the old slap and tickle, and any kind of fleshly contact would be nipped in the minute; and that, as a result, I would go starkers knowing she was in the next room and not being able to get at her.

"We could solve all that," sez she, "by getting married."

It hadn't occurred to me at all to entertain that bit of a notion, as I was only twenty-six, and I'd always looked on matrimony as an activity for fully grown and mentally developed adults, which far from was I. However, when presented with the "I do" unilateral demand, I said, "I will," and set in motion a matrimonial Juggernaut, which proceeded to flatten me and whose terrible consequences took many a year to recover from.

When affianced to another human, it's astonishing what comes to light. I learned the name of this young thing to whom I was about to pledge the lifelong troth was actually Louise Clara Wachsman. Her mother and father were divorced; the mother was remarried to Carl Friedlander, and the father, Bill Wachsman, domiciled in L.A., had had six or seven more ladies pledge their troth to him.

An astounding little fellow he was, the father, a designer of some sort of interiors, restaurants, I think, a fringe of white hair around the shining pate, a gap-toothed smile, and Chaplinesque feet, which only by sheer force of will operated in tandem with each other. Yet he nonetheless charmed a fair sampling of elderly, well-to-do widows.

I also learned that my soon-to-be life's companion had been wed before, to someone named Lance, in a Presbyterian ceremony; that she had converted to Christianity; and that, as a result, she still had a valid marriage in the eyes of a good many churches. Consequently, "they," the ubiquitous "they," would not allow us to marry in any of their more orthodox churches, so plans were made for the old civil ceremony at City Hall.

The mother had to be informed of the acquisition of a daughter-in-law and instructed that the bed be prepared for two bods for the hols, and the welcome mat laid out for the new bride. Making the decision to travel by ship, as the Cunard Lines were doing good business in the transatlantic passenger trade, I booked two one-way, first-class tickets, the port of Cobh to be the actual disembarkation spot, the place from which I left on June 12, 1952, tearfully, with a sense of desolation in my heart, feeling I would never see Ireland again.

Birth certificates, some finery, an engagement ring, a wedding ring, and a bit of a reception had to be organized, plus a place to live upon return from the honeymoon. There was no time, it seemed, for anything.

Josh Reynolds was to be the best man, and a young woman friend of Linda's, Ellen White, maid of honor, a function she had filled at Linda's previous marriage, a fact of which I was not aware.

Came the day, the City Clerk said, in a very high-pitched voice, "Do you, Louise . . . ?" and she said, "I do."

"Do you, Malachi . . . ?"

I said, "It's Malachy, and I also do," and dat was dat.

A small reception, then off to some hotel—kept secret for no good reason—dinner at some French restaurant, and desultory talk about who was and who was not at the reception. None of the parents were there: Her father was still charming old ladies in L.A., and her mother and stepfather were not invited due to Linda's lack of filial affection. My mother was in Limerick, and my father was probably still rising up in wrath and getting put in prison in Coventry for another cycle of thirty days for drunk and disorderly conduct and assaulting constables. The brother Frank did not attend the wedding on account of hostile salvos launched and threatened by his then fiancée, The War Department.

The conversation dried up, and the rather obvious thought struck me: "I've naught in common with this young woman. I like her enough, but, lo, the pitty-pat and the thumpety-thump of the heart is noticeably absent, and what were we going to talk about for the rest of our lives?"

THE NEXT MORNING, A TAXI TOOK US TO THE CUNARD Lines on the West Side Piers to board the *Saxonia* for the voyage. To my delight, I discovered the Irish U.N. delegation was traveling home for the Christmas holidays on the *Saxonia*, too.

There is a great sense of excitement and wonder at the seeing off of folks embarking on a sea voyage: the band playing, luggage and cargo being loaded, champagne parties all over the place, the little tugs tootling about, getting ready to push the behemoth liner into the Atlantic, emitting ship-shaking blasts from its horn. The huge hawsers are unloosed and hauled aboard, whistles, commands, and shouts go up, and the ship inches away from the pier. We wave to the folks on shore who've come to see us off, and we are away.

Then, the exploration of the interior: a roomy cabin with a view of the sea, library, dining rooms, cinema, and, of course, innumerable bars. It was a luxurious life then, with every need attended to, except, as we got out of sight of the land, a bit of a gale blew up and sent a lot of greenish-hued faces skittering to the ship's rails.

A swift stop at Halifax, Nova Scotia, and off we went again into the tumultuous seas. Yes, the Atlantic was stormy on my honeymoon, but, being a fairly good sailor, I wasn't stopped from the drinking with the Irish crowd. Though we didn't know it, Linda was pregnant, and between morning sickness and sea sickness, the poor thing knew no peace. I partied on, regardless.

There were some British naval types aboard—an admiral and some captains and commanders—and it was not long before they dropped their naval reserve and decided to join our jolly group.

First-class tradition called for the dinner garb for the evening meal: black tie, or, as P.G. Wodehouse described it, "the soup and fish." I'd wander with abandon to second class, to the crew's quarters, or wherever there was the sauce. The supply of beer was depleted on the third day out—or so we were told; I later found out that the crew had their own stores—so everyone perforce had to drink spirits, aperitifs, and wines. It didn't bother me: There wasn't one night I arrived at our cabin sober, with the new missus looking at me with those why-are-you-doing-this-to-me eyes. My response was, "There is, first, no sense or benefit to the world if both of us are miserable. Further, I grew up midst disease and death, with three siblings snatched to premature heavenly rest, and a dozen or so classmates and playmates coffined and slid 'neath the verdant sward, so mild indisposition, like sea sickness, suffered by the well-brought-up well-to-do evokes no sympathy from me. 'Smatter of fact, I have no toleration for illness in myself or others, unless it's fatal, but that hasn't happened to me yet, as far as I know. When you've grown up in a community where the hawking up of bloody tubercular phlegm, scabby, pus-filled eyes with warts and bursting boils decorating the skin is the daily norm, it's hard to pay attention to whining about coughs, colds, flus, and sea sickness."

Then, having dealt, I felt, with my responsibilities to the new wife by explaining myself, I would grandly concede, as I drifted off to sleep, "I suppose I could do with a bit more compassion for the other bod's pseudo-suffering."

————

ON THE LAST NIGHT OF the voyage, the *Saxonia* pulled into Cobh Harbor and dropped anchor a couple of miles from the town, as the water was not deep enough to dock there. The tender was scheduled to come out in the morning and ferry the Irish passengers to shore, then the ship would continue on to Southampton.

Conviviality and jollity were the order of the night. The drink flowed, the songs were sung once again, and the recitations were delivered as if never uttered before.

Bonds of eternal friendship were forged, and addresses exchanged, and promises to look each other up were made. It was loud and merry until, at 11 P.M., the barman's voice crested over the noise with the dread words of last call: "Time, Gentlemen, Please." We, of course, had a good laugh at this barman's whimsical humor. We soon found out that the man did not speak in jest. He refused all further orders of the sauce, because we were in Irish waters, proclaimed he, and local licensing laws must be obeyed.

An appeal was made. "In the name of the suffering Jesus, man, is it the way you think that the local Garda are going to commandeer a cutter and speed stealthily the two miles, board this craft, come in here, and arrest you for serving and us for drinking after hours?"

There was no stirring this stoic Brit. It was pointed out to this obdurate guardian of morality that, for eight hundred long and dark years, the Brits had slaughtered the Irish, ravished their women, and sold their children into slavery. They starved us during the potato failure in the 1840s, deprived us of due process of law and of government representation, and now you, great yahoo you, are going through a hypocritical motion of pretending to observe Irish law, depriving returning exiles of the welcoming drop. As well as that, you benighted eejit, Irish law has it that if you are a bona fide traveler that is more than three miles from home, you are entitled to refreshments for your journey.

The man said he didn't know about that, and his orders were to close down the pub.

Ignorance of the law is no excuse either for breaking it or observing it. This Thomistic appeal to the brain-scarred barman produced an uncomprehending stare and a repeat of the old refrain, "Time, Gentlemen, Please."

Conor O'Brien and Maire McEntee departed a bit too willingly, thought I, as did everyone else. Then I, seeing the battle was lost, decided to leave too.

But wait! The keys have gone missing! The liquor cabinets cannot be secured, the doors cannot be locked, the cash registers cannot be safely shut: a first-class emergency!

The Chief Purser was summoned, who proffered the opinion that one of the Irish crowd had snaffled the keys. I nosed around a bit on deck and approached Conor Cruise O'Brien, future special deputy to U.N. Secretary Dag Hammarskjöld, future Chancellor of the University of Ghana, future Minister of Posts and Telegraphs of Ireland, future occupant of the Albert Schweitzer Chair at N.Y.U., and obliquely asked if he knew anything about the whereabouts of the keys.

As is the wont of the Irishmen, who don't look at each other when speaking, he gazed intently into the dark waters of the harbor of Cobh and said he might perhaps know the location of said keys.

I thereupon ventured the query that if I could negotiate a reasonable supply of stuff from the Chief Purser to continue the night's celebrations, did he think the keys would be returned?

Still not looking at me, he nodded in what I took to be an affirmative.

Back to the purser went I, to impart the info that I had met someone who knew someone who had heard that the keys could be found if a sale of liquid refreshments could be negotiated.

"Oh, no," sez your man. "They must be returned, or else I'm going for THE PADRE," a threat that is supposed to strike terror into the heart of the priest-ridden Irish.

I informed him he was backing the wrong jockey in this ride, as the shower of shites that I represented was a collection of agnostics, apostates, lapsed Catholics, retired Catholics, and (as Brendan Gill termed himself) collapsed Catholics, "and, I Sir," sez I, "am an atheist, thank God. So there is no point in getting the man with the collar on backwards out of his celibate bed. But if you could see your way to selling me a few jars of the jar, then all our problems will be solved."

He reluctantly agreed, and pulled out the cardboard box for the dozen or so bottles needed for the night ahead. "And throw in a couple of cases of beer, too, while you're at it. And don't tell me you don't have any, because there's plenty down in the crew's quarters, ye cute hoor."

He glared at me, but complied, totting up the bill, which had all the appearances of Great Britain's national debt. "What's this?" sez I.

"The bill," sez he. He had charged me the regular old shore prices instead of the duty-free, to which we were accustomed on the high seas.

"Stuff this up your armpit," sez I.

"It's the law," he bleated.

"No duty-free, no keys. That's it," sez I.

He relented, and I said I'd return with news of the keys. O'Brien told me he had heard they were in the First Aid box on A Deck, and I passed that news on to the Chief Purser, who found them and finally got his beloved bar shut and locked for the night.

Away we went for a high party in the low sea.

It was as a boy of eleven in Limerick, Ireland, that I had my first serious drink, with my pal Jackie Adams, a man of the cloth these days. Jackie had pilfered some pounds from a little cache his brother had in a wee hole in the wall. Off with us to local pub, Bowles's, into a part reserved for women, a discreet spot with a door and a sliding panel, through which clawed hands could be seen taking whiskies and beers into the darkish confines, commonly called "the snug."

'Twas early in the day, so there were no women in the snug. Our eyes were barely at bar level, but if you were in possession of the coin of the realm, and were not armed with a howitzer, 'twas no trouble to order a couple of half pints of an alcoholic beverage known as "Bulmer's Cider," a potent brew that, if the memory has not been soddened by the sauce, was crushed out of the apples in County Tipperary. A crisp, tart sort of beverage, this cider was causing a John Wayne—like wince as it trickled past our taste buds, warming the tonsils, and easing its way into the bloodstream.

We finished the one, and rapped on the sliding panel for the refill.

We sat there acting like men, pretending to ourselves that this was something we did all the time, and all we needed was a couple of Meerschaum pipes emitting clouds of smoke to complete the picture of two wise men engaged in deep discussion on the condition of the world and things beyond. Of course, the impartial observer would have seen two small boys in short pants, snotty-nosed and scabby-kneed, with hair that might have been cut with a knife and fork, a bit on the dirty side, and wearing shoes with unsaved soles.

A great feeling of peace and contentment floated out of the heavens and wrapped itself around my being, softly and lovingly clothing me in spiritual finery and the understanding that I was the best boy in the whole wide world, and there wasn't anything I couldn't be or do in this life.

Adams cleared his throat and said that a half a pint of porter would go down well on top of the cider. I couldn't get over the sheer brilliance of Adams for this idea. I was struck silent by it, and all I could do was nod assent. He rapped on the sliding panel again, which now looked to me like the one in a confessional, and when the barman slid it back, I thought Jackie was going to say, "Bless me, Father, for I have sinned," and I had a fierce time stifling the cider giggles rising to the lips.

When we secured the two half pints, or "glasses," as they are known in Ireland, I told Jackie my thoughts on the confession deal, and we both nearly expired trying to contain our laughter. Then peace reigned again, and my euphoria began its spectral climb once more. What great stuff this was, and if a half pint could induce such power in a boy, wouldn't a pint do twice as much?

Adams agreed, and once more the benign barman/priest was called on, to serve us two pints of porter. More reverie, and no more talk. And when the two pints were mere foam in the bottom of the imperial pint glass, I rapped on the panel for our man's attention. I'd read somewhere in some English book of etiquette that it was all right to address the serving class, and, indeed, all one's social inferiors, with the sobriquet. "My good man." So, when our friendly padre slid open the panel once more, I addressed him expansively, with as much superiority as I could muster.

"My good man," sez I, "would you kindly refill our tankards with more of this refreshing brew?"

He looked at me as if he had just been bitten in the penis by a king cobra. I remembered and added a phrase I'd once heard a chinless wonder of an English officer use on a slow-witted enlisted man. "And hop to it, fellow," sez I.

Yer man turned the color of a Trinidad sunset, and I wasn't sure whether it was his gurgling or death rattles I was hearing, but the words were unmistakable: "Jasus Christ Almighty in Heaven above! 'My good man,' is it? If the two of ye don't hop out of this fecking pub, 'tis the way I'll be coming around to the door of that snug, and if I find it still being contaminated by the presence of two poxy, scabby-eyed, guttersniped Kaffirs from the dirtiest lanes of Limerick, I will drive the toes of my shoes so far up each of yeer arseholes, that I will be forced to wear ye as shoes until God calls me to account on the Judgment Day. Fuck off out of here!"

I worked to explain to this hostile chappie that he ought to know his place, and ought not to be speaking to his betters in that fashion. Adams, sensing the imminence of instant death for both of us, dragged me out the door and into the bright, sunlit St. Joseph's Street, and there we went into an hysterical, incoherent fit of laughter, staggering, falling, and clutching each other, to the amusement of passersby who were not aware that we were fluthered.

Jackie said we'd never give that pub our business again, a remark that caused more eruptions. We composed ourselves, and off with us to another pub on Henry Street, and again we did the cider routine, followed by the porter routine, and then we ordered a Baby Powers, a little bottle containing about three ounces of Irish whiskey, which we took carefully down by the river Shannon, and as the gulls swooped and squeaked, and the sun began its trek to Australia, we sampled the whiskey.

We fairly passed the bottle back and forth, as do the most practiced of street drinkers, and then new spiritual vistas were opened up for me. I was hypnotized by the flow of the water, and the gentle, insistent lapping sound against the dock wall. Then, as I closed my eyes, I felt myself being assumed into a higher place. Slowly, gently, exhilaratingly gently, I was being held up by some soft but powerful force as I moved among the clouds. The feeling of exhilaration grew 'til I was nearly exploding with joy, with the rapture of freedom from the poverty of the world.

I was singing from my heart, from my lungs, from every pore of my body, and my song became a paean for everything beautiful in the world of God's creation, and my song was an offering to the Most High, and, as He kept Himself invisible, I knew my offering had been accepted, so I soared again through the heavens, higher and higher, feeling finally that, should I go any further, I could not come back. With the greatest of reluctance, I returned to earth to find myself alone in the darkness on the dockside.

Once more, I was just a scabby-kneed, snotty-nosed Limerick laner, and still poor.

On the way home, I was thinking that whoever they are might erect a shrine where I had had my vision, like they did for the kids at Fatima and Lourdes.

In all my years of drinking, I never achieved the same euphoria again. The peak was always missing: It was either ahead of me, or behind me, but never quite there again.

———

WHEN WE TOOK THE TENDER to shore, Maire McEntee's father, who was a minister of something in De Valera's government, was harborside with several cars and drivers. I got my first taxpayer-paid ride in Ireland up to Limerick, the blighted city of my childhood. Lapsing into the wandering thought during that ride, I lazily asked myself what in Christ's name was I doing here in Ireland with a wife I hardly knew, going to visit a mother I didn't particularly like, in a city that filled me with alternate bouts of rage and nostalgia. I know I wanted to show off what an important man I'd become: a television talk-show guest star, an off-Broadway luminary, owner of the most popular saloon in New York, married to a beautiful girl from Park Avenue. In my opinion, there wasn't a party in New York City that was complete without my wit, my erudition, and my exuberance, not to mention my presence.

We arrived in Limerick and were dropped at the mother's council house, as public housing is called in Ireland. A bit of foresight on my part had secured the place for the mother and the two bros. I'd done a merit badge in the boy scouts on public health, and I knew the examiner was the doctor in charge of the whole public health biz in Limerick. Subsequently, I wrote to him from New York and told him that the mother and the two brothers, Mike and Alphie, were living in squalid conditions. A wave of his pen got her a very comfortable house with three bedrooms, a parlor, and kitchen cum dining room, and a bit of a garden in front and a bigger bit in the back, plus, wonder of wonders, a lavatory with bathtub inside the house itself.

The mother was glad to see me, but the set of her lips indicated a certain disapproval of the new daughter-in-law. A too-casual, rather obvious attempt to elicit information about Linda's religion, where we got married, and the name of the priest was met with my evasions.

Then came the poor old, shure, begorrah, close-to-the-grave, Irish mother act. She was about fifty-one then, but decided to act eighty. She pitched her voice into the high register of the ancient ritual of keening, as practiced by the women of Ireland mourning the dead: "Will ye not, in my declining years, ease the tortured mind of an old woman, tottering on the edge of the abyss of eternity, by getting yeerselves wed in the embracing arms of the Holy Mother Church? There's many a priest in this town would be glad to rescue ye from the furnaces of Hell that ye are condemned to fer living in sin, for a marriage not blessed by the Church is not blessed by God, and ye will have no luck, and every seed and breed of ye will wander in the darkness until yeer return to Rome!"

This, mind you, from a woman who had never heard of, not to mind read, the plays of John Millington Synge. My beak was agape at this flow of eloquence from the mother, and I almost acceded to the plea to seek out a priest and have the marriage religionized, but, of course, I couldn't. If Linda had remained Jewish, her previous marriage wouldn't have been considered valid by the One Holy Roman Catholic and Apostolic Church, to give it its full, self-bestowed title. But, no, she had to tear off and get herself baptized a Presbyterian ere she married the bedmate before me, and that baptism was valid, according to the Holy Mammy, the Church, as was, therefore, her marriage.

Odd how Jews, Hottentots, Muslims, and Tutsis didn't count in the lexicon of the to-be-saved, on account of not having had water dumped on the cranium, accompanied by the words, "I baptize thee, in the name of the Dad, the Son, and the Spook, etc." However, Linda, having chosen Presbyterianism over Limbo, had queered our chances for eternal bliss, at least in the eyes of my earthly mother. Now, there was a woman who had railed all her days against the Church for favoring the rich and ignoring the poor and for being interested only in power and money. Now, suddenly, the Church was the Way, the Life, the Truth, because I had chosen to marry outside its power base.

Memo to Thomas Wolfe: You can go home again, but don't be bringing Jewish Presbyterian wives with you, especially at Christmas.

What we didn't know then was that Linda was preggers with our firstborn, Siobhan. She thought she was having a residual sea-sickness hangover. We argued all the time, with the righteous me roaring at her: "Don't blame me! You knew what you were doing when you married me! You were the one who insisted on coming to Ireland with me, and now you are spoiling my fun and fucking up my holiday."

I booked tickets for us for a New Year's Eve dance thrown by the Young Munsters Rugby Football Club, a black-tie do. But come the night, she was too sick to go out, so I suggested I'd go by myself to the festivities.

Whereupon the portals of Hell blasted open, and roaring torrents of hellfire lava poured over me, leaving not a screed of my body, soul, mind, or my antecedents unscorched. If there was anything left unsaid by my honeymooning beloved, I do not recall it.

I still, however, attempted to don the soup and fish, but a swift grab by the weak and ailing wife, and I was left holding less than half a dress shirt with a cufflink in the sleeve, whilst Linda held slightly more than half, as she had the part with the studs and one cufflink.

At this point, the mother entered the bedroom in a great state of agitation, announcing she was firmly on my side in this war, always had been, and would be forever. Apparently, nobody had ever taken the trouble to inform her that, statistically, more police officers are killed intervening in domestic disputes than in any other arena of law enforcement.

Linda and self promptly became allies and told the woman who bore me to mind her own bloody business and not be interfering in ours. She beat the hasty retreat, leaving us like two collapsed balloons. Shirtless now, I conceded defeat and skipped the festivities, grumpily staying home.

Linda was well enough to go out the next night though, and we arrived home around midnight to find one of the martyred mothers of Ireland on her knees, scrubbing the kitchen floor, January First being her birthday, and I'd forgotten all about it.

There was the mother, lower lip quivering with self-pity, on a floor which had not welcomed a knee since my brother Mike did his imitation of Al Jolson singing "Mammy." It was so absurd and clichéd, and having had more than a few beakers of the spirits that cheer, I could only laugh, thereby ruining the tableau of Mater Dolorosa with Bucket, Brush, and Cloth.

The wife was shocked at my insensitivity, and the martyr was furious and flung a scrubbing brush at me, followed by a big bar of Lifebuoy soap, and a wet, soapy cloth, which hit me in the gob, shut off the laughter, and sent me scampering up the stairs, fleeing the wrath of an uncorked Joan of Arc.

'Twas time to move on. In winter, Limerick had all the charm of Siberia, and none of the winter sports, so it was to Dublin we hied: pubs, theaters, actors, merchants, barristers, conversation, and, most of all, the most savage gossip in all of Europe. Be a person deceased, or 'twixt life and death, the more elevated the personage— be it Joyce, St. Francis of Assisi, the President, Jesus, or a government minister; be they archbishops, nuns, or the bogtrotters who came from Cork and made a living by fleecing good Christian Dubliners— the more ferocious the flaying of the skin, the more satisfying the destruction of the character.

The woebegone missus sipped the beer while I downed the bottles and, as she liked her cigarettes, she wasn't too unhappy puffing and sipping.

Then it was off to London. More of the same, except that Linda ended up in Charing Cross Hospital, threatening a miscarriage. She was in one of those huge, old-fashioned workhouse-type wards, with about forty other people in beds around her. She'd been passing some blood, but the Brits saved the day, the wife, and my to-be daughter.

By now, the business partners in New York had decided I was away too long, and that it was time to stop the funding of my holiday honeymoon. I had cashed a number of checks in Limerick,

Dublin, and London, thinking that my partners were depositing the money in my account. They weren't, and there was a fluttering of bounced checks across the Atlantic, causing yelps of anguish from assorted friends and acquaintances who had vouched for my fiscal integrity with various banks. One furious fellow from Dublin tracked me down in London, howling about treachery, trust, and so forth, which is how I found out about the partners' decision to cut off the funds.

We had some pounds, but when it came time to check out of the hotel, there weren't enough to cover the tabulation, and no more readies being available, 'twas over with us to the U.S. Embassy, assuming they would be glad to fork out goodish quantities of quids so we could continue our honeymoon.

We were referred to some society for the Relief of Indigent Americans, where we were interviewed by two granite-visaged daughters of the British Empire, who clearly disapproved of the existence of Americans and Irishers.

After a lengthy interrogation, the ladies decided we were worthy of the sum of five pounds, which at that time might cover a dinner for two, with a goblet of vino, which is what the money was spent on.

I explained to the hotel that my funds were blocked in New York, but I would see to it that the bill would be paid in full after my return to the U.S.A. and consultation with my attorneys. Being, then, more innocent times, I was taken at my word.

Next was to get back to Ireland. It should be noted that I had booked only one way on the ship, not having the money for the return then on hand, but having instead great faith that it would miraculously appear. But that miracle was slow in coming, and we had now not even enough for return passage to Ireland. We hied ourselves to the railway station and got into a first-class carriage on a train bound for Holyhead, where the overnight ferry departs for Ireland.

I proceeded to convince the train conductor that our tickets had been mislaid. I had taken the precaution of ascertaining the first-class fare—of course, we always traveled first class when we couldn't afford steerage—so I was able to pop that piece of info when the canny conductor laid that query on me. (As noted before, specificity will often pass for veracity.) I gave him my name and address and told him, as I had the hotel, that the bill would be paid in full on our return to the U.S. He let us stay on the train.

The next hurdle was the ferry. We were referred to a clump of officials seated at a table off to the side. Ahead of us were three people, males all, claiming to have lost their tickets. They allowed one fellow to get on the ship and told the other two to come back when they had tickets.

My turn: "Gentlemen," said I, "I am aware that you have heard all the stories about lost tickets, stolen tickets, and torn tickets, and I do not have any unusual story, except my pregnant wife and myself seem to be without our tickets, and we are traveling first class, and you may be sure that when I get to Ireland, naturally all will be taken care of, as my funds are there, rather than in London."

It was high-fallutin' horseshite, but it worked, and we were not only ushered onboard, but were given a cabin, so there was no mixing with the peasantry and the laborers in lowly third class.

———

SO, IT WAS BACK TO Dublin and to borrowing the pounds to get the grub and the pint and what they so eloquently term in Dublin, "the ball of malt" ("whiskey" to you, sir or madam).

In the City of New York, among the Irish Catholic crowd, family members are defined and noted by their parish. For example: "Do you know Terry Moran?" "Ah, yes. He lives in Holy Name parish."

But in Ireland: "D'ye know Terry Moran?" "Ah, yes. He drinks in Eric Lynch's public house."

Every pub in Ireland has its fixtures, both human and crafted.

Indeed, the humans were more of a fixture. Like a lot of outsiders, which I had become, I was looking for colorful and brilliant characters in the dark recesses of the pubs, and if you stayed long enough in one of them, you'd find lonely, unwashed men, dark-clothed, dark-visaged, repeating age-old clichés with vehemence and passion, giving them the sheen of newly minted oral brilliance.

The wife was fascinated by the pub life, the low decibel level, the ritual of pulling the pint, the subtle nods with which Irish men communicate: the wee forward nod, to indicate another pint; the very little nod over the shoulder, to show what man ("yer man") they're talking about, who could be Pope, President, or Prime Minister, or, if recently in the news, Haile Selassie.

Irishmen don't look at each other when they speak—they are usually squinting at an imaginary ocean—and they do not like touching. One of the rarest sights in Irish communities is a glimpse of the palms of anybody's hands. It is likelier you will see a bared penis or a breast than a palm. The swiftest motion in Ireland is a handshake, because of its being a fleshly endeavor, and according to Jansenist dicta, it could be an occasion of sin.

Of course, there were also the elite joints: the Shelbourne Hotel, the Gresham Hotel, Nearys, and Davy Byrnes, which were lighter and brighter, a trifle noisier, and more expensive than the pubs we spent our days in. For after hours, there was Grooms Rooms, near the Gate Theatre, a hangout for judges, actors, writers, I.R.A. men, and the detectives who were paid to shadow them by government ministers. A grand place entirely.

The main product of Dublin at the time was talk. You met the friends for the drink and the chat, and then you'd make another appointment to meet them later for the drink and the chat, and groups would move from pub to pub, seeking each other out, absorbing the news and newness, ending up at Grooms after all the other places had tolled the sonorous "Time, Gentlemen, Please. If yez don't have homes to go to, yez can't stay here."

Drink, cigarettes, and talk, never ending. Did anyone work there? Bits of it for survival, if it couldn't be avoided. Underlying Irish insouciance is the knowledge that when Adam and Eve got turfed out of Eden, it was for sinning, and the punishment was, for Eve and all of womanhood, pain in childbirth and having to put up with dopey males sticking their wee-wees into them. For Adam and male-kind, it was tending the land, with thorns and thistles sticking in their hands, and pulling up frightful boulders to make the land arable. In other words, "work," earning your bread by the sweat of your brow.

The Irish said, "We didn't do it, for Christ's sake. We don't even know God, not to mind piss him off, so why should we work, when all our sins are before us?" So, as a general rule, you will find Irish workers leaning on shovels, facing the same way as the cows, or they will be on strike or in the pub. Being at work means confessing to having sinned. Lucky for the vacationing prodigal, the Irish are always ready to down tools or pens and enjoy a jorum.

Peremptory summonses were arriving and being forwarded to me, to essentially get my arse back to the job at Malachy's, as they had no intention of paying me until I returned. The classic rock-and-hard-place dilemma faced me: no money until I got back, no money to get back to get money. I'd run out of personal checks, so I was now creating my own out of oblong pieces of brown paper, which when vouched for were accepted and cashed. The sight of the fragile, pregnant Audrey Hepburn–like person that was Linda often helped soften the heart of a steely-eyed bank manager, as well.

At that time, it took two or three weeks for a check to clear, and I prayed I might get back ere the brown paper checks fluttered to the earth, especially as good friends were doing the vouching.

So I big-shotted my way around Dublin, begging, borrowing, and bouncing checks, a successful "big deal" from New York, buying drinks all 'round, and sweating whether I'd ever be able to get spouse and self out of Ireland. Then it was back to Limerick, to the mar-tyred mudder, who'd no idea of my dire financial condition.

I threw parties in my mother's little council house, with good food and booze "on tick," as they say. The old pals rallied 'round: Mickey Kenihan, Jackie O'Brien, Tony Gaffer O'Brien, Eamonn "Smacky" Tobin, Paddy and Alice Egan, and Ger South, whose brother Sean had just been killed in a raid on a police barracks in the North and who had had possibly the biggest funeral ever seen in Ireland. Sean Costelloe, our next-door neighbor, had written a lament for him.

Most Irish songs are paeans to defeat. Always outnumbered, always heroic, noble, and brave, our lads fought undaunted against the savage Sassenach, the Saxons, who, by treachery and weight of numbers did us in and crushed us. But then, had we been victorious early in our history, we would have produced masses of bookkeepers, brokers, and bankers, instead of poets, bards, writers, singers, and musicians, not to mention warriors of the field.

To make the good wine, it is necessary to crush the grapes, and the English crushed us Irish, hence the vintage wine of words:

> 'Twas on a dreary New Year's Day,
> As the shades of night came down
> A lorry load of volunteers
> Approached a border town.
> There were men from Dublin, and from Cork,
> Fermanagh and Tyrone,
> But the leader was a Limerick man,
> Sean South of Garryowen.

> As they moved along the street,
> Up to the barrack door,
> They scorned the danger they would meet
> The fate that lay in store.
> They were fightin' fer old Ireland's cause,
> To claim their very own,

And the foremost of that gallant band,
Was South of Garryowen.

But the sergeant foiled their daring plan,
He spied them through the door,
Then the Sten guns and the rifles,
A hail of death did pour,
And when that awful night was o'er,
Two men lay cold as stone.
There was one from near the Border,
And one from Garryowen.

No more he'll hear the seagull cry,
O'er the murmuring Shannon tide,
For he fell beneath the Northern sky,
Brave Hanlon at his side.
He has gone to join that gallant band,
Of Plunkett, Pearse, and Tone,
A martyr for old Ireland,
Sean South of Garryowen.

'Twas odd having a childhood friend who was now a national hero. It was like being on good terms with Patrick Henry.

———

IT WAS GER SOUTH WHO one night shared with me a half pint of poteen, a great illegal spirit, whose pronunciation had been an issue for one Carroll O'C., but whose consumption was currently not as easy to swallow as kissing the soft lips of the beloved. Though a highly intoxicating drink, it is slow to induce drunkenness. It seemed to awaken all the senses slowly, a spiritual stretching, if you will, the eyes gently orbing to the light, the lips parting in the kissing smile, the nose receiving the delicate aromas of life, the ears opening for the music of the air, the mind filled with great thoughts of breath-taking scope.

With that inside me, I couldn't sleep, so out with me into the fields near the house, where the Traveling People (tinkers to you) were grazing the donkeys, jennets, and horses. I selected one of the steeds to ride. However, he didn't select me, so a chase ensued, until I finally cornered him. But the silly equine thought he could escape by running at me.

There are moments during total inebriation when great clarity descends on a person, as it did then me, and the world moves in perfect slow motion, as did this charging horse. Remembering my rugby days, and the instructions for tackling—"Get your man around the forward leg, wrapping your arms tightly, and fall back, thus bringing him down"—I brought down my mount. (American footballers crash tackle, a fine technique if you're getting paid.)

I managed to soothe him with soft words, and got him to his feet. I rode him home, and parked him in my mother's kitchen, which did startle her somewhat when she came down in the morning. She ran to the neighbors next door and said there was a horse in the kitchen. Having gotten used to my presence and its consequences, their reaction was roughly the equivalent of, "Oh. And will it rain today, do'ya think?"

The horse was led out quietly and returned to freedom, and with a shovel the mudder took care of the evidence of the horse's kitchen reign. I awakened at noonish, bruised and sore, very muddied and bloodied, and more than a bit thirsty.

I kept very active on outside activities during the honeymoon, such as going to rugby games, drinking, going to dances, drinking, going to parties, drinking, going to pubs, and drinking, all with money I didn't have; but in Ireland, like the miracle of the loaves and fishes, where there is no money for food or rent, there are always the necessary funds for the gargle. As Brendan Behan said, to eat was an accomplishment; to get drunk was a victory.

Of course, the whirl of social activity kept me from communing with the missus, as she was apt to complain a bit about the lack of amenities, the perennial shortage of money, and question the how and when of getting back to the United States and hot showers.

The partners in New York, Roland and Hal, finally relented and booked the airline passage for us on Aer Lingus, on a propeller plane. There followed a bumpy twelve-hour journey, but it was one of relief to be returning home.

BACK IN NEW YORK, IT WAS MARCH, AND IT WAS BRIGHT and sunny, and it was green ghetto time again: St. Patrick's Day, with its "Shure and Begorrah Brigades," and the beer and bagels dyed disgusting shades of green.

The whole affair is run by a "comishee," composed of members of the Ancient Order of Hibernians, or "Hibernates," as I prefer to call them. Paul O'Dwyer, the great unabashed liberal, sez they are guided solely by the question, "Who can we keep out of this parade?" Consequently, my brother Frank remarked, "If you threw a bomb at this ghastly assemblage, you would wipe out the cream of Irish mediocrity."

The poor, benighted narrowbacks don't know the difference between a parade and a procession. There are no floats, no evidence of Irish culture, just militaristic kids with guns trying to act like soldiers, horrible, ersatz Irish music, and thousands of ma-faced micks, grimly plodding up the avenue in search of sin and wrongdoing in others, to the doting looks of yer Man, who, having condemned transvestites, homo-, and bi-sexuality, stands there on the steps of St. Patrick's Cathedral, in full ecclesiastic hypocrisy, clad in gorgeous red and basic black, with sashes, rings, jewelry, and Gucci slippers, all of which causes envy to surge in the everyday crossdresser, who hasn't the readies for such finery.

Joy is forbidden on that day, as it's an occasion of sin, but hypocrisy is the order of the day, as the sheep shaggers, pious adulterers, fornicators, swindlers, thieves, wife-whackers, pudpullers, and the divorced pound their righteous way north, practicing Catholics all, else you can't belong. No fags, queers, pansies, poofs, or fruits allowed—not even Gay Licks can get into the act. Yet, there I was, on that return from Ireland, hoping that it all would have changed, which, of course, it hadn't, and once more I got caught up in the green flow of bile honoring the foreigner who fucked Ireland up.

As a lark, the brother Frank and self and Tony Hendra, an ex-Benedictine monk of total Brit extraction—later an editor of the *National Lampoon*, actor, comedian, and wine critic for *New York* magazine—decided to march with the Limerick Men's Association. The bossman of this assemblage was a malevolent martinet named Geary, armed with a blackthorn stick, who had obviously studied the training manuals of the S.S. in detail.

Hendra's Brit accent was noted at once, and several burly chaps moved up close to him, in case he might read a proclamation of fealty to the Queen while en route.

As we marched, Geary came up behind Frank and ordered him to take his hands out of his pockets. Frank said, "I can't."

"Why not?" sez Führer Geary.

"I have pneumonia," sez Frank.

"Aha," sez Geary triumphantly, "ye shouldn't be marching if you have pneumonia," and switched his attention to me.

Due to the television appearances, I had garnered some attention from the spectators, who did the bit of waving and shouting to me. Naturally, I waved and shouted back.

"Stop that waving and shouting," sez Geary. "You are on parade! Keep your eyes front!"

It struck me that there was a certain negativity about that man. There came out of his thin-lipped face hole a series of "no's," "don'ts," "stops," "can'ts," "not-alloweds," "no-goes," "not-permitteds," "forbiddens," "prohibiteds," and "verbotens" in such a flow as to make one think that they could form their own procession up Fifth Avenue, without any help from we reprobates atall.

"In the name of the crucified Christ," sez I to him, "it is supposed to be a joyous day of celebration, and here you are, shillelagh in your hand, casting gloom on the day." This Unter-führer called over a panoply of police to fling us from the procession for disorderly conduct, a charge that couldn't be proven there and then, so they refused to remove us, and I continued on the hoof.

Had we been ejected, we would have joined an illustrious bunch of other rejects: Mike Quill, the greatest and most honest labor leader ever, who got the heave-ho in the 1950s, and then the gregarious, wildly funny Brendan Behan, a diabetic alcoholic (or was it the other way round?), was thought to be a potential disgrace, and thus was not admitted.

And, of course, years later I.L.G.O., the Irish Lesbian and Gay Organization, tried to march, but after one year, when they marched under the protective banner of Div. 9 of the Ancient Order of Hibernates, they weren't allowed to march again.

The year they did, a group of us decided to march with them in support. When our mob got in front of the reviewing stand, didn't the top-hatted, morning-coated Grand Viziers of the assemblage, as one person, turn their backs on a bunch of gay men.

"By God, sir," sez I to myself. "If yer man Freud was about the premises, wouldn't he have a word or two to say about turning the old arses toward the alleged perverts?"

But that was yet to happen, and it is with a certain sadness that I have to relate that I was never turfed out of the doleful do up the avenue.

THREE

DUBIOUS LUXURIES

I never thought of my mother and father as married, a thing that only happened to people in the newspaper or in the fillums. They were just the mam and the dad and nothing more. Of course they behaved as a typical Irish couple. There were no words of love ever exchanged in my hearing, nor did they ever hug, kiss, or let out any hint that they might like each other, not to mention have a flicker of passion. When the mother was angry at the man she referred to him as "your Pop," he on the other hand always said "your Mother this, your Mother that." They never went out together for a walk, nor did we get out anywhere as a family.

My mother loved the company of anyone, be it man, woman, dog, devil, or child, whilst the pater was a loner who disdained idle talk and gossip. I'd heard him say once that a married woman should never be seen in public without her children and that no working man should be observed carrying parcels or packages on the street.

They were polite enough to each other, and indeed they often shared a laugh at the doings of the neighbors. When he got the temporary job

and drank the pay, she'd call him a mad cruel bastard, and he'd say in
his Northern Ireland accent, "Ooh now, Ange, don't use such language
in front of the children," and for days there'd be silence between them,
until finally she would declare the truce by offering him a cup of tea.
It was no example for the growing lad, as it appeared that for them,
as for many other Irish Catholics, marriage was an occasion of sin, so
all outward appearances of it must be avoided.

———

'TWAS THE SPRING OF 1959, and I was twenty-eight, and life was
very peculiar for me as a married man. Every morning, I'd return to
this tiny apartment on First Avenue and Sixty-sixth Street, over an
old saloon, to find the same pregnant young thing in my bed. Sometimes fluthered, sometimes sober and weary, I'd push into bed beside
Linda, mutter "Good night," and sink into something akin to a
blackout. I do believe I was quite dotty in those days, as one night
I came home and found the spouse asleep, with the light still on.
She seemed to be smiling in her sleep, and I, in my sozzled state,
was convinced she was dreaming of some ex-lover, and worked myself into a huge tidal wave of rage, waking her up to my vicious
tirade of accusations because of her morphiatic infidelities.

The poor girl didn't know what in God's name I was yowling
about, and couldn't even remember her dream. I'm inclined to think
that this was the first rock to scrape the bow of our little ship of
marriage.

The brudder Frank was then engaged to the woman we knew as
The War Department. The outbreaks of hostilities were frequent,
so one night he came to stay at our apartment. Later, at around 2
A.M., there was an insistent banging on the door, which I opened to
find two gents in wide-brimmed hats, flashing F.B.I. badges. They
informed me they were looking for a naval deserter, and was he here?
"No, he is not."

"Who is here?"

"My brother Frank."

"We'd like to talk to him."

I awakened Frank so that the Hoover boys could have a look at him, bugger off and let us sleep.

"Aha," sez one of these agents, "Jesus Fernandez! Come with us!"

"I'm not Jesus Fernandez. I'm Frank McCourt."

"It's O.K.," sez the lad of the F.B.I. "We have you, and there is no getting out of it." They produced a blurred picture of Jesus and tried to make out that my mick brother had turned into a Hispanic naval deserter overnight.

As it happened, I recognized the picture as one of the many visitors to the gay chap next door. Being Irish, from a fifty–fifty tradition of heroism and treachery, I wasn't inclined to inform on the neighbor. I came close, but only to save the bro from the hold of a ship's dungeon. Fortunately, Frank had enough I.D. to prove his farness from naval desertion and to send the lads on their way.

Soon thereafter, to teach him a lesson, his War Department fiancée decided to marry someone else, rather rapidly, much to Frank's consternation. But she divorced the guy after about ten minutes and returned to wed Frank, a marriage that made the Thirty Years War seem like a mere squabble between friends.

In the meantime, brother Mike, who had been brung over by Frank and hied himself off to service in the U.S. Air Force, was now suitably discharged and in the market for gainful employment, so we trained him at Malachy's both as a barman and a drinker. A wonderful, insightful observer is Mike, of the eccentricities and peccadilloes of the human species, and the best storyteller you'd ever want to meet. But he is a moody man, too, and when the mood descended upon him, he was given to glowering at "assholes," as he would describe anyone of ambition, wealth, and social position.

One night around tennish, I was strolling from my apartment after dinner with the wife Linda, who had persuaded me to stay a bit late and have the dinner with her. 'Twas a clear night, with a splendid full moon stuck to the sky, smiling that inane smile betokening no understanding of the chaos and lunacy erupting all over this mad orb.

"Oh, oh," sez I to myself. "That accounts for my staying home for dinner, and now I wonder what the rest of the night will bring." There was no need to prolong the wonder. As I turned onto Third Avenue from Sixty-fourth Street, I perceived two figures locked in combat outside the portals of Malachy's. A more specific and detailed inspection revealed that both of the combatants were blood relatives of mine. In fact, they were my brothers, Frank and Michael. Mike was roaring drunk and in a towering rage, and upon my intervention, Mike turned not one but two bloodshot eyes on me, and, in his inimitable and most eloquent manner, proceeded to loose the full force of his inner rage on me.

Beginning with Adam and Eve, he verbally leapt through the ages, like a balletomaniacal mountain goat, holding me responsible for the Fall, the Plagues, the Wars, and all genetic defects, ending with the statement that I was the closest thing to an Englishman he had ever met.

Other upstanding Irishmen, like George Bernard Shaw, Oscar Wilde, and Samuel Beckett have been accused of being English, but it is still the vilest insult that can be offered a Hibernian, and coming from a brother made the cut immeasurably unkinder.

Needless to say, Mike soon resigned from Malachy's under pressure, and my partner Roland gave him a job at another venue, The Minute Tavern, where he attracted a coterie of the brilliantly demented, like Montgomery Clift, Sidney Chaplin, Orson Bean, and others. But that's another yarn, and Mike's, at that.

THE YEAR OF 1959 SLOWLY DRIFTED BY, WITH LINDA TRYing to conceal the bulging evidence of an approaching new citizen, vainly and in vain, and having to put up with the devil-may-care me, a man who felt shackled by husbandhood and terrified at the prospect of fatherhood.

Summer in New York City, with the high heat and humidity and yellow-tinged miasma befogging the streets and building tops is not a fit climate for any living thing, and there was something about then-mayor Robert Wagner's face and demeanor that seemed to indicate he was presiding over a morgue rather than a vibrant city.

The opposite was the governor of the state, Nelson Rockefeller, an irritatingly, indefatigably cheery kind of fucker, who behaved as if he were presiding over a nursery school and all that was needed to run the joint were cheerful songs and diaper changes.

So we endured the city during a hellish summer. I did get a television job that year, my first, and it was live—an adaptation of

Billy Budd, starring Don Murray and, originally, Jason Robards, but he left over artistic differences with the director, Robert Mulligan, and was replaced by Alfred Ryder. Joe Papp was the stage manager, or the equivalent thereof, and he got upset at my utter lack of professionalism. He complained angrily to my agent, Joan Scott, who, in turn, upbraided me for not being ready for call, not being made up, not being dressed, not being on time, and not being an actor.

What they didn't know was that I wasn't being unprofessional; I was suffering from the ravages of the twin demons, arrogance and ignorance. I was under the impression that the rules of the trade did not apply to me.

Nonetheless, it was exciting doing "live," as any thespian will tell you. At the wrap party, bods from other shows appeared. Roddy McDowall was there, and so was Kim Stanley, who was feuding with Eric Portman; they were all appearing in O'Neill's *Touch of the Poet*. Stanley and Portman despised each other, and the night of the wrap party, Portman, one of the most viciously funny gay men I'd ever encountered, insulted Ms. Stanley at a curtain call, and she whacked him across the beak just as the curtain rose for another bow. There is nothing like a feud on Broadway to get wonderfully vicious gossip going, and tickets selling, too.

The great Helen Hayes was in that cast, and blithely went about her business, ignoring the battles around her and quietly upstaging them all; while the others delivered their lines, she pretended to be dusting the furniture with an eye-catching snow-white cloth, which the audience couldn't help watching. This proves my contention that great acting is attributed to many people who have done nothing more than grow old, remain ambulatory, get vertical on a daily basis, remember a line or two.

Sardi's was the center for the Broadway stars, with its walls covered with Hirschfeld cartoons, and the illustrious Vincent presiding over his empire, always remembering the names of the elite. Jackets and ties, the old dress-code bogey, were required for the men in those days, so I rarely went there.

The rank and file of the biz hung out in Jim Downey's. Downey was very generous to the starving actor, and you could get a steak dinner with the baked spud and the veg for $2.65, and a grand piece of meat it was, too. 'Twas in Downey's I met Edward Mulhare, a man from the city of Cork, who replaced Rex Harrison in *My Fair Lady*, and went on to do *The Ghost and Mrs. Muir* on television. Begod, Sir, you'd never think the man was from Cork, atall, atall, with his impeccable manners and his Oxonian accent. But then, we have to recall that it was another Irishman who wrote *Pygmalion*, from which came *My Fair Lady*, so why not have an Irishman in the lead after all? Look what we've done for that leaden language!

The opening night party for Brendan Behan's play, *The Hostage*, his first on Broadway, was at Downey's, and what a triumphant night that was for the Irish. We awaited the reviews, as was the custom, but there was nary a bad one. Behan was not drinking that night, as his lovely wife, Beatrice, was with him, as well as his various relatives, and he was on best behavior.

Jackie Gleason was uproariously sozzled and trying to get Brendan to start on the sauce. People kept telling Gleason to lay off, but he persisted until he got so out of hand we had to eject The Great One onto the sidewalks of New York and lock the door behind him. It was a bizarre sight, watching him leaping and hopping like one of those balloons in the Macy's Thanksgiving Day Parade, shaking his pudgy fists, the face contorted with what we presumed were curses and imprecations flowing out of his face hole, as we could hear nothing with the door being closed.

He eventually faded away, and a very proper party simply wound down in a quietly joyful, sober way. 'Twas not long, though, before Brendan was on the piss again, leaping on the stage to the consternation of the actors and the delight of audiences and news reporters. 'Twas great fodder for the papers, and great business for the play, because people hoped to be there when Brendan did his bit. As it is, people who would have been around two and a half years old at the time tell me they were there once when the bould Brendan harangued the actors for mucking up his play.

There always seemed to be small, flashing demons darting around Brendan's head. When sober, he had a lovely, modulated, working-class Dubliner's manner of speech, and a not-quite-shy way with him—"uncertain," I think, would be the way to describe it. The Yahoos and the drink were omnipresent in his life, and it was hard for him to resist the adoration of the one and the taste of the other. He was a diabetic, subject to blackouts from lack of insulin and too much whiskey: a lovely man with a small body of work. When he died in 1964 at the age of forty-one, he was reputed to have said to the kindly nun who was mopping his fevered brow in the hospital: "May all your sons be bishops!"

AFTER MY ADVENTURES ABROAD, I HAD BEEN RECEIVED A trifle frostily by the partners upon my return to Malachy's. But being my charming and repentant self, and scared I'd be turfed out of a job with a wife and a new life on the way, I buckled down to the tedious life of the ersatz Irish saloonkeeper.

The most successful saloonkeepers in New York rarely drink. They turn up on time, can be counted on to stay the night, and are as unctuous as a full barrel of grease, the Irish ones, particularly. They compliment the women, remember men's names, and do a fair imitation of Pontius Pilate in the hand-mangling department. That's what I did for a while, until I got fed up with being hemmed in by places, people, sobriety, and propriety, and my demons invited me out again.

From my occasional contacts with the spouse, I perceived she seemed to be expanding in the belly area, and resigned to the fact of being married to a bachelor. There was many the night I wouldn't return to the marital bed, as there would be the bed of a nubile, adoring young thing to be tried for the resiliency of its springs, and whose walls needed acoustical testing.

I didn't feel deeply about these fleshly contacts, and it was understood there would be no commitment, due to my being a married man with a need for the outlets, or the inlets, for the Lust. And I would explain to anyone inclined to listen that, while I had engaged in infidelity, I had never been unfaithful, as I still loved Linda.

———

BACK IN IRELAND, THE MOTHER, Angela, was living in a new council house with the brother Alphie, and having a hard struggle because we three in the U.S. were neglectful about sending her money. Alphie, a very intelligent, well-read, and talented lad, was doing well in secondary school, the first one of the family to make it that far. Indeed, it is noted that the brother Frank was the only high school teacher in the New York school system not to have a high school diploma.

But Alphie made it, thus honoring himself and all the family, though he still lacked the necessities of life.

Frank had married his War Department and so was busy trying to keep from being slaughtered on the battlefield. Mike's black moods kept me at bay, his whole demeanor having become that of my father, which brought back the horrors, the loudness, and the embarrassment of the child at the lunatic antics of the out-of-control parent.

My father could skulk for days after an episode, but we had to face the world, schoolmates, playmates, and put up with the taunts, insults, and vicious jibes that children have patent rights to. Of course, I didn't make the connection at the time. All I knew was that I didn't like Mike's behavior when we were drinking.

Linda decided she was going to have the baby without anesthesia, but under hypnosis, a vogue of the time, so she found an obstetrician of Indian origin for this bit of a lark. The man sounded like a roadshow Svengali, with the earnest singsong intonations, and the certainty that the hypnosis was working well. After he thought he had brought the trance to fruition, he would leave the room to tend another "trancee." Thereupon, my mischievous spouse would open one of her eyes and inform me 'twasn't working, but she didn't want to make him feel bad.

"Look here," sez the suddenly responsible me, at one point in the proceedings, "this is no joke. Having a baby can be painful," but Linda laughed and said, "I can always get a shot."

"Righto," sez I.

Then came the day, September 1, 1959. The labor pains, the swift bundling together of clothing and toiletries down the stairs to the taxi on First Avenue, and off to the French Hospital, on Thirtieth Street and Eighth Avenue.

Hustle-bustle into the hospital bed, settling in, then the pains, and settle again. As anticipated, the hypnosis didn't work, and Linda got the painkiller.

I had hoped to be present at the birth, but in those unenlightened times, was absolutely not allowed, and if I had thoughts of storming the delivery room, they had some security folks standing by who would remove my bod from the premi, so I stayed out.

Then came the word that the baby had arrived—a girl, six and a half pounds, everything in place: ten fingers, ten toes, eyes in their sockets, one ear on either side of her head, a mouth directly under her nose, and the nose centered in the middle of the most beautiful face ever to meet the light of day.

As for all first-time daddies, it was a time of joyful tears, and a reassessment of the past life and a firm resolve to mend my ways and be a great father, a loving husband, and an upstanding citizen. After all, I was almost twenty-eight, and had, in my view, accomplished buggerall in that long life stretching behind me, and all I could think then was I had a great past ahead of me if I continued on my present road. So the resolutions were made, sworn to, and made sacred by the birth of my daughter, Siobhan (pronounced "Sheevawn") Elizabeth McCourt.

The first order of business was to leave Siobhan, the fragile little being of the lovely little lips, the wondrous eyes, the tiny waggily hands and feet, and the pale, wan Linda, who was in post-birth trauma and severe withdrawal from cigarettes and coffee, and head north to gather the chums for the celebratory grog. I handed out cigars, of course, and accepted every congratulatory drink proffered; of course, I got wildly sozzled, weaving my way around town from watering hole to watering hole, rising to new heights of intoxication at every stop, then slumping and beginning the quest again.

I never knew the object of my quest, but Linda and the little one did not see my face again for days.

WHEN LINDA ARRIVED HOME WITH LITTLE SIOBHAN, TO our tiny papier maché apartment, I felt joy and irritation in equal proportions. The odor of the used diaper hung in the air, and there was the need to feed a yowling infant every few hours, regardless of our need for sleep. We slept in the tiny living room, whilst Siobhan commanded the whole bedroom.

I think I put another nail in the marriage coffin when Linda told me she felt depressed and trapped in this domestic role. My brilliant response was to say I couldn't help her—it was something she'd have to handle herself, and off I'd go to the bars, leaving her to face the long nights by herself.

And, to keep the old pot boiling, I decided to invite my mother, Angela, and the brother Alphie over for the holidays. "Where will they stay?" sez Linda.

"Here, of course," sez I.

"It's too small," sez Linda.

"Are you making my family unwelcome? Besides, it's only for a few weeks. Surely, we can put up with that."

———

IT WAS ALL VERY FESTIVE when the mother and the brother Alphie arrived, just before Christmas, and we were prepared to suffer the overcrowding in our one-bedroom apartment. Linda and myself slept on a pull-out couch in the living room, and the mother slept on a small bed in the bedroom, with Alphie on the floor, whilst Siobhan slept in the crib.

But I neglected to inform the mother of the time limits on the stay, so she stayed and stayed and stayed, until birds were returning from their winter sojourns, while my mother still was not. My gentle hints about going back to Ireland were met with how lonely it was over there and how 'twas more pleasant here.

The woman who bore me had this romantic fantasy that America was a permanent party land, a fairyland, a place where work was incidental to the business of having a good time. The fact that I was in the saloon biz hobbing and nobbing with the gentry and the quality only illuminated her fantasies to the point of the absurd. Nothing would do her, only to park her not-insubstantial body in the confines of Malachy's and have her highballs—whiskey and ginger ale—and chat with all and sundered. The erudite sophisticated polished witty me was a bit embarrassed at the presence of the peasant mother, who wouldn't know a fish knife from a scimitar, but then people began to say how charming she was and how wise she was, and she was never averse to singing a song after a few jorums, to the delight of all, so my bit of shame abated somewhat. But still she stayed too long; like a barnacle on the hull, she was hard to dislodge.

Conjugal relations with Linda had ceased as, between tending to a young baby and the constant presence of the other bods, there was no time for such goings-on. Tensions rose and angers flared, but still the mother remained, and I took to coming home later and later until I was staying out altogether.

Finally, leaving the country seemed like a good idea, so I took Alphie on a rugby trip to Canada. On the way back, the immigration crowd told him his visa was good for only one entry, so they put him off our bus. He was returned to Montreal, where he had to stay for a year before being allowed back into the U.S.

The mother, though, had overstayed both her visa and her welcome, as any semblance of family life in our tiny apartment had disappeared, so upon my return I practically had to deport her myself, which I did, with the promise that I would bring her back for the following Christmas.

Then Linda announced she was again with child.

I, a grown man, said "How did that happen?" but larger quarters still had to be sought.

Linda's small trust fund, about ten thousand dollars, had finally been turned over to her with the birth of Siobhan; her mother and stepfather had refused to release it till then on the assumption that I was a fortune hunter. We moved to the West Side of Manhattan, Broadway and Ninety-third Street, a big, spacious place with a maid's room, so we got a maid and, with the last of the money, made a down payment on an eighty-five-acre farm, with two houses and a trout stream, and never stayed there once. I also bought a used Cadillac, which I proceeded to wreck while driving home drunk that same night, smashing into a Lincoln Continental going in the opposite direction, nearly killing the occupants.

———

Now we had a safe and secure apartment, with doormen and help, and I felt free to roam without remorse, guilt, or regrets, all duties as husband and father discharged. The trouble was that Linda did not see it that way, nor did she take to the life of a wife on deposit.

Show biz had ground largely to a halt, though I did get one job, a television drama, which, I believe, involved the first use of videotape on location. We shot it on a ship in Bayonne, New Jersey. 'Twas there I met Peter Falk for the first time, and Val Avery, a wonderful character actor.

I distinguished myself on this production by turning up too late to take the company bus, and having to get a very expensive taxi to Bayonne, arriving to the cheers and hoots of the assembled company. I thought I was being eccentric and colorful, but when you are costing a corporation money, you'd better watch out, 'cos the little blacklist cometh out, and you get on it.

It's an odd country, this U.S. of A. Corporations have exactly the same rights as a human being, but let the average punter assert that his body, the only equipment he has to live with and by, is becoming aged and less sharp, and the I.R.S. will say, "Come off it, Mac! No depreciation allowed for the body of man, even if it leaks the soul."

IT WAS THE END OF THE EISENHOWER ERA, AND VIETNAM
was still a "Where's that?" to most people, even though Spellman,
the Cardinal of Vaseline, Lord Dick of Trick Nixon, and that crowd
of thugs in Saigon were trying to get Ike to drop "the Bomb" on
Hanoi. The French had gotten their comeuppance at Dien Bien Phu
in '54, and yet the U.S. blundered in, trying to make up for lost
time in the colonialism department.

I knew this stuff vaguely, but it wasn't as important as the hedonistic pursuits of my daily life.

Linda trudged on, having to endure the heat of another summer
pregnant again, and take care of the infant Siobhan as well. I only
wanted to be around when the baby was smiling.

The 24th of August, 1960, was the day of Malachy William
McCourt's arrival on this planet, again at the French Hospital. Also
again, they wouldn't let me in to witness the birth of my firstborn
son. There was no hypnosis this time, just regular old knock-out-
the-pain stuff.

He was a lively lad, this Malachy William. He arrived with a great yell, I was told, and I know he didn't stop yelling for quite a long time again, clearly his father's son. Off I went for another celebration, sentimental and weepy about the new life that had come into mine, and I envisaged great prospects for my children. Drunken dreams of glory rampaged through the mind, as I strode from saloon to saloon, roaring through the walls—Frank has noted that I never seemed to use the doors—frightening bar owners, and delighting bartenders, because of the munificence of the tips.

'Twas about then the partners in Malachy's decided this laborer was not worthy of his hire, and the business could do very well without him. The partners offered me seven thousand dollars for my twenty percent of the biz, and they would pay me at the rate of a hundred dollars a week for seventy weeks, not much for a piece of the flourishing enterprise that bore my name. Even worse, I accepted these payments in post-dated checks and without interest.

I had swaggered around New York City, the bigshot owner of one of the most successful saloons in town, an actor and television personality, and now here I was, with a wife and two small children, despairing and despondent of ever working again, as I approached the ancient age of thirty.

Humiliating as it was, I got a job bartending at the behest of Joe Allen and John Cobb, at their popular spot at Seventy-third and Third. I had by now taken an intense dislike to the job of barman. I felt trapped, and subject to the beck and call of any and all idiots, fools, imbeciles, defectives, deviates, arseholes, and inferiors; the fatuous, the stupid, the moronic; all of whom seemed to seek me out and torment me with the aridity of their talk and the emptiness of their lives.

Day in and day out, I was raging within, and when someone gave me some pills, ostensibly to lose weight, that cloaked the rage with a kind of jittery euphoria. I took to them like a baby to the breast.

I was on the day shift, so I'd start with coffee, cream, honey, a dram of Hine cognac, and one of those little pills, and during the passing of the day, I'd keep the euphoric fire going with more drams of Hine.

I shifted to another John Cobb enterprise up the road on Third Avenue, but a small matter of neglecting to pay the rent led to an eviction. The marshals pulled everything out into the street, and when they crowbarred the bar itself off the floor, all the beer taps sent geysers of the amber stuff up to the ceiling, where it foamed and sudsed for a mo', ere returning to drench the bar wrenchers, leaving them smelling like an abandoned saloon.

A whirl around town to celebrate the loss of income was indicated. I staggered home the next morning at 3 or 4 A.M., and announced to the worried partner in matrimony that I had figured it all out. Due to my national prominence and great talents as an actor, I would hie my way to Hollywood and see which one of the studios or networks would meet my requirements. "Yeah," sez this doubting lady, "but, in the meantime, what are we going to do for money?"

"For God's sake, woman! Stop this negativity! Expunge it from your mind! Toss it into any of the four winds! Boot it out the door, for as soon as I land in Hollywood, vast fortunes will come tumbling in so quickly that we will be in need of professional bank tellers to count and keep track of it! Now, let us to bed."

I could see she didn't share my enthusiasm for this venture, but the ingestion of the pills and the alcohol had imbued me with certitude and a vision of the righteousness of my new economic and artistic crusade, which would ensure the well-being forevermore.

Two phone calls—to the father-in-law, Bill Wachsman, the flat-footed, diminutive Lothario of seven wives, to arrange to sleep on his couch, and to the airline, to arrange the cheap flight on the propeller plane, with donut and coffee—and off I went.

After F.I.L. Bill picked me up at the airport, I called Peter Falk, who put me in touch with Sandy Lieberson at William Morris, who in turn told me friend Richard Harris was in town, doing a remake of *Mutiny on the Bounty*, with Marlon Brando and Trevor Howard. A call to Harris brought an invitation to his home.

Harris was then married to the former Elizabeth Reese Williams, whose father was Lord Ogmore. She was preggers with their son Damien then, and very beautiful. 'Twas a lively household, with bodies coming and going all night and all day, and parties coupling at the drop of a cork. A very handy heated swimming pool helped the sobering-up process, and there was a nice little pool house complete with bed, where I often laid the head when the night got too advanced to be thinking of getting back to F.I.L.'s.

Despite hanging out with established bods in the biz, I still couldn't get an agent to represent me. I had no pictures, no résumés, no car—and not having a car in L.A. leaves you helpless as a baby, but between shanks mare and the laughable bus system, I managed to get around if I began my journey prior to the dawning of the day. Yet somehow I convinced myself I was nothing like your average, ordinary actor seeking work in Hollywood.

I finally got a job for a week on some silly series—I think it was called *Surfside Six*—a reprieve from total penury.

While I was off doing this show, Harris had to relinquish the rented house in Beverly Hills to the owners, two spinsters named Crumby, since their other house had been damaged in one of those California brush fires.

I didn't know Harris was out of there and now ensconced in the Bel-Air Hotel. So, on my return, I meandered up to the old house after the water holes had closed at 2 A.M., doffed the entire body-inhibiting clothing, donned a pair of water wings in case of sinkage, and in full, glorious nudity, hurled myself into the soothing, warm waters of the welcoming pool. A desultory attempt to swim was soon abandoned, and I just floated about in a semi-somnambulistic state.

My reverie was gratingly interrupted by the sound of a harsh voice, bellowing in *Wehrmacht* tones, "Outa da pool! Now!" I opened my eyes to see the pool ringed with what seemed to be a division of Hitler's troops in the highly polished jackboots. As my eyes traveled upward, I observed belts festooned with handcuffs, pouches, guns, and bullets, and the other mysterious items police lug around.

Further up the shiny button line, I saw grim, sunglassed, Aryan faces, fixed on me with fierce intensity. "Why?" sez I, tentatively, but when I saw some hands move in the direction of the holstered firearms, I decided I could wait for an answer to my query.

No longer nude, I was now naked, and I could see the contempt in the liplines of the assembled constabulary, as they viewed my shriveled three-piece set. They ordered me to put my hands up, which struck me as rather funny, so I tried a little whimsicality: "Would you like to search me?" sez I, thinking they would collapse laughing at the thought of searching a naked man.

"Shut the fuck up, you filthy flasher pervert," sez one of the grim jaws, in what struck me as a fine use of alliteration. I was going to compliment him on his language skills, when I was roughly grabbed and pushed toward the gate of the house.

I managed to grab a towel as we swept out of the pool confines, and off I was taken to durance vile, protesting I was a guest of Harris, etc.

At the stationhouse, I was booked for indecent exposure. It seems the Misses Crumby had been awakened in the middle of the night by the sound of a loud splash, and, upon looking out the window, observed a large, naked, bearded man floating in their pool. After a decent interval, they called the gendarmes.

I was also charged with criminal trespass and theft of the water wings. I was exasperated beyond endurance at this point, because every time I tried to explain my presence in that location, I was told to "Shudafuckup." I was roughly shoved into a cell. The mattress on the cot was covered with abstract stains, and had an aroma that did not involve Estee Lauder, and there were neither blankets nor sheets nor pillows for the weary felon to lay the pulsating cranium.

When a new shift came on, around 6 A.M., I finally got the ear of one of my captors, who got on the blower and ascertained that I was telling the truth about Richard Harris having rented the house and then moving out. This compassionate cop thereupon rang up Harris at the Bel Air Hotel and told him they had in custody a "Malarky McCord," who claimed to be a friend.

My chum Harris told the cop he had never heard of me and hung up, leaving my newly found champion livid with me for lying to him. That afternoon, Harris did swing by to bail me out, and he was very amused at the sight of me, lepping up and down outside the police station in the bright sunlight, clad only in a minuscule towel and still wearing the water wings.

I liked hanging out with Harris. He had an enormous capacity for whiskey, and sublime taste in wine and food, so he always set a gourmet table, complete with tastefully arranged flowers, candles, and service. He was a wild man in many ways, and if the facts of his many stories were fictitious, he nevertheless always wove a good tale.

————

I NEXT LANDED A JOB as a combination Brendan Behan and Dylan Thomas, in a film with Robert Mitchum and Shirley MacLaine. Harris was an old chum of Mitchum's, and told me to make myself known to him as a friend. A bit reluctant to approach the star, nevertheless, up with me to him, and I stuck out the paw and announced I was one Malachy McCourt, friend of Dickie Harris from Limerick.

A hearty greeting was extended by this Hollywood legend of sauce, pot, and evil, with an invitation to come and have a jar in his star's dressing quarters, as he had been holding a special brew for a special time and a special guest. "All is in conjunction now," sez he.

"Right," sez I, following along, as ordered.

In the quarters, the suave Robert unearthed a cache of quart bottles of Guinness—there seemed no end to them. Then he opened a bottle of Powers (Three Swallows brand), and poured two large beakers of same, and then expertly poured two pints of the wine of Ireland, and set them in front of us.

I averred it was a sight to gladden the eyes, the heart, and the internal organs of any decent man walking the earth this day.

"Stop the yap," sez the bould Mitchum, "and get it inside of you." He had done a few movies in Ireland, and therefore knew the lingo and how it could interfere with the quaffing.

It took very little time to mollify the tonsils with the water of life and the black-brew chaser. A few more gargles, and the surroundings got comfy and friendly, and we chatted about that and this, and he didn't seem to mind me repeating a yarn that one R. Harris had laid on us.

In the city of Dublin, within the confines of the actor's outpatient clinic, otherwise known as a pub, this long-gone, hallowed place named Groom's, there came an evening when the cast of the movie Harris and Mitchum were doing assembled at said haunt. Mitchum was a man able to hold his own in the talk department, even with the fierce competition yer likely to run into in Dublin. (Jasus! Wasn't it a well-known fact that Shaw left because of the competition?) Anyway, in the course of the evening, a butty little Dublin jackeen arrives under Mitchum's elbow, tugs it, and announces that his wife wants an autograph.

"Not now," says R. M.

"Why not," sez the little man.

"'Cos I said 'not now,'" sez Mitchum.

"Is it the way you tink you can come over here and act like Lord Muck, and refuse to sign your shagging name for a decent, hardworking little woman who is too shy to ask you herself? Who in the name of the suffering Jasus d'you tink you are?"

Mitchum sez, "Give it to me," signs the bit of paper, and resumes his yarn. The butty man takes it without a word of thanks and brings it back to his wife and friends at a table. When she looks at it, she lets out a strangled shriek, and faints. Her butty husband then takes a geek at the autograph and, in a flash, bounds toward Mitchum, whirls him with a classic uppercut, and knocks our movie hero unconscious.

What he had written on the grubby piece of paper was, "Fuck you, Kirk Douglas."

Mitchum did not affirm or deny the yarn, but he smiled.

There was a tap on the door. "Come in," sez the host. It was Frank Sinatra, who was on a break from filming *The Manchurian Can-*

didate next door. A quietish kind of fellow was the Hoboken lad, and a bit reluctant to tackle overflowing glasses of Powers and Guinness. It was hard to see him behind the pint, him being so bereft of flesh. They talked about things I knew nothing about, and I listened noddingly, trying to look as if I comprehended.

Sinatra left, and then came a series of knocks.

"Mr. Mitchum, you are needed on the set."

"Fuck off."

"Mr. Mitchum, the first assistant director here, Mr. Wise, says you are due on the set now."

"Fuck off!"

"But Mr. Mitchum..."

"FUCK OFF!"

Some more drinks, and he decided 'twas time to return to the vineyards and do the labor. We left his dressing room and headed toward the set. Almost there, he stopped. "Sing 'The Bold Fenian Men' for me," saith this grand actor, and together we sang:

> *As down by the glenside, I met an old woman,*
> *A plucking young nettles, she ne'er saw me coming,*
> *I listened awhile to the song she was humming,*
> *Glory, O Glory, O, to the bold Fenian Men.*
> *As I passed on my way, God be praised that I met her,*
> *Be life long or short, sure I'll never forget her,*
> *We may have great men, but we'll never have greater,*
> *Glory, O Glory, O, to the Bold Fenian Men!*

> *Some died in the glenside, some died midst the stranger,*
> *And wise men have said that their cause was a failure,*
> *But they loved dear old Ireland, and never feared danger,*
> *Glory, O Glory, O, to the bold Fenian Men!*

"QUIET ON THE SET, GODDAM IT!" came a very annoyed, stentorian voice. It was the first assistant director. He came over and told Mitchum to get to the set, and informed me that I was fired.

"Hold it! Hold it!" sez Mitchum. "If he's fired, so am I. Come," sez he to me, "let us get back and resume where we left off."

My ticker felt as if a large, mailed fist had grabbed it and was squeezing hard. "Fired from my first movie," was all I could think. "That's it for me in the fillums!"

Concealing the fear, the disappointment, the feeling of having made a first-class, ocean-going ass of myself, was difficult but necessary in the face of R. Mitchum's insouciance. He didn't care: 'twas just another job to him. He told me not to worry, as worry spoils drinking, and, sure enough, a summons came for me to go see the director, Robert Wise, "the giant of helmers," as *Variety* would say. He talked to me sternly about booze, hanging out with stars who had nothing to lose, about professionalism and punctuality, and he told me to get back on the set and behave myself. Mitchum then rehired himself and that was how *Two for the Seesaw* got made, and why it disappeared from view forever.

———

RICHARD HARRIS WAS FINISHING HIS tempestuous sojourn on the Bounty. He used to infuriate Brando by doing savage imitations of him and deriding his acting techniques. In one scene, Brando was supposed to strike him for his insubordination, but only gave him an effete little slap. Harris said, "Would you give me a good whack, for Christ's sake!"

Brando said he didn't think Harris could take it, and, besides, no one was going to tell him how to act. Or whack.

The encounter ended with Harris asking Brando for a kiss and stalking off the set. Some years later, Brando got his revenge by doing a superb imitation of Harris and his Limerick accent in *Missouri Breaks*.

In the end, Harris's part in *Mutiny on the Bounty* was cut to practically a walk-on. The night the film premiered, with the names Brando, Howard, and Harris above the title with star billings, Mitchum rang Harris in London to tell him his name was on everyone's lips.

"Oh gosh, golly, gee, wow," said the suddenly modest Harris. "I didn't know I was that good that everyone would be talking about me!"

"It's true," sez Mitchum. "They're all saying, 'Who the fuck is Richard Harris?'"

But, I leap ahead. To say good-bye to Hollywood, Harris was throwing a party in the Montecito Hotel, a somewhat tawdry place, patronized mostly by New York actors. Harris had moved in there after his wife Elizabeth had gone back to Blighty. He decreed that the theme of the party would be sadomasochism—he was a bit ahead of his time. A visit to the property shop at the studio, and a judicious handing over of quantities of dollars, secured a supply of whips, manacles, handcuffs, straitjackets, and executioners' masks, as well as some skulls and assorted body parts, and a supply of fake blood.

Harris spent an afternoon directing some bemused hotel staff on how to decorate a hotel suite to resemble a torture chamber and on how, precisely, to smear the walls with fake blood. The effect was completed by using big heavy candles as the only illumination.

The guests were not informed of the theme, so it was interesting enough to watch their faces as their eyes lit on the paraphernalia on the walls and chairs. Most tried to behave as if it were normal to stroll into a room that looked as if it were leased to the Spanish Inquisition, but try as they might, they couldn't resist staring at the stuff.

The average stay at this party seemed to be as long as a finger stays in a flame. Many, many people suddenly had emergencies at home, or other unforeseen appointments, so it was necessary for them to leave. Some diehards—and some possible potential S & M fans—stayed, and as the drinks relaxed them, the questions began. Harris regaled them with stories of orgies and other frightful goings-on, which, like a lot of his stories, bore no resemblance to the truth, but a good story well told is a good story well told.

Most of the parties I attended weren't quite so extreme. At one of these, I plunked myself down beside an elderly, somewhat dissolute-looking woman puffing away on a small cheroot. Thinking I was being kind to an old woman, I complimented her on being alluring and sexy. "I am having a most difficult time," I told her, "restraining myself from carrying you off in my arms to a gondola. If only such a craft could be found in L.A."

She fixed me with a rapt gaze, and appeared to be absorbing all I was babbling forth. When I had exhausted the flowery speech, I stopped, waiting for her to give vent to her gratitude that such a charming young man had taken the time to flatter her. Generous lad that I was, I added that a night in bed with her would satisfy my desire for eternal happiness.

If her tongue had been made of sandpaper, it couldn't have done me more damage. She ripped into me for being patronizing, insincere, and idiotic. She said that throughout her life, she had been complimented truthfully by the best, and, though my compliments were adequate, they were hurtful, as older women have enough trouble accepting aging, without some nitwit telling them they weren't.

Suitably chastened, I complimented her on her tongue-lashing abilities, which made her laugh, and we proceeded to have a great chat. That is, she asked me questions, and I responded at length. She did tell me that her name was Dorothy, and that she had "written some little things." We parted on the best of terms, and later I found out my new chum was Dorothy Parker. I regret we never met or talked again—until after she died.

The executor of the Parker estate was Paul O'Dwyer, a great, indomitable man of decency, compassion, and civil rights. The unclaimed urn of Dorothy's ashes ended up in his office in downtown

Manhattan, and one day, while visiting pal Paul, I asked to see it. There, for the first time in my life, I spoke to an urn full of ashes. I apologized for not knowing who she was, and for not having read the "little things" she had written, and then I bid her *au revoir*.

———

THE MISSUS WAS GETTING RESTIVE in N.Y.C., due to my prolonged absence and no funds in sight; the F.I.L. was getting restive at my prolonged occupation of his couch, as it was interfering with his dipping of the wick into wealthy widows.

The loving calls to the wife were not being fielded with any great enthusiasm or energy. Beyond the "How are yez?" and "How are the children?" there was a definite chill in the air.

Though I'd gotten a few jobs, I was mostly not working, and of the little money I earned, much less flew back to Linda. She was forced to drop the pride and ask the parents. They, in turn, battered her into insensibility with a barrage of "I told you so's."

Despite the financial exigencies, I was having a good time at parties, and the missus resented that. Here she was, up to her nostrils in the acrid stink of the dirty diaper and up to her knees in small children, and it was not at all surprising that my ill-advised recounting of my social leaping and divings were not great news to her.

Finally, after a long spell of no work, I reserved a seat once again on one of the donut-and-coffee twelve-hour specials for ninety-nine dollars, cadged from various friends and acquaintances.

THE AERIAL DONKEY CART ARRIVED AT IDLEWILD AIRPORT an hour late, and when I got to my door at Ninety-third and Broadway, it was after five. There was a perfunctory greeting from the beloved, who offered me her cheek instead of the lips for the welcoming kiss and slipped rapidly away from the all-too-fervid embrace.

Siobhan and Malachy, after a bit of getting used to me again, clambered all over me as if I were a great oak. There was a great fatigue upon me after that rickety flight, so I said to the cool spouse that I'd take a nap and then have a bite of food, and then, sez I, "You never know what might happen after the children are asleep."

When I awakened and came out to the living room, my brother Alphie was present with Linda. She said he had been staying there, as he had need of temporary quarters. I said that was fine. Then, she said we were going out for dinner, and she had invited Alphie along.

I tried to be amusing at the repast, but no success attended me there. Linda's ermined lips and plucked eyebrows looked like angry slashes in a carved mask. The brother was polite, and not realizing he was being used as a pawn in her fend-off-Malachy game. Finally, I said I'd collapse on the floor if I didn't get home to bed, but the woman said she thought we should go out on the town to celebrate my return.

I replied I was too weary, and, anyway, I thought the best way to celebrate was to get to bed.

No takers, so I rose and said, "I'm off to bed." I fell into it and into a deathlike sleep, from which I didn't awaken until the a.m. around nineish. Refreshed and in a good mood, I sought out my wife and, once again, she evaded the embrace, saying she was busy when I suggested a return to the bedroom.

"Is there a bite of food in the house?" sez I.

"What's here has been paid for by my parents," sez my former bedmate, frostily.

Fighting the rising fear in the heart of an approaching wreck, I said, "Could I have some?"

"Get it yourself."

"I see," sez I, not seeing, because I didn't want to see, and off I went to get dressed and think. I hadn't yet unpacked, so, in a simple action that changed my life, I picked up the suitcase and walked down the hall to the entrance door.

Linda came out and said, "I hope you know what you're doing."

"I don't," I said, and off I went into the day, not realizing that that was the last civilized exchange of words we would have for many a year.

I dawdled at the elevator, hoping she would come after me, then left.

The rest of that day was spent going through rage, remorse, contrition, sorrow, grief, questioning, soft sentimentality, nostalgia for what never was, belated paternal emotions, desire for revenge and, above all, self-pity.

The internal monologue ensued: "Who the fuck does she think she is anyway? I married her and gave her two children, an exciting life, the chance to meet all sorts of people. I took her to parties, and she basked in the glory of my fame, and that's the end of it for her: no social life, no more parties, no more fun, no more trips! She's stuck, and no one will ever have anything to do with her, as they'd be too afraid of me. How dare she leave me! Does she realize who I am? Everybody loves me except her, and she doesn't have any judgment anyway. She knew what she was getting into when she married me! She knew how I live and act, and that my life is un-shackled and unfettered, and it was her insisted on getting married, all because of one fucking trip to Ireland. She'll see! There are thoughtful loving women who understand me, and who won't be-grudge me having a bit of fun and a drink or two!"

A friend, John Cobb, always man of the moment for a huge coterie of needy lunatics, said I could stay at his pad, and not alone that: He gave me a job bartending in his place in the financial district.

I brooded all the subsequent days at my dismayed departure from the unwelcoming hearth and heart, talking to myself, sending tele-pathic messages to make it right, and drinking—petrol to the flames. A conflagration was inevitable, and one night, after ordering people to stay out of my way in various saloons, and being refused service in several others, I found myself on the street at about 2 A.M., bereft.

I stood for a while, and then a peace descended on me. I suddenly knew what to do. I would call her up, explain the whole thing, and straighten it all out. I found a phone and called.

"What do *you* want?" she sez.

"I'd like for us to work this thing out."

"There's no point. I don't love you anymore."

"What!"

"And I want a divorce."

I felt like I'd been plonked on the noggin with a halberd. Through my daze I heard her say, "I've talked to my parents' lawyers, and the separation is drawn up. All you have to do is sign, and we can begin the divorce." Every word she spoke was like another blow with the halberd, alternately smashing my skull and piercing my heart.

"You've been talking to lawyers!" I screamed. "Behind my back! You didn't even have the decency to tell me!"

"You knew our marriage was over," she said, and then my dime ran out, and we were cut off, as I'd no more change.

Roaring and whimpering like a wounded, blundering buffalo, I charged an off-duty taxi, whose driver tried to wave me off, but I succeeded in getting in and threatened his life if he didn't take me to Ninety-third and Broadway. The poor, terrified man begged me not to hurt him, and said he would take me anywhere, for free, if I'd leave when we got there.

We arrived at the building and I breezed past the doorman—I was a good enough actor to appear to be normal—got our spare key from over the door, and let myself in. I burst into the bedroom, switching on the lights, bellowing at the frightened woman, "No divorces, no separations!" and demanding she do her duty as a wife under Napoleonic Law.

I rampaged from there into the living room, where the brother was groggily getting up from the couch. I accused him of conspiring with my enemy. I went and got the maid, and informed the assembled group that anyone who wouldn't obey my laws was to get out, and get out now. They gathered up the petrified children, and fled over to the parents' place on Park Avenue, never to return, except to pick up cribs, clothes, and ties, and for the rest of that mad night, I wandered from room to room, speeching and orating to the furniture.

Of course, I'd gone totally bonkers. I'd reclaimed the home, but driven out the family that made it one. As the dawn came, I lay down, fully clothed, and wept myself to sleep.

———

THERE WAS MY DESCENT INTO slow, calculating lunacy then. I'd bartend during the day and, at night, fearful of going to the apartment that echoed emptily without human beings, I went on mad rounds of pubs, parties, and brawling. Barmen feared my coming, and I got the reputation of being a foul-mouthed lout and a danger to all. On the inside I was a mass of gray granite pain at all times, and I responded by lashing out to hurt anyone I could.

Immune to any physical pain, I fought with savagery, and bloodied all my opponents. I hopped from bed to bed with a variety of women, lying and deceiving, not knowing who they were, and certainly not caring if I ever saw them again.

Going into bars became an adventure again. I'd sit beside the biggest guy in the place, and no matter what he ordered, I'd remark, "Only fags drink that." Minutes later, the man would be on the floor, and I'd announce to the room that the guy had no sense of humor.

There was one night when I met up with the brother Frank, who was always the man of the big heart. He'd quietly comfort me and counsel me, but I wasn't about to hear him. That night, I happened to encounter him on my way to a party at someone's East Side apartment, and invited him to join me. After a few drinks, we took a cab there, and the elevator up. In the hallway outside the apartment was a group sitting in a circle, for what reason I do not know. I kicked over one of their drinks on the way in the door, threw a perfunctory "Sorry" over my shoulder, and joined the party, in full swing.

"Greetings," "Hellos," and "Good to see ya's" all floated my way, but there came the nagging feeling of something missing, and indeed there was: the brother Frank. Out to the hallway with me: no sign of him or the sitting circle. I went thundering down the four flights to the lobby, where a circle of yahoos was pummeling the bro, on his knees but still getting off a good punch or two.

I was in my element: A swift appraisal of the battlefield showed a ratio of five yahoos to one McCourt, who was battling bravely, dodging fists and shoes and boots, and unleashing the odd punch as best he could.

I dived in, and they turned to deal with a howling lunatic. Renewed by the reinforcement, Frank got to his feet and inflicted a fierce amount of damage on several of his cowardly attackers, and I did likewise, enough so that four of them fled, leaving only one of their number behind. Trapped he was, in a corner.

I fixed him with a look, as he cowered against the wall, whinging and mewling, with lips and limbs all trembling at the prospect of what was about to happen. I icily eyed him, and with all the cold malice in my heart, I plotted in slow motion what I was going to do to him. First, with my left hand, I would grasp his old school tie and collar. I would then kick him in the shin, and as his head jerked forward in pain, I would hit him in the right eye and smash him against the wall. I would then give him a knee in the area of the family jewels, then jerk him forward again, to smash him in the left eye, and after that I would slowly smash his nose, his teeth, and, of course, his lips, which seemed ideal for splitting.

All my thoughts were methodical and easy, but, as Robbie Burns says, "the best laid plans of mice and men gang aft agley." My plan to lay this thug out went badly agley. I grasped the tie, and delivered the kick, but instead of jerking forward, according to my plan, he jerked to the right, and instead of my fist connecting with his right peeper, it smashed into the wall, sending a surge of pain up the arm, so that I dropped the yahoo, who fled his place of execution.

Frank and I ended up at the emergency room, with no injury except my broken arm, which was put in a cast and made grist for another fanciful tale for Siobhan and Malachy.

I'd regularly arrive at Linda's new apartment on Fifth Avenue to pick them up for the Sunday visit with black eyes and a swollen nose, and regale these two little tykes with stories of my battles. After I'd taken them home in the evening, the terrible loneliness would descend and I'd hie myself to a bar and start the whole savage business again.

———

So it went—me surging about New York City at night, brawling, roaring, bellowing, raging, and tipping hugely, so that barmen were becoming schizophrenic. "Oh, Christ! Here comes McCourt! Trouble in the offing! But he does tip well, so fuck it, we will put up with him for a bit."

I'd go to P.J. Clarke's at first, but that stolid place put up with no nonsense. The Blarney Stone, a chain of Irish bars noted for a uniformly bleak decor, was for serious drinkers, and any rowdiness quickly ended with me being ejected. There were a couple of places that put up with me because of the bit of fame, but gradually the welcome mats were being pulled from the door.

I would on occasion contact Linda, and crawl and squirm and beg and plead for her to give me another chance, but all she would say was, "I don't love you anymore." From my mouth, then, would pour, "I will always love you, no matter what," and off I would go to the nearest drinking hole to prove my love by getting completely pie-eyed and having another fistfight.

One night I was holding forth at a bar, decanting a story of some dimension, complete with the necessary lurid language. Absolute rubbish, of course, as bar stories of sexual conquest usually are, but nevertheless the tale amused myself, as I couldn't wait to hear what I had to say. A tap on shoulder from behind interrupted the ribald tale. I swiveled on the bar stool, and came nose-to-nose with a laddie who saith, "My woman don't like the way you're talking."

"Tell her not to listen, then," sez I.

"Look, asshole," sez he, "The lady don't like the way you're talkin', so cuditout!"

I said, "If your woman was a lady, she wouldn't be listening to other people's conversations, and she would not be going out with an idiot like you!"

After a suitable pause, he invited me to join him outside.

"Be back in a tic," sez I to the chums. "Don't bother to get up, as this will be the work of a mo'." My opponent-to-be went ahead and, as I stepped through the front door, musing on my tactics, the night abruptly went completely and utterly dark. Sometime later, I was awakened by an ache in my jaw and, when I tried to open my eyes, all I could see was a reddish haze through the left one, and pinpricks of light coming through the gauze covering the right.

I was in New York Hospital, and a Peruvian surgeon was trying to correct severe damage resulting from a well-aimed Italian shoe, which I gather had popped the unsmiling Irish eye. It took nine stitches under the lower lid. The surgeon told me the tear duct had been damaged beyond repair and in later years I would have trouble with tearing.

I wouldn't have to wait to have trouble with tears. I'd get to bed many a night crying in drunken self-pity, and I'd talk to God and tell him, "Listen, You. Can You get Your arse up to Fifth Avenue and tell that woman she has to love me again? If You do that, I'll return to the Church and become a shining example to all. I'll raise the children as Catholics, and I'll get Linda to convert. Now what do You say to that?"

No answer.

Then a mad bellow, "Did you hear me, God? I'm talking to you, you old Fucker, and why don't you answer me? At least give me a sign that my request is on the calendar!"

Nothing. Silence.

When I was growing up in Limerick, my ambition was to come to America and become a convict, because in prison I'd have shoes, a bed to myself, with sheets that no little brothers had pissed on. There'd be no lice or fleas, and there'd be showers all the year round, and I wouldn't have to wait for the summer to wash the whole body. They would give me food several times a day, and a tin cup to bang on the bars, and we would talk out of the sides of our mouths, plotting escapes and beating up brutal wardens, and I'd have a number all to myself, and there would be a prison library, where I could read to my heart's content, and if all went well, I'd get to die bravely in the electric chair after the grandest last meal a dying man could hope for. Maybe I'd meet James Cagney, Spencer Tracy, George Raft, Humphrey Bogart, and Brian Donleavy, and we'd all riot together and the governor would come and see how rotten we were being treated, and he'd reform the whole system, and I'd get to marry his beautiful daughter and be put in charge of the whole works.

It's different from the movies, real life is.

———

CAME THE FRIDAY EVENING I took the visit to Fifth Avenue into my own hands, after a night of drinking at the Men's Bar at the Biltmore. I was drinking gin martinis that eve and, in a spirit of childish rebellion, and against all the rules of the house, I bellowed every dirty ditty I could think of, and if I couldn't think of them, I composed them on the spot. After several hours of raucous concert, it occurred to me to phone the wife.

The maid answered the phone and said that Mrs. McCourt was out.

"Out where?" I roared. She said she didn't know.

I accused the poor woman of lying, and of neglecting my children, and of things she'd probably never heard of, let alone done. I then returned to the bar to continue my rantings. After another couple of hours, as the clock showed the approaching hour of midnight, I phoned the spouse again, and again she was amongst those not present, which led to another wave of verbal abuse from my mouth. All sense departed me, and I left the Biltmore, leapt into a taxi, and headed for the bode of the estranged spouse on Fifth Avenue.

I have no memory of how I got past the uniformed majordomos at the portals of this building, but get past them I did. I rang the apartment bell, and the maid asked from the other side of the door who it was. I roared at her that it was me and to open up the fucking door. Of course, the poor, terrified thing refused, and I found myself gently tapping on the door with a handy oak chair from the lobby.

After the chair was smashed to smithereens, leaving the door still intact, I sat down on the floor to plot my next move. In a fit of drunken cunning, I figured out that the maid would have rung the spouse's parents, and that perhaps the stepfather was on his way up, so I kept quiet for the decent interval and then rang the doorbell. When the maid asked, "Who is it?" I said I was Mr. Friedlander.

"Thank the Lord," sez she, as she unbolted the door and ad-mitted one raving madman. I pushed the little woman out the door and locked same. Siobhan and Malachy were in their respective cribs, and I made sure they were asleep before I started on my search for evidence of the wife's involvements with other men. I went through drawers, cupboards, and closets, but found nothing but some old photographs of happier days, which I proceeded to tear in two when-ever there was the picture of us together. I went on a systematic rampage in the bedroom. I removed all the drawers, and dumped out the clothing. I emptied essences, perfumes, creams, and lotions all over the floor. I removed anything on the wall, tore anything I could to shreds, jumped up and down on a guitar, and tore off the Venetian blinds.

After I'd done the job on the bedroom, I decided to do the living room. The children seemed to sleep through all this high-decibel mayhem, and I kept checking to make sure, as I didn't want them to think I would do them any harm.

I was surveying the living room, preparatory to kicking in the television set, when the door was suddenly opened, and I was buried under the charge of a heavy blue brigade, an assortment of N.Y.P.D. lads, followed by a distraught wife, a determined stepfather, and a very angry maid, shouting "Check the children! Check the children!"

In very little time, I was handcuffed and ordered to keep lying face down on the floor. When it was ascertained the children were unharmed, I was pushed out the door into the elevator, and out into ye olde paddy wagon, and off we went to the Twenty-third Precinct, where I was lodged in a cell with a transvestite, arrested for trying to sell his bod to an undercover cop. The transvestite lad complained bitterly about not being allowed to dress as he liked, and the un-fairness of a system where you can sell everything but yourself.

I sympathized with him, and thought it a perfect demonstration of how hypocritical is the capitalistic system. That set me off on a filibuster, wherein just about every thought I ever had was mentioned and every speech I knew was summoned. Lincoln at Gettysburg? Too short for my purposes. Songs, poems, speeches, orations, bits of drama, quotations, demands for justice for transvestites and the working class, an end to the right of women to walk out on marriages, no more immediate custody for mothers, even if the father had no place to live of his own and was an alcoholic, and other such demands and declamations flowed from my cell in a mad gin-fueled rant, with no sign of the gauge pointing to empty.

Our Laddie of the Cross-Dressing, bludgeoned by my heavy speech, put the cups of his brassiere over his ears and shrank into a corner, whimpering. Shifts of the boys in blue came to the cell to be entertained and have a bit of a giggle at my expense.

Finally, myself and the cellmate were shackled together and transported downtown for the arraignment. I was charged with attempted murder, attempted kidnapping, burglary, malicious mischief, resisting arrest, verbal abuse, breaking and entering, criminal trespass, and disorderly conduct. The missus told the judge she was terrified of me, and His Honor gave a long lecture on people who create disturbances in Fifth Avenue apartments, and how they shouldn't be allowed on the streets of civilized cities, but reduced the charges to one of disorderly conduct, with bail set at $1,000.

I was tossed into the infamous Tombs of New York, and sent word to Tom O'Malley to come bail me out. I lingered all day Saturday and Saturday night, with a cellmate on his way to twenty-five years at Sing Sing for murdering someone who informed on his drug-dealer pal. He was quite proud of himself, and didn't seem too perturbed about his looming quarter-of-a-century stay upstate. However, when morning arrived, with slivers of sunshine descending on us from high slits in the walls, he became a trifle irate at the inequity of life. One of the guards brought in the Sunday papers, and the *News* and the *Mirror* had accounts of my doings. Here he had committed a perfectly good murder in Prospect Park and got barely a mention in some Brooklyn throwaway paper, yet I, a drunk in for a disorderly charge, was practically hogging the headlines. I think he muttered something about writing to his congressman about unfair press coverage.

The day brought bravado to my various incarcerated colleagues, who shadow-boxed, deep-breathed, did push-ups, walked about briskly, cursed, swore, and threatened each other. They were almost all awaiting transportation to upstate penitentiaries for murder, robbery, rape, and other such offenses, and when they asked what it was that was holding me in the Tombs, I was quite diffident about saying it was disorderly conduct, so I added that there was a chance of having the "attempted murder" reduced.

Days in prison are lengthy, and toward evening I was informed that bail-held prisoners were to be shipped to Rikers Island at dawn. The heart plummeted into the footwear at this bit of news. Where in the name of the Almighty God, his Son Jesus, and the Blessed Mother, was the old chum, T. O'Malley? Here I'd spent an eternity of penal servitude awaiting the springing, but no savior in sight! I began the prayers for succor to St. Anthony, St. Jude the Little Flower, St. Blaze (though he specialized in curing sore throats), St. Alphonsus Liquori, St. Gerard Majella, St. Therese of Liseaux, and any other of the vast multitudes of sainted and beatified bods that popped into the quivering cranium.

O'Malley arrived with a bail bondsman at about sunset. He had forgotten all about me, as he'd had a few drinks and was only reminded of my status when he turned on the television and the word "bail" was mentioned. He was more amused at his memory lapse than I was, but I wasn't giving vent to any tirades against my bailer, lest he find it ungrateful of me and bugger off.

Back to court the following month for the trial. Fierce testimony from the spouse, the maid, the stepfather, a neighbor or two, the doorman, and the arresting officer, all alleging some rather serious criminal activity by me. I'd secured the services of a lawyer, who told me to plead guilty but say I was riddled with remorse at the moment, which was true.

His (dubious) Honor also knew people who lived in that Fifth Avenue building, and said it was unconscionable that a ruffian like me would be allowed to run wild in respectable habitations in the middle of the night, creating fear and havoc among the denizens of this high-rent joint, so he was going to sentence me to six months.

"Six months!" gasped I, a man defeated, as I collapsed on my barrister. I felt like Dreyfus upon being sent to Devil's Island. "Six months," repeated the judge, and then he reopened the doors, with, "Sentence suspended!"

The calcium returned to my bones, and I heaved myself off my defender, vowing there and then to devote the rest of my life to charity, chastity, good works, and abstention from strong drink.

The estranged spouse squeaked her objections, and the assistant D.A. said something that sounded like a demand for the death penalty, but I did not linger for a change of His Honor's mind. I fled the court like a shot off a shovel, and in no time I was seated in a warm hostelry, bending the elbow, regaling all who would listen with fearsome tales of my brush with capital punishment.

Despite my vows to sacrifice the self in the cause of humanity, 'twas not long ere I was leaping in and out of the fleshpots again.

————

AFTER THE BRUSH WITH THE law, it was into the flaming hell of family court with me. My transgressions were laid out by the wife's barrister, to much head shaking and tsk-tsking by the judge. I didn't have a chance to respond before I was given about as lacerating a tongue-lashing as one could get. Eloquent as she was in her description of ruffianism, spouse-abusers and property-wreckers, she was particularly vehement because, like every judge in America, she knew someone who lived at the wife's Fifth Avenue address. I'd read about rowdy lads in the poorer areas doing more damage than I, but the

judges never seemed to comment on the inviolability of those premises.

She wound up her peroration by ordering me to undergo a psychiatric evaluation. "In the meantime, you will not come within one
mile of complainant, her children, or her residence."

It took six months for the psychiatric evaluation to be arranged
and the results to be presented to the court, and I was in agony at
not being able to see Siobhan and Malachy. If I had so much as
picked up the phone to call them, I would have been arrested, so I
chose instead to spend my time immersed in the pain-dousing spirits,
the bed-hopping, and the fisticuffs.

When the results of the psychiatric exam were presented to the
judge, she wasn't a bit pleased. The doctor said I was a sane lad,
disappointed in love, missing his children, with a bit of a problem
with alcohol. So, thence forward, I was to be allowed to visit the
offspring for three hours every Sunday.

FOUR

WHIRLED AFFAIRS

My father came and went throughout my early years. I was ten or eleven the last time I saw him in Limerick, and I wasn't to see him again until I was a big man.

He had been gone and we had been evicted from our rotten old house for nonpayment of rent. Afterward we had moved in with a drunken sot, a cousin of my mother's, and twasn't long before she was sharing his bed despite his cruelty to her and to us. Part of the deal, I suppose, for giving us shelter.

One night the disappeared father arrived home, only to discover there was no home anymore. I was at my retarded uncle's rundown abode, a little place lit by a gas lamp, and my father happened to find me there.

The drunken sot of a cousin heard he was back, and came looking for him. When he came in the cousin gave me a whack that sent me flying, and then punched my father—who made no attempt to defend himself or me—practically unconscious. After he was done with us, the swine left, like the king lion having downed his adversary, stolen his mate, and whacked his cub for good measure.

There was silence in the little room, and then my father looked at me and said, "See how well I kept my temper?"

I wanted to scream at him about the patriotic nonsense he preached at us about dying for Ireland. How about defending your own son instead of Ireland, I wanted to shout in his face.

But I didn't, and even though my ear was still ringing and my skin still stinging from the whack I had received, I nodded agreement that he was terrific at self-control.

———

CAME THE DAY, SOON AFTER, I met again an old acquaintance from the lockjawed set, who mentioned the possibility of some work involving considerable travel in far-flung places. You'd wonder how a place could be "flung" at all, but I wasn't going to chomp the claw that was about to feed me, as my finances were in a sorry state and travel seemed like just the thing right about then. He arranged for me to meet my boss-to-be at a coffee shop in the quiet of the after-lunch recess on Wall Street.

Paul Brown, the employer, can best be described as nondescript. Your eyes passed over him as it would the wallpaper, and I believe that suited his purpose. He was a smallish man, and wore rimless spectacles over ever-watchful eyes, a greyish suit, an unobtrusive shirt, black shoes, and a tie that sported either a vague design or leftover-food stains. Speaking through what appeared to be a repaired cleft palate, he informed me that he was in the business of moving gold about the world, and asked about my availability for travel, my passport, etc., which I assured him were all in place. When could I take off, he asked.

"At once," sez I.

He told me to go to the Indian Consulate General and secure myself a visa to visit that spectacular country. Thrilled was I to get a chance to go to India, a country I'd felt an affinity for since I was a little fellow. For some reason, I'd ploughed through a history of

India when I was barely in school, and I always suspected I was a reincarnated Hindu.

I sojourned to the palatial building that housed the consular folk. It was a very simple process. I plunked down the necessary spondulicks and the passport and was told to return in a day to pick up same. My new boss told me to get packed and to meet him at Idlewild that eve, as we were going to leg it to Switzerland—Zurich to be precise.

The first rule of packing is that everything you need is at the end of the road, so I took nothing more than the toothbrush, the book, the sock or two, a pair of drawers, and a bit of this and a bit of that, and with a light bag and a lightened heart, I hied my way to the airport after lying to all and sundry that I was off to Europe to do a film.

I was nicely fluthered by the time I met up with the boss at the airport, who wasn't delighted at my drawing attention to myself with the chumminess toward Swissair folk, indeed, toward most every passing stranger. He told me to board the plane to Zurich without acknowledging his presence. When we arrived I was to check into the hotel and wait for him to contact me. Good old cloak-and-dagger stuff.

There was a bit of a wait, so I toddled off to replenish the fuel, which was wearing thin a bit. A few more whiskies got the engines going again, and all looked rosy and warm, but when the Now Boarding call came and I sauntered off to the designated gate, a small matter of a missing ticket and a boarding pass prevented me from getting on the plane. Search as I might, retracing my steps, the items seemed to have taken flight all by themselves. Fortunately, Brown was still on terra firma, reading the white-collar criminal's instruction manual, the *Wall Street Journal.* It occurred to me to launch into a tale of being assaulted by a roving band of robbers who specialize in airline passengers, but time was passing, so I tapped him on the shoulder and simply said I'd lost my ticket.

He sputtered and fumed, but he couldn't alter the fact that my dockets were not available to me or him. A mad dash to the ticket counter secured the necessary, and after I was admonished about drinking and carelessness, we separated and boarded, to journey to the land of yodeling cuckoo clocks, secret bank accounts, and neutrality.

Having forsaken booze at that point for close to an hour, and now that we were airborne and outside the three-mile morality limit, 'twas time for another drink. I ordered four of the wee airline bottles, which I estimated to approximate a single real drink. At fifty cents each, they were still a bit of a bargain.

A tendency prevailed among the Swiss plane staff to press food on me, but I expostulated in strong terms that I never ate on an empty stomach. After the dinner was served, the cabin lights were doused, and the skimpy blankets and doll's pillows were distributed, in observance of what seemed to be a general desire to sleep. This would not do at all! I ordered another cluster of the wee bottles and, now fully oiled up, I decided to become an impresario and get an onboard concert going.

To start matters off, I roared out a couple of the more bawdy songs I knew. It being singer's choice, I tried to pick the next entertainer. I studiously avoided the boss—who was studiously avoiding me—but every single person onboard, man and woman, declined to stand up and do their bit. This was long before hijackings had terrified the traveling public, but these bods all had that petrified look. To make matters worse, the stewardess now refused to serve me any more clusters of bottles, and the captain soon forsook control of the aircraft to come back to have a word with me.

He might have been a good pilot, but as a conciliator he could have brought the Swiss out of neutrality and to the brink of war. *Threatening* the man was! With talk of restraints and premature landings to have me arrested! Here we were, high above the Atlantic, and all I could imagine was plopping down on the waves, and them hailing a passing police boat to take me in.

"Will you stop talking shagging rubbish," sez I, "and get me the gargle?"

"Nein," sez he.

"Fuck thee," sez I, and fled to the lavatory, from where I announced I would thump the walls and sing all night if they didn't serve me. The olive branch was stuck under the door, and an agreement was reached that on condition I shut up and sit down, they would let me have one cluster of bottles every hour. I asked for them to be served sans charge, which they refused, but at fifty cents each I wasn't going broke.

In Zurich, it was a drizzly morning as we got off the plane to board a bus for the terminal. The other passengers avoided me, and who would blame them, as I reeked of used whiskey and unchanged socks. I retrieved the bit of baggage, went through customs, got into the taxi, and off to the hotel.

The noggin was pounding a trifle as I tried to focus the peepers on the passing scene. Everything was neat and symmetrical and orderly, and not a thing in sight to disturb the color scheme. Flowers, shrubs, and plants all clipped and leaning in unison to the direction of the unseen hand. There were people washing and hosing pavements, cleaning windows, polishing bells, painting walls, and generally doing violence to the natural order of things. A weed poking its cheery little head up through a crack in a footpath would be cause for mobilization of the Swiss Army and their knives.

After checking in at the hotel, I plonked myself down on the bed, where I stayed until I was awakened by someone whacking the door. It was the irate Paul Brown, lugging a largish case. He plunked it on my bed and opened it up, to reveal layers of gleaming gold bars, twenty of them, a kilogram each. They were all stamped with the name of a bank, the weight, and some indication of the purity. Also in the case were a length of canvas, scissors, thread, and what appeared to be sail needles. My goldman—Mr. Brown had been transformed to Gold, and would henceforth be known as the goldman—told me to get my shirt off, and when I raised the querying eyebrow, he said he had to measure me for the gold-carrying corset.

Not alone was the man a financial wizard, but an expert seamster as well. He measured me and began cutting and sewing, nipping and tucking, threading the needle, shaping shoulder straps, and attaching hooks and eyes. Amazing what you can learn reading the *Wall Street Journal!*

Then he had to make kilo-shaped pockets to nest the gold bars in. He hummed and whistled whilst doing all this sartorial service, and once in a while, dropped a pearl of wisdom about Indian people, such as that they are very curious about your business. There were four public phones in Bombay, he said, and two of them would be out of order at any given time. Upon arrival, I was to find one that worked, telephone the Laimeck Trading Company and announce I was Haaji Khan, and they would tell me what to do.

"What if someone answers the phone and doesn't know Haaji Khan?" sez I.

"Stop creating difficulty where there is none. Small company owners in India do not allow the menials to answer the phone," he huffed. He then pulled out two little ball-peen hammers and a newspaper, which he spread on the floor, and the two of us squatted there, flattening all identification on the bars.

My financier seamster slipped the bars into the pockets, and hoisted the whole load onto my bod, over a T-shirt. I donned another T-shirt, then a dress shirt, jacket, and tie, and being a hefty class of lad anyway, it didn't seem to make a whit of difference in my girth. But Jesus, it made a difference in my gait! Tentatively, I strolled about the room, a newly enfeebled person.

I bid an unfond farewell to my goldman, hopped onto the handy bus to the airport, and off with me to the stopover in Rome. There I checked into the little *pensione*, blithely slipped the gold under the mattress, and got on the blower to Sandy Lieberson, an old chum who was agenting in the Eternal City. He introduced me to various fleshpots and traveling actors, like Gordon MacRae, and we generally did the old *dolce vita* bit.

I also ran into Russ Rooks, an old Clavin's denizen, who wanted to know what I was up to. I responded that I was in the export–import business, a catch-all phrase that I didn't understand but that seemed to cover my situation. "Ah," sez Russ. "You're into that gold-smuggling scam." Speechless, he left me.

A couple of days cavorting in the Pope's town, where I went to confession in St. Peter's Basilica, to a non-English-speaking priest. I thumped the sternum and proclaimed a vigorous *mea culpa, mea culpa, mea maxima culpa!* Like my father before me, I was observing the outward form of the religion and having a bit of fun jabbering all kinds of sins to a bewildered Portuguese priest. I think my penance was one Hail Mary, which I duly said:

> Hail Mary, full of grace, The Lord is with Thee. Blessed art thou amongst women—or, as I misheard it as a child, and still say to this day on occasion, Blessed art thou, a monk swimming—Holy Mary, Mother of God, pray for us sinners, now and at the end. Amen.

Of course, it was slightly sacrilegious, if not blasphemous, to be participating in a sacrament for the fun of it.

Rome was such a cheerful city, where Catholicism, Communism, and Hedonism were an accommodating trinity for the most morally frail; unlike Limerick, where the rains and the sermons brought gloom and despair to the quivering victims of Jansenist tyranny. That took all the fun out of sin!

The current prisoner of the Vatican then was Angelo Giuseppe Roncali, a.k.a John XXIII, as decent a man as ever wore a satin slipper, who was promulgating the novel theory that you could have a reasonable relationship with your God. You could even be joyful in the knowledge that your Higher Power loved you, without lacerating your spine bones with a steel-tipped cat-o'-nine-tails to prove that you loved him. Angelo's dance card was a bit full whilst I was sojourning in Rome, so he never did get to meet me.

A good amount of the vino was taken aboard the day of my leaving for Bombay. The plane was due out at 7 P.M., and I arrived at the airport to find the bloody flight had left without me. I was quite indignant, as I was only forty-five minutes late! I had assumed that Italians had the same philosophy about time as the Irish: When God made time, he made plenty of it, so wherein is the hurry?

So, back to the fleshpots of Rome again, until Wednesday. I was relieved that I missed that plane, as it crashed in the Bay of Bombay with the loss of all on board. That was Monday; Wednesday saw me head out again for the airport for the seven o'clock flight. Fortunately, this one left at eight o'clock, which was more in keeping with my ideas of life and time.

Now encumbered with the gold bars, I had a vague notion of how a pregnant woman feels awaiting delivery. I groaned at the prospect of being trapped on a droning craft for an eternity of hours, weighed down with the stuff that supposedly drives people mad. It indeed does, if you don't own it and you have to carry the fucking stuff all over the world.

Sitting down was a problem, and getting up was a problem, as you can't remove the stuff. I had a vision of the plane crashing, and my skeleton found years later still wearing the canvas vest with the gold intact, making me one of the richest corpses in the world.

I was saved from going completely bonkers by a stop in Beirut, where I discovered, to my delight, a copy of J.P. Donleavy's *The Ginger Man*, a book as dear to my beating heart as anything by P.G. Wodehouse. To make it better, it was being sold as pornography in a plain brown wrapper, from under the counter. At an airport shop, mind you.

I had decided, in the interests of clarity and safe smuggling, 'twere better I remain sober and, back in the air again, I was thrilled to be going to this exotic country about which I'd read so much. Without the drink to divert its wanderings, the mind would travel back to New York City, and the broken marriage, and the children, and the blasted tears would start again. Then, back to the present and the fear of being caught, and the anticipation of the great adventure.

It was a smoothish landing on Indian ground, but the ticker was doing a fandango as I approached the immigration booth. My gold-man had instructed me to be precise and specific in my answers, as doing so reassures the authorities and produces less paperwork, though Indians love rubber stamps, so you could never tell. The country resounds with the sounds of things being stamped. I shouldn't be surprised if they didn't stamp their wives' bottoms to show the time of the last entry.

"Purpose of your visit to India?" The singsong cadence of the Maharashtra native velveted my ears.

"I am a tourist and I want to sea the Elephant Caves in Bombay and the Taj Mahal in Agra," sez I, confidently, having prepared.

"How long will you stay?"

"Ten days."

"Where will you be staying?"

"At the Taj Mahal Hotel."

"Thank you."

"Indeed. Thank you."

Done with immigration, retrieve the battered portmanteau, face the last obstacle to my freedom: Customs. Now the heart begins a sprint, toward what, I don't know, but sure as shite, I thought I radiated guilt in every direction, which in my case causes an eruption of hubristic horseshite. Quelling my tendency toward the *furor loquindi*, I just answered the questions simply.

"Do you have enyding to declare?"

To my astonishment, I didn't parrot Oscar Wilde, and the olde "Nothing but my genius" response. I simply said "No."

"Do you have foreign currency?"

"Yes."

"How much?"

"Three hundred dollars."

"Please open your bag."

A perfunctory shuffle though the bag, and a "thank you," and I was safely done. But as I attempted to close the bag, a shoe fell out onto the floor. I wasn't sure if I could bend down and retrieve it without toppling over from the cargo I was carrying, so I ignored the shoe and pretended to smooth out items of clothing, hoping that some polite person would chance by, pick up the shoe and hand it to me, which is precisely what happened. A bearded man in the raiment of the Mohammedan did just that, saving me the possible embarrassment of landing on my nose, not to mention any subsequent quizzical looks, impromptu investigations, and subsequent arrests. I thanked him profusely for his kind act. I made a mental note to begin an intensive study of the teachings of Mohammed and seek a discreet bookshop where the Koran could be purchased for my perusal and possible conversion.

Of course, I had to reconsider that course of action, as it would mean a lot of ablutions during Ramadan, plus the fasting and the task of remembering where the East lies for the morning and evening prayers, and at the time my sense of direction was on a par with my moral compass.

Then there would be the sad farewell to the sausage and the rasher, and also the prospect of never raising the high-proofed beverage to the puckered lips again, and the nipping over to Mecca every hour on the hour, and once there explaining how a Mick became a Mohammedan, lest I get the infidel treatment, i.e., Scimitar + Infidel = No Head.

Gratitude does lead one to thoughts of great intention, but action is another matter, so I never did become a follower of Allah, and, being no muladi, I remained an atheist. Thank God!

I closed up the old bag, and with a charming smile to the assembled Hindu custom lads, strolled in the general direction of public transportation. In short order, the bag was taken from me, and a horde of smallish people began pushing me toward a specific taxi, rather like a fleet of tugs pushing an aircraft carrier into safe harbor. I began swatting at these midges wildly, as it belatedly occurred to me that their little paws were coming in contact with the bars of precious metal festooning my person. Little did they know the craft they were propelling carried such a cargo!

The things you have to think about when you are a low-level gold smuggler! You can't patronize water fountains in public, where they are generally situated. The options for picking up the shoe have already been related. You can't allow diminutive strangers to place their paws on your person. Sitting down is a matter of struggling against gravity, and standing up is a foretaste of the infirmities of advanced years. Assuredly, spontaneous sex is almost always out of the question, unless with a golden calf, or yourself, or ye old *bulla aurea*, if that's your predilection.

The fury of my counterattack chased off my little helpers, and I managed to get in the taxi and sink back and relax. I issued the instructions to the driver, and off we chugged toward Bombay. But not so fast! A bit down the road, one of those red and white barricade bars dropped across our path, and from a little hut there emerged three khaki-clad lads. One looked at me through the left window, and the other peeked in the right, and number three stood in front, to make sure of no movement.

"This is it," sez I to myself. "I'm fucked. The little fuckers back at the terminal copped to my cargo and reported it. Jesus Christ Almighty! You can't be up to them Indians! They lull you into the arms of false security, playing with you, and letting you through, while meanwhile outside they have hordes of ill-clad midget detectives, frisking you and patting you down for contraband under the guise of getting the taxi!

I made a mental note to bung off a letter to the *Times* of India on the unsporting nature of their law enforcement procedures. India being a cricket-playing nation, you would expect more than lip service paid to sportsmanship. But what can you expect from a nation that learned everything from the Brits?

Anyway, one of the about-to-be-captors made the circular motion for me to crank my window down.

"Would you kindly step outside, Sir," sez he.

"Right," sez I.

The taximan opened the trunk and my khaki-clad lad sez, "Do you have any alcohol, gin, viskey, wodka, or vine?"

"Whaa?" sez I? He repeated the question.

"No." I almost turned that word into a *Te Deum*, a paean of praise to the Almighty. "No," I sang again, and launched into an attack on drink, drinking, and drunkenness, and how it had ruined so many lives and countries and cultures. I had never touched it, and never would, let alone bring such poison into the pristine purity of a sober India.

The khaki-clad one put up a hand to try and stem the flow of verbiage, and wearily told me I could proceed. I shook hands with all of them; in my exuberance, I shook hands with my taxi driver as well. I felt so relieved, I forgot the gold, and sat down too quickly and heavily into my seat—fortunately not observed by the law lads—and off we trundled.

BOMBAY, THAT ANCIENT CITY-STATE, IS SPECTACULAR, teeming with life and squalor and thoroughly polluted by industry. The American Civil War helped bring it to the fore, when it became the main supplier of cotton for the world; before that, Bombay was H.Q. for the British East India Company, a mob of Brit thugs, who polluted and perverted India with drugs and terrorism, with the blessings of the reigning monarch and House of Lords. To this day, many Indians are afflicted with Anglophilia, thinking they are worthless because of a dark skin, eternally damned to be W.O.G., and wishing to emulate that squealing, betraying scum, Gunga Din.

My driver, a loquacious man, still bemused by my hearty handshake, dropped me at the Taj Mahal Hotel. He tried to charge me triple the fare on the meter, but I was having none of that rip-off-the-sahib stuff, so I robbed myself and gave him a mere double the fare.

The hotel, a pile of architecture built a hundred or so years ago, was designed so that the front part would face the Gateway to India, a huge archway, and the Bay of Bombay itself. The architect, 'tis said, was very happy with his design, and betook himself back to Europe ere construction began. The contractor, 'tis said, turned the blueprints upside down, and proceeded from there, with the result that the magnificent frontage faced the slums of Bombay, and the servants' quarters and kitchens all had the magnificent view that was to be the reward of the rich who stayed there. At the grand opening, the architect returned and, aghast at the incredible blueprint blunder, he checked into his suite and caused a housekeeping crisis by blowing his brains out with a revolver. Or so I am told.

Inside the place was a cool marble marvel with huge fans doing the air-wafting duty, and a most-anxious-to-please staff in uniforms and turbans of the Raj period. The daily rate was fifty rupees, which came to ten dollars at the exchange rate of that period, and that included three full meals. The place was not awash in Michelin *haute cuisine* plaques, but the fodder was sufficient unto the needs of an adventurous eater like myself, who wasn't used to much anyway. I had been warned to avoid the water, but having grown up in the lanes of Limerick, Ireland, was I not immune to all the tropical diseases known to medicine? Besides, when you ordered any bottled drink, the brilliant servers used ice of local vintage, thinking, no doubt, that ice killeth all bacteria, germs, and viruses.

However, that was not the immediate problem confronting me. I had perforce to get on the blower and call the contact firm to let them know that Haaji Khan was in town with the metal. Keeping said metal on the body, I ventured out to the railway station to use one of the four known public phones in Bombay. There must have been more, but that was the dish on it for the nonce.

My progress was impeded by a festive group, marching in some kind of parade, complete with drums, cymbals, and anything else that could be whacked noisily, with lots of leaping and burbling and singing, and all the participants dressed in the most astonishingly beautiful garb: a joyous occasion indeed for 11 A.M. of a Bombay morn. I got to the phone, followed by a vast array of brown Lilliputians, displaying an extraordinary wealth of disabilities: armless, legless, lacking in the standard quota of orbs.

Burdened as I was with that fucking gold, I was still adept at the two-step of avoiding entanglements with the suffering underclasses, God help them. Dropping a few *nai paesa* coins into the ancient coin box of the telephone booth, I dialed the number, and to my satisfaction, it did ring, and it did ring, and ring, and ring.

Soon, the scene was this: a large, red-headed, fully-bearded hulk of a man, a perturbed, not to mention pissed-off look on his Irish visage, standing up in a glass booth, a strange-looking black yoke stuck to his ear, the booth surrounded by brown faces, pleading eyes, and upturned light-colored palms for as far as the eye could see.

There was no answer at the Laimeck Trading Company, so I hung up and retrieved my *nai paesa*, which I flung in the direction I was *not* going, and took off at a briskish pace for the safety of the hotel. There, a survey of the huge bathroom showed the tub was encased in marblelike paneling, and with the screwdriver on my trusty Swiss Army knife, I got a panel unscrewed and the gold safely deposited in a trifle longer than a jiffy.

I never did get gold fever in the usual way; instead, I became sick of it, weary of it, and tired of it, and if it had been human, I would have strangled it. Of course the thought had come to me to decamp with the stuff, but the process of disposing of it and facing my goldman in Zurich seemed more wearying than delivering it to good Abdulla Laimeck and his company.

When it came time to call again, I was tempted to use the hotel phone, but the goldman's huffed warning came back to me: "Don't use the hotel phones. Indians are very curious, and they eavesdrop all the time." So I hied myself off to the railway station, followed by my now-familiar retinue of God's blasted children, hobbling, scrambling, limping blindly, groping, crawling, hopping, fingertips (if they had any) fluttering like hummingbirds, on and off the lips, whimpering for *baksheesh! baksheesh!*

'Twas the same old routine at the phone booth: *nai paesa* in old coin box, dial, hear ringing, survey the brown sea of visages, some sloe-eyed, some no-eyed. The inexorable, nonanswered ringing, and the nonbusinesslike inattention to the job almost provoked me to a phone-booth-destroying act, which would have drawn unwelcome interest from the khaki-clad lads with the badge of office.

Again, hung up, withdrew coins, flung them in the direction I was *not* proceeding, and hoofed it off toward the hotel. But not so fast! The more hobbled of my retinue, being incapable of the mad dash for the pence, surrounded me beseechingly. This was the legless, totally crippled-below-the-waist brigade, and they grasped everything that could be grasped of me: shoelaces, socks, trouser legs, and the occasional wandering paw exploring the possibility of a grip on the three-piece set dangling 'twixt the thighs, a move I firmly discouraged at all times.

Stuck I was, unable to take a step, disabled by the disabled. The usual defense I employ against immense and emotional compassion is to get ferociously angry and to berate the victims for coming to me with their troubles: "I didn't have anything to do with your mothers, so I'm not responsible for your plight. Find your fucking fathers and make *them* pay up and look after you."

The *nai paesa* chasers had now returned, so the ranks around my Gulliverian frame were legion once more. As I realized I had a bit of time to spare—indeed, going by my absent partners in the gold-smuggling biz, Indians seem to have the same attitude toward time as the Irish—I decided to make the most of this chance situation. One bright-looking, one-legged lad of indeterminate age seemed to have the English language in hand, so I asked him if he or any of the gang knew any songs. He did, they all did, and that started our mini-concert in the railway station in Bombay.

I sat on a bench, and my gang of beauties sang for me. What they were singing, I don't know, and maybe they didn't know either, but, Jesus, it was lively. I gave each of them a rupee, a lot at that time (the head barman at the hotel got sixty rupees, about five dollars a month, and considered himself fairly well compensated), and we were quite pleased all around.

One of the khaki-clad lads with badge had strolled over at one point to disperse the *chanteurs*, but a few rupees suddenly endowed him with a profound appreciation for the street songs of Bombay.

I was still in a dilemma re the fucking gold and disposal of same and what to do next. Once back at the hotel, lying on my half acre of bed and staring at the ceiling, doing a splendid job of waiting, I hit on the solution. I had solemnly vowed to my goldman in Zurich I would not do any quaffing of spirituous liquors until the job was done. But, reasoned I, by now the job is done in theory, 'cos it's not my fault those fuckers at Laimeck Trading Company weren't answering the phone, so now I can have one or two drinks. I consulted myself in the mirror, and got an affirmative nod: "Go to it, lad! You deserve it!"

Donning the appropriate apparel was a small and joyful task, and off I went, down the huge staircase at the Taj Hotel, doing an inept imitation of James Cagney tap-dancing down the stairs of the White House in *Yankee Doodle Dandy*, the movie about that chauvinistic, union-busting old Fascist, George M. Cohan.

I repaired to Brown's Hotel next door, one of those more sedate old Brit places, reeking of colonialism, with the heads of butchered wildlife stuck on walls—tigers, and elephant tusks, and wild boars, with tame bores harrumphing in their leather chairs. They never leave, these old colonials; they form clubs, drink pink gins, and die of liver disease and attacks of painful gout.

I asked a turbaned nabob, who turned out to be a waiter, how to get a drink. He directed me to the bar, which was crowded with well-to-do tourist types as well as a large number of obviously wealthy but ailing-looking Indians and resident businessmen. This was explained by the fact that all of India was under some form of Prohibition, and in Maharastra province, wherein lies Bombay, in order to drink one had to possess either a tourist permit; a resident permit, for Europeans and other permanent outsiders; or, for Indians, a medical permit from a physician, attesting to the fact there would be dire results if these well-to-do Hindus were suddenly deprived of the squeezings of Bacchus.

Seated behind a desk at the end of the elaborately carved fifty-foot-long bar was one of the khaki-clad lads of the Customs branch of government. The three legacies the Brits leave to any colony are Bloodshed, Snobocracy, and Bureaucracy. They pretend they are pulling out, as if it is a Colonial Coitus Interruptus, but the reality is that they are giving every country a royal fucking, leaving behind the seeds of their particular perversions. Here was a customs man in a saloon, for God's sake!

And what was he doing, sitting on duty with rubber stamps by the dozen lined up neatly in front of him? He was there to ensure that the procedures for buying a drink were properly observed, and all the necessary papers were stamped and verified.

PROCEDURES:

1. Go to bar; order drink (Vodka gimlet, this time)
2. Barman requests passport and tourist card
3. Barman proceeds to customs man and ceremoniously hands over documents
4. Customs man peruses passport and whacks the tourist card a few resounding thumps with one of his rubber stamps
5. He hands passport, tourist card, and a long form he produces from the desk to the barman
6. Barman sails in my direction, tacking in the wind of others' alcoholic pleas for more drink, and hands me documents

7. He instructs me to sign the long form, which sez I'm entitled to 27/27ths of spirits, or nine quarts of Indian beer, per week. I'm allowed to order one drink at a time, which equals 3/27ths. I sign, and off he is, gone again

8. More frantic stamp thumping, and the barman sails back to me again and hands me the thumped form

9. He proceeds to mix the vodka gimlet (a handy drink if one is in imminent danger of coming down with scurvy)

I resisted the urge to down it at one gulp. I just sipped and told my friend, "I'm ordering the next drink now, so please begin the procedures." To ensure good service, I slipped him the equivalent of one week's wages, and off he went to get me the next 3/27ths, and indeed, much more.

As the evening progressed, I did my sociable bit with some of the denizens, who, in turn, wanted to invite me to various homes, but I said pressure of business kept me from making any future engagements.

At last, fatigue and jet lag and 15/27ths of a vodka bottle caused the lowering of the lids, the closing of the ears, and the spaghetti-izing of the limbs, so that I had to be assisted to my suite next door. So ended my first day in Bombay.

NEXT MORNING, I WAS AWAKENED BY THE TAPPING ON the door. A "Come in" brought a turbaned laddie with the brass buttons and the white tunic and the golden sash, bearing a tray with toast, butter, marmalade, and tea. Great stuff, as I realized I had not allowed any solids past the teeth the previous day. But, wouldn't you know, in deference to another dopey Brit tradition, hadn't they denuded the bread of its crust, the best part of the bread. Brits were fifteen years out of India, and they were still decrusting the bread, a practice almost as heinous as peeling a potato.

A stern lecture to the turban, tempered by a generous tip, and I was assured that never again would I be served uncrusted bread.

One problem I had with alcohol was the fact that, beyond a mild feeling of debilitation, 'twas a rare time I'd experience "hangovers," as they are called. If you are going to ingest the toxin, then 'tis well after having extracted the benefits of inebriation to dispose of that lethal leftover waste. So, before retiring, I would find a convenient porcelain altar, bend the knees to the floor, and do the reverse of Communion, in that it is better to regurgitate than to receive.

Having cleared the bod of toxicity, 'twas nothing at all to resume the imbibing the next day, and again after that and so on. There wasn't much of a problem eating food in the a.m., either, so all in all, I was on pretty good terms with myself in the morn and, by the eve, under or over the influence.

So after ingesting the proffered comestibles, it was up and out with me again, to my favorite telephone: same crowd, same routine, same singing, and still no answer.

I casually mentioned to the khaki-clad lad with badge that I had difficulty in contacting a businessman whose name had been given me. The cop smiled benignly and said it would be impossible to contact anyone, as most businesses were closed to celebrate Krishna's birthday: a popular lad, Krishna, raised by cowherds as opposed to cowboys, particularly kind to *gopis* (milkmaids), having, 'tis said, slipped the divine flute into several hundred of them, simultaneously causing hundreds of orgasms and a tumult of shrieking on the subject of spilt milk.

'Twas no wonder he had a great reputation as a deity, adept at the use of the flute in all its aspects. Whatever Krishna, avatar and eighth incarnation of Vishnu, did with his flute and the gopis and the cowherds, he wasn't doing me much good in my business. There was one more day to go of the Krishna hooley, and myself filled with anxiety about the golden burden hidden beneath the bathtub.

Some wandering about Bombay, a bit of desultory sightseeing, interspersed with swift and frequent returns to the hotel to check on the booty, did not make for the serene and carefree tourist.

The ferocious heat was getting to me, so I couldn't stay on the streets, and I was making an attempt to stay reasonably sober, so that I'd have my wits about me and not be depleting my weekly 27/27ths too abruptly. So, no drinking 'til after dinner.

Back at the bar, the usual mob had assembled: head barman @

sixty rupees a month; customs khaki-clad lad with badge; pink-ginned Brits; some too-loud Yanks; a goodly number of very ill Indians with prescriptions; and assembled Arabs and others. A swift exchange of documents, the thunk of the customs man's stamp, the proffering of the five rupees per drink, and, lo, I had my vodka gimlet in front of me in five minutes this time instead of ten.

As the stuff trickled into the parched crevasses of my soul, the peace that passeth all customs barriers took over, so 'twas time to order another. I got to chatting with some business types—a German, a couple of Walloons, and two very sick, sari-clad Indian ladies, with prescriptions and the red dots over the hidden oculi. Charming they were, and very amused when I offered to buy them a drink. It could not be done, according to the law. One of the Walloons absented himself with one of the sari-clads, and I suggested to the remaining one that she accompany me to the adjacent cabaret-type room, whence the tapping sound of the tabla and the enhanced sitar sound crept around corners, demanding attention. Pots of tea were ordered, as we listened and watched the cross-legged musicians bend and sway and nod and smile. Very delicate stuff, this Indian music, structured, but highly improvisational, using bansuris (the ancient bamboo flutes), kantals, cymbals, and the stringed sarangis and tambouras, all of which was explained to me by my new companion, whose name was Yoni.

She told me these music sessions sometimes go on for up to ten hours, and, indeed, the music-hungry populace will rise up in wrath if the performers get weary too soon. I suspect the public admiration for these minstrels was as much for their ability to sit cross-legged for hours, without getting a cramp, as it was for their musicianship.

After a lulling few hours of music, I hinted to Yoni that a trip to my quarters should be undertaken. "Oh no, no," she said. There would be terrible things said about her if she were seen accompanying a man to his room. "I will give you my key," sez I, "and you can let yourself in, then I will follow, and you can let me in."

She approved of the plan and off she went.

After a suitable and proper period, I signed for the tea, tipped the tabla three, and forced myself not to leap up the staircase. I tapped on my door, which was opened by Yoni, who was now clad only in what Vishnu and the other gods had given her, a lovely brown skin. No false modesty here, no downcast eyes, just a gentle, lovely girl, who proceeded to undress me and get me into the huge bathtub, where she washed every part of my epidermis, with special attention being paid to the upstanding part.

Just an inch of porcelain separated us from the Mammon beneath, and I almost blurted out that little fact, but through the vodka mists arising from the marshes of my brain, came the warning voice of my goldman in Zurich: The Indians are a very inquisitive people, and many of them are paid for information. Do not trust anyone. So I stifled that idiotic impluse.

We dried each other with huge, soft, white towels, and ambled our way toward the half-acre bed, and clambered aboard, where Irish–Indian relations were cemented forever.

A deep sleep was enjoyed, and when I was awakened by the turbaned tea bearer tapping at the portals in the a.m., there was no sign of the saried one. I never knew what she did, who she was, and why a seeming Brahmin would share the bed with a wandering, pixilated Mick.

Anyway, she was gone forever, leaving me facing another day of Krishna lepping, dancing, and fluting, and my 27/27ths were nearly exhausted. So, I stayed in bed, and when the eyes opened again, it was tiffin' time. The poor Indian upper crust liked lunching at the Taj, even though the food was the height of Brit cuisine, i.e., vegetables burnt to the cinder, chops rancid, and beef boiled to anonymity, accompanied by oil-soaked chips. On the other hand, there were the meals of India: the curries, the chutneys, the dahls, the breads, and the yogurts, but diffidently offered to the Caucasian.

Another stroll around Bombay in the heat of the day, walking off the effects of tiffin', followed by my legion of the legless, who had now taken to singing loudly and heartily whenever they saw me approach.

Back at the hotel, one of the turbaned staff, upon my request, took out my "soiled linen," as the Brits would say, to be laundered. That laundering took place across the way, where the washerwomen dipped dirty shirts into the dirtier water of the bay, and then would go on a shirtocidal rampage, whacking the inoffensive clothing into insensibility with rocks; not an inch was spared. It only cost a couple of rupees to have my shirts ruined by professionals. Fortunately, I'm not the fastidious lad in the french-cuff department.

The next a.m., fortified by the morning oolong and toast with crust and marmalade, I bounded out of the bed and into the shower, agog with the prospect of getting the gold to its destination.

What could the goldman have done if I absconded with the stuff? Nothing, really, as he didn't seem to have access to thugs and knee-cappers, so again I cogitated on the possibility of stealing the booty and saying I had to bribe the entire government of India just to be allowed to take off in peace.

The inner voice said, "Don't be a fucking eejit and thief. The man trusted you, so do your fucking job and be straight about it."

"All right! All right! I'll do it—just shut up," sez I to the clamoring voices in the head.

I donned the lightweight haberdashery and, with all the insouciance of the man about to be relieved of a burden, I stepped out in the direction of the phone booth in the railway station—a wee spot now familiar to me as the bed. Dropped coins in box, dialed number, and, Glory Be to Jesus, Vishnu, Buddha, Allah, and Mary Magdalene, the phone was answered and a voice, a soothing, friendly Indian voice, said, "Good morning. Laimeck Trading Company. Can I assist you?"

"Bejasus, you can, dear man, for this is Haaji Khan."

"Yes, sir. How may I help you?"

"My name is Haaji Khan."

"I heard you sir, and now would you state the nature of your business so that I may assist you?"

Desperation seized me and—along with being confined to an airless booth in stifling heat—caused me to spurt rivulets of sweat in every direction, making the hands so slippery I could hardly hold the telephone.

"Let us begin again," I said, holding down the savage urge to scream and rant at this brainless fool, who should be on the streets seeking baksheesh instead of fucking up the lives of honest, diligent gold smugglers.

"I was told simply to ring you up and tell you my name and you would give me further instructions as to my next step. Do you understand?"

"No, I do not, sir, but if you would be so kind as to tell me your name and business, perhaps I could assist you."

I inhaled as much of the fetid air as I could and, suddenly inspired, I imitated the Goldman of Zurich's speech pattern. Speaking in his tortured inflections, I snuffed:

"Dis is Hawji Cong."

A delighted voice rose into the treble range at the other end. "Why did you not say so, Mr. Khan? Here's what you must do this evening. A man will meet you at the Gateway to India at nine o'clock, and he will tell you what to do."

"How will he know me?"

"You have been observed going from the Taj Hotel and endeavoring to contact us on the telephone, so we know your appearance."

"Why in Christ's name did you allow me to wander around for three days like a lost sheep?" I sputtered.

"Dat is a good one," said the voice. "A lost sheep in Bombay. Very amusing. I hope I may use it. But, you see, we do not transact business during the celebrations, as we are not Hindu and it would draw unnecessary attention to us. You will be met tonight. Good day, Mr. Lost Sheep. Ha ha ha," and he was gone.

A few minutes prior to the appointed hour, I unscrewed the panel on the side of the bathtub and took up my golden burden once more. I'd forgotten how weighty it was! Donned same, slipped on the shirt and jacket, looked in the mirror, a pat here, a pat there, and Bob's your uncle.

The Gateway to India is a huge *Arc de Triomphe*, erected to their majesties by grateful, slavering slaves, to thank them for the privilege of being robbed by the Empire. An eerie stillness falls over certain parts of Bombay at night, where people just lie and sleep on mats, wherever they'll not be stepped on. In the dark, you hear quiet talking, and ghostly figures clad in white float past, making no sound, except sometimes the whispered word, "Baksheesh," but never as insistent as during the sunlit hours.

I was wondering how my man was going to find me in this Stygian darkness, when a young fellow accosted me. He was leading an older man, whose hand was on his shoulder. He shone a torch on the face of the older man, who promptly pulled down his lower eyelids to show me he was bereft of eyeballs, retinas, pupils, and all the other stuff that goes with them. "My father," sez the younger fellow. "He cannot see, he cannot see."

I assayed the opinion that he could hardly see without eyes and laughed at my own tasteless jape, as did the two baksheeshers. I immediately felt bad about laughing at the eyeless one, and overcompensated with the *baksheesh*, handing over ten rupees. Instantly, I was almost buried under a torrential wave of beseechers. I was saved by a voice, an insistent voice, saying "Haaji Khan? Haaji Khan?"

"Oh, Jasus, yes! I'm yer man! Get me out of here before they find out I'm made of gold!"

Whatever he said to the Baksheesh Brigade, they melted into the darkness. "Follow me," I was told, and into the dark I followed him, and where I was that night is still a mystery to this day.

"Wait here," and he was gone. I couple of swift whiskeys would have stilled the leaping nerves, as I stood there with strange rustlings and movements about me. Then a strange monster loomed over me, nearly stopping the heart. Thinking I was about to be attacked, I cowered against the wall, covering up the visage as boxers do. The beast lumbered by and, to my utter relief, 'twas only a sacred cow.

My guide reappeared and walked me into a building and up a flight of stairs. A little white-haired Caucasian woman, clad in the basic black dress, with a white lace collar, a cameo brooch and pince nez, stepped into the room and shook hands with me.

"Do come in," sez she, "and make your choice." She had the perfect Brit accent. I was a bit bemused by this until it dawned on her that I was there on a mission.

"Oh, deah! I'm so sorry! You must be the courier."

"Right," sez I.

"When you have completed your business, perhaps you will pop in and examine our wares."

"What wares?" sez I.

"Beautiful girls," sez she.

"Right!" sez I again.

I followed my guide into another room, where I divested myself of that fucking gold, which had weighed me down, literally and metaphorically, for a seeming eternity. I skipped down the stairs and found the grande-dame brothel keeper, and asked for my private preview. She seated me, poured me a vodka and lime on the house, and paraded the beauties in front of me. Lovely they were—slim, demure, the red dots and all, clad in the sari.

Not wanting to hurt anyone's feelings, and really not knowing what kind of inspection one should conduct, all I did was give a little squeeze to the passing breasts, a fraction of a fondle on the buttock, and a run of the hand up the thigh to the promised land.

This procedure was going well until, running the hand up the velvety thigh of a particularly beautiful young thing, I was jolted into an upright position by contact with a three-piece set. I pulled my hand away as if I'd just been hit with electricity, and, not believing what my hand was telling me, I touched the things again, and then I yelled for the grande dame.

"What do you think I am, sending this whatever-it-is to me?"

"Oh deah me," sez she. "Sometimes people are a bit bashful about stating their preferences, so we like to give them a choice without being too obvious. And so many of our fellow Britons do prefer boys, as they are more used to them than girls, as it were, don't you see?"

"I'm not a 'fellow Briton,' madam, and I'm not much used to boys," sez I, and then I made my choice and off we adjourned to the playpen. Milady took off my shoes and socks, the nether garments, and the rest of the garb, and put me down on a comfy bed, where she proceeded to wash me with water, laced with Lysol, and then caressed the whole bod with a scented sponge.

I was enjoying her feathery-fingered ministrations, 'til I opened my peepers, and there, high up on the wall, was a large painted reproduction of that famous Sacred Heart of Jesus, with yer Man pointing to the thumper encircled by thorns, and erupting with the flames and the blood dripping.

The upstanding member fell over on the thigh like a shot giraffe, and all thoughts of mounting my lady of the gentle sponge evaporated. The dusky maiden eyed the collapsed member, and made a unilateral decision to apply mouth-to-head resuscitation. I waved her off and told her to fetch the madam, who came in and, not at all fazed by my nakedness, listened to my problem. Of course. Many of her Catholic clientele—both clergy and lay people—had the same problem, so she would transfer me to another room.

"Why don't you remove that picture altogether, and not be giving practicing and collapsed Catholics palpitations in their sacred hearts?" sez I.

"Several of our girls are Catholics, and they have a peculiar devotion to the Sacred Heart, as they are from Goa, where St. Francis Xavier converted their ancestors. He was a Jesuit," said this learned brothel keeper, as if that were sufficient explanation for all the obstacles I was encountering on my way to the holey land.

The transfer to the other room was effected, and there, under a picture of a Lord Krishna avatar and eight incarnations of Vishnu, the wick was dipped, and more good work for Irish–Indian relations was intercoursed.

———

MY GUIDE WAS AWAITING ME, and 'twas a lighter journey back to the Taj and into the bed, where I slept the sleep of the uncaught criminal.

As my association with Bombay was with hot days and anxiety-ridden nights, my inclination now was to get out of India rather than continue the tourist farce. Anyway, there were too many impediments to procuring the drink, unlike the young Indian maiden.

I sent the coded telegram to my goldman in Zurich, to the effect that my sister had just delivered a fine, healthy boy, and all were doing well, the sort of innocuous messages that must immediately arouse the suspicions of the authorities.

My airline ticket at that time allowed for extra cities, so side journeys were in order. I opted for Nairobi, for no particular reason, except that I'd been reading and admiring the doings of Jomo Kenyatta, a Kenyan of the Kikuyu tribe.

Jomo led a band of lads called the Mau Mau, who were not a gentle crowd. They went after the wealthy white settlers in the highlands, the robbers and pillagers who had seized the lands of the Kikuyu and the Masai and caused frightful privation, starvation, and death among these native folks. So when the Mau Mau took their revenge and tried to get the lands back, it was called "savagery," which, of course, is different from colonization.

Jomo had studied in England, and when the Brits reproached him for ingratitude, he is said to have replied: "I thank you for helping me learn how to think, but I reserve the right to determine *what* I think."

I, of course, admired Jomo and thought there would have been a chance to meet him if I popped into Nairobi—much the same chance as one would have to meet Her Majesty by popping into London.

Once the Kenyans found I was Irish and from America, rather than a Brit, it became a longish running party. I drank strange concoctions out of gourds, and 'twas well not to peer in at the contents, as there were strange, reptilian creatures floating about, but the effect was glorious.

There's not much I remember about Nairobi, but I knew I'd been there, because it said so on my passport.

Of course, if I were not passed out with the drink, the little black demons that come just before dawn would begin gnawing at the soul, reminding me of the family wrecked by my insanity, and two small children saying, without prompting, "I love you, Daddy." Ha! Me loved. Me daddy. Impossible, and if it weren't, I made it so.

I'd cover the head again, and whimper like an abused puppy. Curse God again for the bad hand dealt me. What did I know about family life, the duties, the responsibilities, the love, the honor, the fidelity? Didn't any idiot know that it's not a good thing to say wounding, hurtful words to the loved ones? Didn't I know that no amount of good intentions can make up for a father's absence?

But it wasn't my fault; it was her, it was circumstances, no, it was God Himself.

"Now look, God, here's the deal: You tell her to reconcile with me, and I will be a great husband and father. I'll settle down and reduce the drinking to a tolerable level, and I'll stay home more. All right, God," I said, "All right! Did You hear me, or are You ignoring me?

*Well, if You are not listening, up Your bucket and get stuffed, You
mangy ol' fucker! It's all a goddamn myth that You exist and are all-
powerful, for if You did exist, You wouldn't deprive children of a loving
father and a united family."*

Silence.

———

ONTO THE JET TO FRANKFURT, change to a local for Zurich, and
report to my goldman all the details of the trip. He handed over
my money, three thousand dollars, and asked if I would like to go
again. "Yer on," sez I.

He told me to get some passport pics taken again, and meet him
in my hotel room. He had another American passport in the name
of Mark Silverstein, from which he expertly removed the picture and
replaced it with mine, hit it with the seal, and lo and behold, I was
now Mark Silverstein. There was no end to the talents of this man!

Off to the Indian Consulate for the visa, which was ready in two
days. My goldman appeared with the kilos, and once more we were
tapping out the seal on the bars to disguise the bank's name and
city. The routine was to be different now, as I was to fly to Bombay
via Calcutta, another city I wanted to see, as it was the home of the
scientist, J.B.S. Haldane, a redder-than-red Communist, who had
fought against Franco, Mussolini, and Adolf. He had decided to
devote the last years of his life to helping the destitute of Calcutta.
He had written about that wondrous city with love and compassion,
as well as anger at the horrors, such as the mutilation of infants so
they could be rented out to professional mendicants.

The purpose of coming via Calcutta? Simple—the off-chance
that a sharpish customs officer or immigration lad would remember
my last entry into Bombay a month or so ago.

Another short hop to Milan by train, and then on to Roma for
another swift dip in the fleshpots of that holey city. Then I was

gone again on Air India to Calcutta, with a stop in Baghdad, which brought up memories of all those Technicolor Arabian Night tales from Hollywood, with flying carpets, elephants, magic lamps, genies, beautiful princesses, Ali Baba, and so on. As none of that stuff was present at Baghdad Airport, I wasn't tempted to stay.

Same old routine at Calcutta Airport: Whack the shite out of your passport with the ubiquitous stamps. Purpose of visit. How long are you staying. Where are you staying. And, finally, do you have anything to declare.

There were no bathtub panels in the hotel where I was spending the night, so I had to lug the gold everywhere, and let me tell you, it was unpleasant. But in comparison to the grisly suffering on the streets, 'twas nothing. Deformed people, holding even more deformed wee babies, with eyes scooped out, huge infected sores oozing pus and slime, tiny legs broken so that they bent the wrong way, amputated ears and hands—you'd wonder how anyone could live for even five minutes with such pain. Giving the alms only encourages them to mutilate more babies, while if you withhold alms, then the suffering ones have hunger added to their woes. If you're like Haldane, you do what you can; the rest of us leave it in the hands of whatever deity looks after those born directly into suffering.

I did ring up Haldane's house, as he was listed, but found out he was absent from the city, so I simply left a message that I was an admirer and hoped to meet him one day. I never did, for he died shortly thereafter.

The plane to Bombay was a local, making stops wherever there was a bit of flat ground, it seemed. It was an old Constellation prop plane, which looked as if it had been around for quite a long time. The seats were narrow and, as there was no first class, I was among folks carrying all sorts of small animals and reptiles, not to mention bulky items like commodes and such like. Great arguments ensued, about luggage, rack rights, seats, and where to put babies and bird cages. It was a rickety take-off, with frightful vibrations and engines roaring, so that I was convinced we would lose the wings and go bulletlike for a mile or two, ere we crashed. The old saw about pilots wanting to live did not strike me as pertinent here, as Hindus and Moslems had a more sanguine approach to death than we: Were the pilot Hindu, he would expect to return presently; were he Moslem, he was headed into the arms of the houris awaiting him in Paradise.

But, of course, one survives, and after a five-hour journey, hedge-hopping and popping into various villages, the journey was completed, and, once again I was back in Bombay. This time, I checked into the faded, elegant Brown's so as not to arouse the suspicions of the Taj Mahal staff.

The phone call this time was answered promptly. For some reason, the rendezvous was in a cinema lobby, with those glaring red posters showing anguished-looking Indians clutching each other. Bombay was then a thriving film center and the cinemas were always crowded. Of course, there was puzzlement at the sight of a Westerner attending an Indian film, wherein the characters spoke only enraptured Hindi, but I was saved from any direct enquiries by the advent of a voice close to the earhole.

"Haaji Khan?"

"Yes."

"Follow me."

We went down a stairway, across a lobby with broken marble flooring and burnt-out, decorative lamps: a shabby place of ancient gentility. He pushed open a door, and we stepped into the foulest-smelling lavatory I had ever entered, except for the one in Leamy's School in Limerick. He tried the doors of a few stalls, afore finding one that swung open to his touch, and motioned me to step inside, and he pulled the door shut behind us. We were about as close together as two humans can be without getting conjugal. These spaces were designed for slivers of men to park their slim arses, not for two men trying to pass contraband from one to the other, whilst getting off coats, shirts, and undershirts.

On either side of this aromatic, fly-buzzing hole, I could hear squeaks and groans and sounds of sexual activity, with stifled little screams.

"Wha's going on here?" sez I, softly.

"Men put tings in boy's bottoms here," he sez, very quietly.

"Why are they doing it here?" sez I, *sotto voce*.

"Because the boys are here, awaiting the men," and then he squealed a little, groaned loudly, and gave the stall walls a couple of thumps with his fist. "They must tink we do the same ting here," he explained.

It was a hellish moment: two men struggling, in a tiny enclosure, to get out of clothes, and back into clothes, passing the gold, pretending they are fucking, whilst standing in puke, piss, blood, shit and pus, the air solid with stink and buzzing insects; penetrating the walls, the sounds of pain and pleasure, from those seeking fleeting moments of ecstasy amidst the fetor.

When our transaction was completed, the small man opened the door and stepped out. My shoes gave a sucking sound as I lifted my feet to exit. On the street outside the cinema, there stood a policeman surveying us. He smiled a tight smile and asked if the little man was annoying me. I said, "Not at all—he's giving me directions." The policeman smiled again, as if to indicate he knew where we'd been, and as the stink from my shoes was filling the air around us, he obviously did. I wanted to explain that I was a gold smuggler, not a bugger, but I had to just smile and allow the cop his speculations. I waved "adios" to the little gold carrier, and he sped off into the hot night as if he were carrying no more than a flea on his back.

Much as I thought I hated that gold, there were times I'd get a bit of a letdown after deliveries. There were always the tension, the anxiety, and the weight, but I at least had a mission, a task, an objective, nefarious though it may be.

I hied my way back to Calcutta and the old Grand Hotel. It was a bit monsoony then, and, more often than not, if the city wasn't drenched with humidity, it was awash in rain, which flushed everything and everybody clean. The old Brit Raj buildings had about as much grandeur as the remains of the Third Reich, towering above the street life and death, decaying, but still sneering at the labors of the poor folks eking out the existence on the footpaths of that polluted and unmanageable city.

Despite teeth blackened from chewing betel and lime paste, the street folk seemed obsessive about personal cleanliness. A bit of an odd moiety exists here, very clean persons side by side with very unclean streets. The inevitable sacred cows wander about, pissing and dumping on them at will; but having lived under Brit rule all that time, the people have been trained to it.

'Twas here, of course, was coined the term "Black Hole of Calcutta," to memorialize the spot where the Nawab of Bengal deposited the Brit garrison of the city in a smallish space, and a good many of them suffocated during a warmish night in 1756. After a hundred years of Brit misrule and monarchical terrorism, the Indian soldiers had mutinied. The sensitive British officials preserved their bullets in cow fat (sacred to Hindus) and pig fat (anathema to Moslems); thus each religious soldier was required to perform sacrilegious acts; hence, mutiny. Brutal were the acts of the Sepoys, though they were simply retaliating for colonial savagery.

I'd find myself wandering up a street and down a street, going into dark alleys, and I'd see suffering beyond reason. So I'd go back to my palatial hotel quarters and drink some more, because I'd want to fix up the world, especially its children and, more particularly, mine.

Again, my airline ticket would have allowed me to visit other cities, but I became paralyzed with drinking and despair, so I had no desire to do so. I did chat occasionally with some pukka types and other passing bodies, but mostly I sat and stared and moped in my hotel.

On the street one day, I was snared by a young fakir, a guru-type of lad, with the flowing robes and the beard and the talk. He suggested to me that I was troubled by some personal problem, and told me to write down the name of the person who troubled me, which I did. He said to fold up the bit of paper and give it to him without letting him see the name. He then handed it back to me with a piece of string, which he told me to tie round the paper. He was a deft chap, as he then told me I was pining for a lady name Linda. That astounded me, as I couldn't imagine he could see the writing. An offering of twenty rupees, he then said, would assist him in revealing more.

He described her in general terms—pretty slim, dark hair, tall—and then he told me another twenty-five rupees would help him tell of my future with her. Clever lad. He had extracted enough information from me to be able to feed obvious inferences back to me, and I fell for this rubbish. This seer informed me that the lady was very much in love with me; all she needed was a bit of encouragement and she'd be back in bed with me.

"When will this consummation take place?" sez I.

That answer cost me twenty-five more rupees: She was awaiting my return to fall into my arms. Cheered up no end, I went back to retrieve the old portmanteau and trek my way back to the U.S.A. via Zurich.

———

THE GOLDMAN WAS AWAITING ME in Zurich with my money, my own passport, and my various personal belongings. He wanted me to set off immediately with another illicit shipment, but, agog with the prospect of reconciliation, I told him the mission would have to be postponed. He snuffled something about never trusting women, but he agreed to meet me again in ten days, at the same hotel.

I was in good spirits on the Swissair flight to Idlewild. Rang up one of the chums on arrival, got a bed for the nonce, showered the body, and got on the blower to Linda. No answer. Every half hour I called, but all I got was that echoing, eerie, ringing tone that betokens an empty apartment.

I rang her parents, who weren't handing out any information, and after a few choice vulgarities on my part, the mother ended the conversation. As usual, I sought the solace of the sauce, and before I knew it, it was I A.M., and I was once again on the phone, abusing her parents. They threatened me with the cops; they would make sure I served the six months that had been suspended previously.

My efforts to contact Linda remained futile, so I decided to skip town and go to England, where I had not been for many a year.

While in England in the service, I decided to seek out the man who had seeded me. The last rumor had it that he was laboring in Coventry. Some inquiries in the Irish pubs were met with the shuffling of the feet, the averted gaze, and the scratching of the noggin and vague statements that he'd been seen in various other jobs and places. One man finally blurted out the truth. "Yer father's in prison for drunk and disorderly conduct again."

Off to the jail was I. A couple of quick lies to the warden about being on my way to Russia or something gained me admittance outside of regular visiting hours.

The man who had fathered me was led into the dreary visiting area, which smelled of damp and decay and old body odor. An ill-lit place with broken benches and a sad saggy little table to sit at face-to-face. He was unshaven and the teeth were out. The old tweed suit would have been loose on a man twice his size, and the shoes had no laces, so he dragged them as he shuffled in.

I eyed the suit and raised an eyebrow. "Savile Row?" I asked, and *he gave me a gummy smile. He told me this was his twenty-third or twenty-fourth conviction for drunk and disorderly—that he had to serve a full thirty days for each one, which meant he'd served almost two years off and on.*

He said the warden and the staff didn't like the Irish, but they treated him well enough, and the food was regular, but he couldn't afford cigarettes. I gave him a couple of quid—which the guard pretended not to see—and then there was silence.

I couldn't think of anything to say but the unsayable: Why did you leave, you worthless old sot?

But I couldn't say it, and didn't have to ask. He would only say what he'd always said, that it was the fault of the Brits, and he'd ask me if I was ready to die for Ireland.

Then the guard announced 'twas time to go.

He shuffled off and I was hoping he'd look back and say I'm sorry, but he didn't and I left, blinking back the angry tears.

———

I HAD LIVED IN ENGLAND when I was a teenager, working as a laborer in Coventry. I was a welder of bicycle wheels in Dunlops, shoveled coal in the Coventry Gas Works, and worked in Courtaulds as a sweeper. There were signs in the windows of various houses on Cope Street where I lodged: to wit, ROOM TO LET. NO IRISH PLEASE. They're very polite, the English, annoyingly polite, using courtesy the same way New Yorkers do hostility. They say "please," and they call you "Paddy," even if it's not your name, but it is more polite than saying, "Hey, you," isn't it?

But, it's all different now. Here I am, traveled and moneyed and, in London, I met up with Richard Harris, now son-in-law of Lord Ogmore, a Welsh coal miner, 'tis said, but a lord nevertheless.

When I arrived at the Harris door, I was greeted by his wife, Elizabeth, with, "Hello, Malachy. When are you leaving?" She knew my arrival portended trouble, as now Richard could always say I led him astray—as if anyone could lead *that* headstrong lad anywhere!

Harris and I rendezvoused with sundry old rugby chums—a grand drinking crowd. We'd spend the day in the pubs, talking rugby, the horses, neutral politics, a bit of soccer, and the do-you-know-who-just-died game, and when the pubs closed for the afternoon siesta, we'd adjourn to the private clubs, lest the great discourse be interrupted. Then, a scattering for dinner and a reassembling around eightish, with everyone yelping greetings as each newcomer hove into sight—typical male greetings of high jocularity, as if the person had not been seen for lo these many years.

Some bods nipped off to work for the odd ten minutes or so, but, generally speaking, we were a solid cadre of subjects moving in formation from pub to club and back again.

After a good bit of this, it was time to get back to what I laughingly called work, so I bid farewell and hopped over to Zurich. My employer was spluttering with rage. I was about three days tardy, my corpus was preceded into the room by the aura of alcohol, and, as I had for the nonce adopted the English tradition of the once-a-year bath, the goldman reeled back as if he had been slapped in the phiz with a decomposing conger eel. He was a religious man, having been educated by Benedictine monks, so he never used any kind of profanity. But I could state without being charged with perjury that he said, "Good Christ!" on this occasion.

He implored me to take a shower while he went and got the gold and the new documents. He then returned with canvas, thread, needles, and scissors, and *muy rapidamente* I was fitted for another vest. I'd had to shred the other vests in India, as there are exit customs officers who could be curious about such pocket-filled garments.

My passport said I was John Taylor, and this time my instructions were to pop into Pakistan via Karachi, leg it up to Lahore, cross over by rail to Amritsar, and south to Delhi and Bombay. After a day spent securing the visas, back with me to the holey city of Roma, where I sampled a fleshpot or two, and off again to the airport to catch the flying toothpaste tube to Karachi. In keeping with the Moslem faith, my new code name was "Ali Jinnah," the founder of Pakistan.

The first and only stop was Bahrain, an oil-rich sheikdom on the Persian Gulf. The journey from the plane to the terminal was blisteringly hot *and* scaldingly humid, a combination I'd not experienced before. I was barely able to cover the fifty yards, gasping for air and hydration. This being a Moslem joint, I knew there would be a plenitude of plain old aqua. Spying the water fountain, the terminal oasis, I made rapid steps toward the thirst-slaking water. It was a very low fountain, more fit for a child and, being desperate, I heedlessly forgot I was top-heavy with bullion, so I toppled over, straight into the wall, whacking the cranium and sliding to the floor.

Right opposite where I fell was a row of seats, on which sat as stoic a bunch of Arabian Knights as I have ever seen. Burnoosed Bedouins and veiled hawk-faced Tuaregs, and one cherubic chap with turban, whose eyes gave indication of amusement. Nothing for it but to grimace as if in pain (I was only embarrassed) and claw my way to biped posish number one. Sixteen dark eyes followed my upward climb. If it hadn't been Ramadan, or some other sacred time, I'm sure they would have applauded, particularly as I did bow to them.

There wasn't much to the rest of the trip to Karachi, the former capital of Pakistan. I went to see the tomb of Mohammed Ali Jinnah, my namesake, the founder of the country, and a wander about the city in the evening found me gaping again at British architecture and wondering at the looniness of a people trying to re-create the home country.

My hotel room was not private, in that it had a curtained window looking into the hallway. I was not sure that the curtains totally concealed my doings in the room, so I did all my doings in the bathroom, thank you.

The streets were packed with the usual tidal wave of humankind, different from that in India in that many of the women wore that black garb which envelopes the head and body totally. Some had netting over the eye openings, lest their eyeballs arouse lust. In the minarets, the muezzins called the followers of Mohammed to prayer; in the evenings particularly, they emitted sounds that floated quaveringly eerie over the suddenly quiet thoroughfares.

From Karachi it was on to Lahore, and from there I took the train to Amritsar. My first-class compartment on the train assured me of complete privacy as long as the train was in motion; it could only be entered by clambering up the steps and entering doors from the outside.

It was a relief once more to doff the shirt, coat, and undershirt, remove the gold, and take a cooling breath. It was supposed to be a nonstop journey of about 1 hour, as I recall, but to be on the safe side, and having had no drink to encourage bravado, I put the gold in the portmanteau, put the shirts back on the bod, and read the *Times of India*. The main news was that China was doing a bit of wok-banging to scare India into ceding some territories. I was a trifle nervous about being in closer proximity to the northern borders than heretofore, but my fears in foreign-war areas were replaced by another little fear, caused by a slight change in the train's rhythms, which indicated a slowing down, and then a rattling, chunting, lurching, stop.

A swift return to my Catholic religion, complete with prayers of my youth. "Oh Jasus, Mary, and Holy Saint Joseph, have mercy on my body and my soul, as there's something going on here!" I didn't know whether to dive for the gold, put on my coat jacket, look out the window, gibber, or continue my idiotic directives to God.

A quick dekko out the window did nothing to clear up matters, because the train was halted at a curve. Just as I was about to open the bag to get at the contraband, the left door was opened, and a very tall, turbaned, khaki-clad Sikh swung himself into my once-private compartment. He pulled the door shut and, leaning out, he waved to someone, and the train began moving. He said, "Good day," and I said, "Good day."

He eyed my bit of luggage—suspiciously, I thought—partially opened on the seat beside. I promptly zipped it shut, and with a prayer for help, I hoisted the blasted thing on the luggage shelf o'er the head. My Sikh traveling companion made an attempt to assist in heaving the bag up, but a bit of old rugby tactic "accidentally" knocked him back on his Punjabi arse, with profuse apologies from me about my clumsiness.

We sat facing each other silently for a while, him with a smile on his phiz, and me with a smile that didn't involve my eyes. He is on to me, thought I.

My employer in Zurich had instructed me that if the corner was too tight, I was to offer one kilo of the metal for extrication from said corner. I was about to do that, when the Sikh spoke.

"May I ask the purpose of your visit to India, Sir?"

"Don't you know?" I blurted.

"Oh, no, sir. We are not seers, contrary to popular belief. I am asking this question in my official capacity."

"I am visiting as a tourist."

"Where will you stay?"

"In Amritsar. I want to see the Golden Temple, and learn a little more about Ram Das."

I knew that would get to him, as the Golden Temple is sacred to all Sikhs, and Ram Das, its founder, is one of their ten great teachers. I had also learned that red-bearded laddies get a special nod in the Sikh religion. Being red-bearded put me a couple of hectares ahead of your average smuggler, who wouldn't know Ram Das from a ram's arse. I'd a bit of knowledge from the reading I'd done, and my newfound friend nodded paternalistically as I trotted out the half-baked ideas I had on the man's religion and culture. He did ask to see my passport, and gave me a card to fill out.

My passport remained in his possession, which made me uneasy, but I couldn't demand it back, so there we sat smiling and chatting. An enquiry here and there elicited the information that he was married and had several children; government work did not pay well, but it was secure; he had a good deal of respect for Gandhi, but he was a bit afraid of Nehru's socialistic tendencies; and so on.

A compliment on his English set the man positively beaming. Had I asked for a night with his wife, I was sure of no objection, so pleased was he.

At last, the train pulled into Amritsar and stopped amid a great cacophony of shouts, doors banging open and shut, great luggage carts being wheeled up to be loaded, and people jumping off the train. With a deft move, I managed to get the bag off the overhead rack and acted as if it were a feathery lightweight thing. My friend, Mr. Singh (all Sikhs take the name Singh), accompanied me as I strolled up the platform, blithely swinging the bag, though it nearly tore the arm out of the socket. There, stretched across the exit were a line of the khaki-clads, seated behind a table, going gaga in orgiastic rubber-stamp frenzies, and to one side there stood a queue of people whose luggage was being inspected.

Brazenly, I headed for the customs table to heave the bag onto it, but my friend said to follow him. He laid my passport down, pounded the table, and said something to the man behind the stamps, who stared at me with still brown eyes while he spoke. Slowly, a smile spread over his phiz, and he reached for his beloved stamp, quietly pressed it to my passport, and spoke the grand words, "Welcome to India, Mr. Taylor."

A TAXI TOOK ME TO THE HOTEL RECOMMENDED BY MY traveling companion, where I collapsed on the bed under the best fan in the whole world and slept the sleep of the once-again-uncaught gold smuggler.

Amritsar seemed a prosperous place, with a paucity of paupers, though a sufficient number existed to get on my coattail. There was no shortage of restaurants and I had a goodish evening repast. After dining I set out for the Golden Temple, but could not enter that evening, as there was a bit of a gathering that didn't include the Westerner.

I asked my rickshaw driver to take me over to the Jallianwalla Bagh Park so that I could pay an atheistic homage to the dead. This sacred spot—quiet enough now, with markers and small monuments to remind people of slaughter for peace—was the site of a great public meeting in April of 1919, where Indian freedom fighters, politicians, and professors, along with the peasants and the prosperous, the clean and the unclean, gathered to yell out loud that world-echoing cry: "England, get out of my country!"

The British army, having just finished up World War I, in which there was an abundance of human slaughter for the freedom of small nations—and only incidentally, of course, corporate profit—was now bereft of small nations to free, and, having gotten used to shooting bullets at will, the Brit commanders thought it a jolly good idea to turn their attention to freedom seekers. So they turned their guns on thousands of defenseless, independence-minded folk, who asked nothing more than the right to help plan the destiny of their own nation. The thundering guns, directed by murderous thugs with cultured accents, put paid to many a peaceful Indian's dream.

The bullets thudded into the heads and hearts and bodies of these gentle people, shot down by the King's Own Assassins, whilst overhead circled the vultures, chatting amongst themselves about how delightful the Brits are at providing daily repasts, just when you think you might have to go hungry.

It was somewhat over a year later that a bunch of ebullient Brits, in the garb of Black and Tans, swept into Croke Park, a sports field in Dublin, on their Crossley tenders, turned the guns on the spectators at the football match, and let fly, blowing scores of innocent civilians out of their seats into early graves and hospitals for the permanently crippled. And off they went, where they toasted each other on a gallant action well executed, and drank the health of George, formerly Saxe-Coburg Gotha, formerly Wettin, now Windsor, Commander-in-Chief of the Imperial Assassins.

It's hard not to take massacres personally. One minute you are in Andersonville, Georgia, or Croke Park in Dublin, or Jallianwalla Bagh Garden, and the next thing you are queuing up with thousands of fellow massacre-ees for admission to Paradise, Shangri-la, Nirvana, Heaven, or Valhalla, wondering why the swift, premature summons to eternity. "It's nothing, old sport. Just the Brits superseding God."

But 'twas time to abandon the pain of history, and return to the pain of the present, and get on with the problems of smuggling the ill-got ingots past stamp-mad officialdom.

I booked a sleeping accommodation on the train to New Delhi, thinking I'd have a cubicle to myself. Imagine my wonder, when I was ushered in, to find an American female on her way to New Delhi to work with some U.S. Embassy trade office. There were two bunks, and in a fit of overzealous gallantry, I offered the lady the lower, forgetting I'd then have to heave self and ingots to the one above. How then, of course, to divest myself of same, and even more importantly, how to reinvest myself once New Delhi was reached?

The other dilemma was to divest myself of thoughts of bunking down with the trade lady, friendly as she was. I managed to say goodnight, clamber up a rickety little ladder, fall onto a slablike mattress, and wiggle out of the garb, the gold, and the footwear. The relief of it all was enough to put me into a sound sleep.

Routine getting-off-the-train stuff once there: heading for a good hotel; checking in; tipping the portmanteaux lugger; ushering him out, since he was a bit garrulous. It was so oppressively hot in New Delhi that the short ride to the hotel had me riveting perspiration all the way down to the socks. Tearing off the garments and gold, dumping the lot on the bed, I gamboled nudely into the bathroom and placed the bod under the healing shower, which was surprisingly strong.

After using up nearly all the ablutional waters of that city, I secured a large fluffy towel and, stepping out into the room, I was greeted by a sight that nearly stopped my heart. Seated in an armchair by my door, there reposed a khaki-clad Sikh. He smiled the enigmatic smile of the cat who has blocked up the mouse hole.

"Jasus," sez I, "you startled me. How did you get in here?"

"I have a key," sez the Sikh.

"Oh," sez I. "I see."

He smiled. I smiled. He had me at a bit of a disadvantage, as I was clad only in the towel. On the bed, the gold-carrying vest was almost entirely covered by my shirt and undershirt, but there remained an inch or two of the canvas showing. I sat on the bed and managed to cover it with the shirt. We smiled at each other again. Is he on to me, and is he just playing a game? I couldn't make out from his sparse insignia whether he was cop, customs, or immigration. Not wanting to leave the room to get dressed, which would allow him to poke about, I finally said, "What can I do for you?"

"Nothing at all, sir. I am employed by the hotel to make sure all our guests are happy and secure in their rooms, and it's part of my job to welcome you and make you feel that there is nothing to fear whilst you are staying here. As well as that, it is beastly hot out there, and I thought I could combine my welcome with getting cool in this, your room."

"Gotcha," sez I, "and I hope these twenty rupees will purchase a cooling beverage for you."

"Thank you, sir. I thought you would understand," and he was gone, leaving me with a full load of ingots, instead of a load lessened by one for bribery or by a sentence of five years in prison.

There was an ancient wardrobe in the room wherein one could hang the garments and deposit the footwear. It was about seven feet high, and had a flat surface on top, behind a fancy carved facade. A climb on the chair, and a check for the dust, of which there was a surfeit, assured me the housekeeping staff were not, thank Krishna, a diligent lot. That's where I deposited the booty, then I lay down for a bit of slumber prior to venturing down for the tiffin'.

The evening was a bit cooler, so I decided on some sightseeing and ventured over to the place where Gandhi was assassinated. At one point in my walk, I stopped to look at a squatting snake charmer, doing the old flute routine with the deadly king cobra. The charmer's family, a wife and about a half dozen children, appeared to be encamped behind him. Suddenly a little girl of about three or four years detached herself from her mother's sari, ran around her father the charmer and grabbed the cobra. We, the spectators, all gasped, thinking, of course, this cobra would do her in, but it must have been a defanged chap, because it retreated in defeat into its basket amid whoops of laughter from us breath-holding onlookers.

To keep the man from belting the child, I gave him some rupees, and said it was a good joke; he smiled with his blackened teeth and thanked me, while a few others threw some rupees into his basket, so all was well.

Anxiety about the gold atop the wardrobe impelled the return to the overnight quarters, despite the offer of the driver to secure for me the services of a young virgin who was so adept at pleasing men that I would have no hesitation in paying double the two hundred rupees he would charge. I was intrigued by the apparent contradiction of how a virgin becomes expert at pleasing men without experiencing the dipping of the wick, but it didn't matter, as I couldn't avail myself of the joys of storming the barricades of a maidenhead on that particular evening.

The next morning I was off again, on another rickety prop plane. All this traveling, a day here and a day there, was wearying, but I was obeying the instructions from Zurich. "Jumping about makes your movements hard to trace," he said, "and always give a false forwarding address and every other kind of false information, and they will never catch up to you."

That's what he thought. I can tell you that a red-bearded, red-visaged Caucasian dawdling from Amritsar to Delhi to Bombay is never exactly invisible, but chances must be taken when nefarious work has to be done.

More hedgehopping, and the eventual arrival in Bombay. Another hotel, this one for Indian businessmen. Conceal or carry the gold—I pondered the alternative and then made off for the phone call.

"Hello. Bombay Trading Company. Good morning. May I assist you?"

"Yes, this is Ali Jinnah."

Throwing caution to the storms, I simply said I was in from

Europe and had business to discuss. The voice on the other end said that the gentleman I wanted to reach had been contacted by the authorities on another matter and had gone to Hyderabad to avoid further contact. He was, therefore, unavailable for any business transactions for the foreseeable future.

I queried what to do with the consignment of metal now in the immediate vicinity, and was told it would be inadvisable to bring it to their premises, as their inventory was now being assessed. I took that to mean they were being watched. Did he have any suggestions as to what I should do then?

"None, sir," and he wished me divine blessings on all my future business dealings, then hung up.

I did have the goldman of Zurich's mailbox address for the confirmation cable about having delivered the booty, so I decided to use it for a nondelivery message. "Unable to deliver your gift, as the guest of honor was unexpectedly called away. Any suggestions?" Risky biz, that, what with having to deal with the prying eyes of the post office folk.

Cursing that fucking idiot who had gotten himself embroiled with the authorities, and all other fools who were holding up commerce, I simply parked the vest under the mattress and went off to seek diversion. A likely looking lad in white, barefooted, of course, approached me with the ingratiating grin on his quite-dark phiz. He told me that his name was Francis Joseph and that he was a Roman Catholic—a bit of news that cheered me up, as I knew the man would understand the necessity of gargling the grape.

I explained to the lad that he was probably named after Franz Josef, Emperor of Austria and King of Hungary, whose grandnephew, Francis Ferdinand, got himself assassinated at Sarajevo, thus sparking off the Great War. Sez I to him, "You think you got troubles!"

The poor fellow gaped at me uncomprehendingly as I rambled on with my impromptu history lesson. His face, however, took on a glow when I asked if it were all right to address him as "Emperor," which I proceeded to do. The next order of biz: Did he know a drinking establishment where documents were not required. By God, sir, he did! So—lead on, Emperor!

———

IT WAS A DARK AND odoriferous place, with a paraffin lamp or two, which only enhanced the gloom. The Emperor said he would fetch the drink for me if I would please give him the rupees. I asked for a vodka and lime, to which he replied, "They have only one drink here, sir."

"Then get one for me, with a chaser of lime juice," and he was gone into the darkness.

A furtive look around showed me that there were khaki-clads, white-clads, Western-clads—all quietly sipping and murmuring, in the serene cadence of Indian murmuring. Some of the lads looked as if they were law enforcement types who should be raiding the joint instead of drinking there.

The Emperor returned, bearing the beverages. The drink he handed me had such a vile taste that I could only surmise it was made from used diesel oil. I was caught between gasping and coughing, with the Emperor gleefully thumping 'twixt the shoulder blades.

A couple of dollops of lime juice eased the pain, and I resumed the quaffing. I must have murdered my taste buds, because after a bit, the stuff seemed quite potable, and, indeed, the world seemed quite potable as I leaned back and surveyed the underbelly of Bombay. I have no idea how long I stayed, but when I went to rise from the chair, the nether limbs went on a wildcat strike, and I had to be assisted by the Emperor.

"Well, Emperor, what have you in mind to satisfy the urgings of the flesh?"

"I do not understand you, sir."

I explained that I had a pressing need to share a bed with a willing partner.

"Oh, I see," sez he. "Would you prefer a good clean boy or a good clean girl?"

"A girl will be just grand," sez I.

"I will bring you to the home of two sisters from Punditry, who are very nice and who are both Roman Catholic, and who are saving up for their marriage dowry, which is why they are sharing their bodies at this time."

It was midnight outside and, of course, it was darkish, but the Emperor guided me on my unsteady way. He propped me against a thick wall, instructed me to wait, and he was gone again. Up ahead, a door opened, and I saw him engage in conversation with somebody in the light streaming out. He turned toward me, gesturing for me to join him.

There was nothing meretricious about the little habitation I now entered. An old man sat in a corner, and at the table sat a younger man with what appeared to be his wife and two other women, both young and quite attractive, with the saris and the oculi red on the forehead.

We agreed on a price, and I was told to choose one of the younger women, and a devil of a job it was, too, as I was afraid of offending the nonpickee. After making my selection and suggesting we adjourn to more private quarters, they all smiled. The woman I'd chosen picked up a clothesline, looped it to a nail in the wall, drew it across the room to another nail, and then threw some tattered sheets and saris over it to give at least visual privacy.

She brought me inside our makeshift boudoir and helped me shed the interfering garb, then washed the privates with a cloth and a dish of warm water, into which she had poured the good old Lysol. Sex, particularly sex for hire, ought to be private in my opinion, an impossible desire in the situation I was in. The folks on the other side of the curtain murmured, and continued eating and slurping the tea.

I was still in a sozzled state from the tractor fuel at the speakeasy, and I was sleepy. When she began the feathery ministrations to the most sensitive part of the bod, so soothing was she that I drifted off into a grand and deep sleep. I awoke in complete darkness, not knowing where I was. An exploratory grope indicated the presence of another body, while inside the confines of the head, the Nuremberg rally was being accompanied by a cacophonic off-key rendition of the *1812 Overture*, complete with fireworks.

To divert myself from anguish, I awakened the nut-brown maiden who was sharing the pad and got her to resume the ministrations of the gentle hand, and, after having settled the business I came there for, it was time for me to depart.

Beyond the curtain, where the only source of light was a little red-globed lamp, all the bodies were asleep on mats. The Emperor was still present, though not upright, so I prodded him awake and said I had to go.

Once more, I had lived through a night of stumbling, whoring, and drinking. Again, remorse, the devil's contrition, came galloping in, lance in hand, skewering, accusing, finger-pointing, lacerating the soul; myself whimpering like a dog. But a bath and a couple of aspro, and a night's sleep in my comfortable bed, and I returned to alert immorality.

It did occur to me that I had a specific purpose in India, which I had almost forgotten, and I frantically leapt from the bed to check under the mattress, but my golden cache was gone.

Despair oozed into my heart, nearly bringing it to a tarry halt. I searched everywhere, under the bed, in the wardrobe, on top of the wardrobe, the drawers of the bureau, the bath tub—but no gold! Try and explain this to Zurich!

I wasn't inclined to believe that he had connections with those who break legs on consignment and, for slightly more, shoot you dead. But then, one never knows.

The first thought after the emergency surge of adrenaline had passed was that a drink, even of that malodorous piss at the speakeasy, would do wonders for the jangling nervous system. I still had the smallest bit of good sense left, though, and first went to check the post office to see if there had been a response to my cable. There was, referring me to a new contact at another small local enterprise.

That still left me with the small matter of the boosting of the bullion from my boudoir. While I'm at the P.O., why not send a 'gram to the goldman in Zurich and let him know the stuff had gone poof? How to word it? "GOLD STOLEN! PLEASE ADVISE." Forget it, and get out of the country, as they will be onto you now, so go, man. Why the fuck didn't I think of that before? It could be the police, and now they were playing games with me. Every man on the street was now watching me. Paranoia was the order of the day.

The sweat was pouring out of me, still stinking from the sewer water I'd drunk last night. After informing the reception desk that I was checking out, I dashed up the stairs, and told the man who was cleaning the room to go, as I had to pack. He offered to help, but realizing he could be the thief, I told him his assistance was not required at the moment. If memory serves, my exact phrasing was, "Fuck off, and leave me alone!"

I cleared out the drawers and the wardrobe, dumping everything on the bed, and went to lift the portmanteau off the latticed luggage holder by the bureau. The grasping hand was stayed by an unexpected resistance; I tugged again, and up it came, still heavy. The heart fluttered, and when I set the bag on the bed and opened it, there, snuggled inside, comfy and safe, were all those delightful, shining ingots. I kissed the fuckers, I was so glad to see them, and did a merry little waltz, holding them close to the chest, jabbering to them like a lunatic.

Then the paranoia set in again. Was the gold stolen, and then put back again, to set up an inescapable trap? Were "they" even now, about to burst through my door and pounce on me in all my innocence?

But then it edged back into my mind. When I had returned in my half-stupored state, in last night's fine dawn hours, I had figured out that if I put the stuff almost in full sight, purloined-letter style, nobody would see it, and so I had removed it from beneath the mattress and placed it in the luggage, the first place a thief would look. That was how the heart-stopping mystery was solved.

A tap on the door signaled the bellman coming to take the luggage. "Why?" sez I, forgetting I had told 'em I was checking out. "Tell them I've changed my mind. I'm staying."

"Very good, sir." He stood smiling at me, not moving.

"Ah, yes. The rupees for your trouble."

"Thank you, sir."

———

THE NEW TRADING COMPANY MAN I was to get hold of told me he would pick me up, and we would go to his club, which was in the suburbs—an enclosed place, with tennis courts, a cricket ground, and a few golf holes. I asked the man why we were out here in the open and how was I to get the gold to him.

"Nobody would suspect us doing anything out here at the club, and as I trade with Europe and the Americas, it is only natural I should entertain my business contacts here."

He led me to the changing room and sent me into the lavatory, where I took off the vest and dropped it into a golf bag he then casually carried into his locker. I was spending so much time in lavatories, I was beginning to entertain the karma idea: Maybe this was my destiny.

That exchange completed, I headed back to the hotel. The Emperor was hanging around the premises when I got back, so I instructed him to fetch one of the Roman Catholic dowry girls and dispatch her to my room. Of course, the desk clerk had to be bribed to allow my lady visitor in, since an unbribed hotel desk clerk is a fiercely moral person.

The evening repast was had, and the Emperor took me to another dungeon, where only homemade beer was served, which had a good wallop to it, so 'twas not long 'til the chin started drooping toward the chest and I wended the way back to the hotel.

The next day, I flew to Delhi, braved the various exit customs and immigration officials, paid the rupees to get out, and headed to Rome. But a trifle of engine trouble occurred, so the pilot U-turned and took us back to Delhi. Many nervous people inhabited that plane, including Sarah, a rather nice-looking girl seated next to me. I babbled a bit about it being a safety measure the pilot was taking, rather than an emergency, and that we'd be doing the perfect three-point landing in double-quick time, which of course happened. Somehow, my new friend misdirected her gratitude for her salvation my way, so the formerly nervous young woman gave me a big hug and a rather-more-than-friendly kiss.

There was the usual milling at Delhi Airport, and, of course, the officials with the stamps came out in force. It was a stampers paradise! They had to stamp us all back into India, through customs and immigration again, and then stamp us all back out, as we reversed the procedure a mere two hours later. What a frightful economic disorder for the rubber-stamp and ink pad industry, if we should all just decide to stay home!

Airborne again, I had hopes of joining the Mile High Club, that exclusive group of male liars who claim they've had sexual intercourse with an airline stewardess or someone else they just met whilst in flight. Wives, fiancées, girlfriends, and persons previously known are not counted. My new chum, Sarah, was on her way to join her family in Riyadh, Saudi Arabia, and after the requisite few beverages of the 86 proof variety, I fell in love with her. I suggested she abandon this silly notion of visiting her mom and dad in the god-forsaken country of sand, heat, flies, oil, and harems, and continue on to Rome with me. She appeared to consider the idea seriously, but I wasn't sure. Overcome with temporary amour and alcohol, I secured a couple of those skimpy airline blankets, lifted the armrests, and stretched the pair of us out on the narrow confines of the seats, atop seatbelt buckles and other protuberances. I kept falling off and getting wedged 'twixt my seat and the back of the next row, and only with great dexterity was I able to resurface.

Sarah, who thought it all very amusing, kept up a steady stream of giggles, guaranteed to quell any ardor. Passing stewardesses averted the eyes, as they apparently didn't want to intervene in this love fest. It just got sillier and sillier, and with the pair of us laughing our arses off, any hopes of Mile High Club membership, or indeed any club membership if word got out, faded into the stratosphere.

Sarah bid me bye-bye at Bahrain, and off she went to join her family. I stopped off at Rome again. I'd made a promise to myself that I would make an attempt to really see the Holy City on this stop, and barreling about to basilicas occupied the jet-weary psyche for a portion of a day; drinking, the rest of it.

At least the people who ran that city had the good taste to leave ancient walls and buildings intact. You couldn't hurl a stray bit of granite in any direction in Rome without hitting a church, a cleric, or, in the summer, a native of Cleveland.

The basilica's original purpose, as designed by ancient Romans, was for the tribunals to carry on the legal system, a more civil gladiatorial arena, if you will. The Church then, in its cunning quest for power, built basilicas with similar designs so that the average punter would still be overawed by architectural power and, by association, attribute to the Church legal power.

Later on, of course, outside the city, spreading its grasping holy tentacles ever further, the Church would dominate rural landscapes with churches of different design. Towering spires were the order of the day and, inside the spires, huge bells tolled the order of *your* day: the get-up-outa-dat-bed bell; the Angelus bell; the come-to-Mass bell; the come-eat-your-crust-of-bread-while-we-feast-on-your-tithings bell; and, after your handful of days of all that, your death-knell bell. Inside the churches, huge organs filled the space with triumphal, powerful sound, and there was a panoply of power places—pulpits, thrones, and altars.

Centuries after, the Church passed the baton to Capitalism, when they agreed between them it would be far more efficient: Rather than having the peasants laboring in the field and squeezing from them the tithes, they would do the sweat-of-the-brow bit indoors, and be allowed to take a tenth portion with them when they left.

"But, let's see," said the new Synod of Syndics, "how can we still dominate the landscape and the soundscape and prevent escape? Something like spires. How about smokestacks? They'll not be able to miss *them*. Bells? No place to put 'em. How about blasting steam horns or screaming, high-pitched whistles? Yeah, either will do, so long as it's morning, noon, and night. Organs again? No! Machinery: roaring, belching, dangerous machinery for the power that's in it. Should we keep the stained-glass windows? Naw. Ordinary glass windows will do—they'll get stained soon enough." And so power was transferred from the papal glove to the invisible hand, and there you have it: the gospel according to me.

B ACK IN ZURICH, I WAS TOLD THAT BECAUSE THERE WAS A bit of restlessness in the gold market, we were postponing the next trip for five or six weeks. I was given my remuneration to date and remembered that the brother Frank had suggested that if I had an opportunity, I should visit Ibiza, a Mediterranean island off the coast of Spain, then a popular spot with the jet-setters and itinerant proto-hippies of Europe and the U.S.

It is my belief that all island peoples are cuckoo, and while it is yet to be resolved which of the many theories advanced explain this phenom, it remains a fact that I was able to fit right into the island life. It helped that Brendan Behan had preceded me, because the lunacy of any peripatetic Mick thereafter was measured against his doings, and if his antics had set the mark at 100 percent, then the rest of us were safe, as it was hard to hit even 75 on that scale.

The hotel I checked into was solid with decorative tiles, arches, and marble floors, which echoed even when people talked softly, and it was economical in the peseta-outlay department.

All the expats, plus a smattering of the born-and-bred-on-the-Island battalion, who for some reason did not mind being seen in the company of the runoff of Europe and the U.S., would sit together getting potted, whilst quoruming, which meant having a minyan of at least ten pesetas for two Fundadors, the favored local drink, made from decayed, burnt, liquefied, grapes. Amongst us were Scandinavians, Limeys, Taffys, Jocks, the Mick (me), Krauts, and Eyeties, and we would all foregather and drink the night away. There were some artists who weren't artisting, writers who weren't writing, and actors who weren't acting. Nobody seemed to have a function, a purpose, or a mission, and the focus was on the gatherings of an evening.

The island police, the Civil Guard, not very different from the days when Franco occupied the island in the so-called Spanish Civil War, strutted up and around the Plaza on Sundays for the band concert after Mass. They were impeccable in their uniforms, with shiny boots, brass buttons, leather headgear, and gloves. It was apparently de rigueur to wear the left one and carry the right one in the left hand, leaving the right hand free for the ever-present cigarette, just like the evil Nazi with the University of Heidelberg dueling scar in the movies. The fag-puffing Civil Guard—and they were about as civil as their war—eyed us, and we eyed them, but we were generally left to our fun and our Fundador.

———

STROLLING DOWN THE STAIRS OF the hotel one noon, I got chatting with a smallish couple from England, who informed me they were on their honeymoon. I gave the perfunctory congratulations to the male, and "I wish you every happiness" to the female, and invited them to a celebratory beverage. Noon it was, mind you, and not a smidgen of grub had yet passed the teeth. Nevertheless, a few jorums of beer put the head into the carefree mode, and thence came the graduation to my new friend, Fundador.

The three of us chatted about this and about this, and sometimes touched on that. The groom explained that he had recently been promoted into management in his workplace and that he wanted nothing more to do with unions and their "shower of shirkers," as he put it. It was the usual song:

> *The working class can kiss my arse,*
> *I've got the foreman's job at last.*

Courtesy forbade me from pile-driving him into terra firma for his treason, and a glance at his—I realized now, misfortunate—wife convinced me that she must be rescued from this brainless traitor to his class. We toddled off to another café and another café and another café. At one point, a whispering waiter told me he had some absinthe—then as now not exactly legal—and would I be interested in purchasing some? *"Yo estoy su hombre,"* sez I, having a go at the lingo.

After a few strong cups of the absinthe, I became totally convinced that the young bride was now deeply regretting her premature marriage to the conservative management arsehole, and that her eyes were beseeching me to please, please rescue her from durance vile. I winked at her to show my solidarity with her desire for freedom, and to reassure her that the troops were massing for the mission.

The husband caught me winking at his new possession—although I don't think she herself ever noticed—and, to cover up, I pretended I had something in my eye. By this time of night, around nineish, almost nothing had yet plopped into the still waters of the stomach, and we were so sozzled that the fumes of absinthe and brandy were able to ascend untrammeled to the cathedral of the brain, wherein glorious *Te Deums* were sung in anticipation of victory over Godless capitalist manipulators who lure young girls into lives of corruption and materialistic gratification.

My plan was to keep pretending I was his friend and, by staying close to the working-class princess, I knew there wasn't any possibility of him foiling my plot to liberate his prisoner. They invited me to their room for a nightcap. I sidled up to the sideboard, where the traitor to his class had placed the key, which was attached to a heavy brass plate bearing the room number. I slid it into my pocket, still not knowing what exactly I was going to do with it and, after the drink was had, bid them good night and crab-waddled my way to my own abode up the stairs.

I doffed the sabots and waited what might be called a decent interval, time enough for the oppressor of young womanhood to have gone to his bed for the slumber. I knew the woman was anxiously awaiting my rescue, I'd read it in her doleful face; though we hadn't actually discussed it, I knew what had to be done.

A slurp or two of the burnt grape and down the stairs I slithered. My first attempt to unlock their door failed, because I used my own room key. The next attempt brought near disaster, as I dropped the heavy key and brass plate on the marble floor with a dreadful resounding clang, and I found myself saying "Shhhhh" to the key, as drunks do in the movies. It was a few forays ere I got the key into the hole, turning it as carefully as a doorknob in a Hitchcock film. I slipped into the sitting room and stood waiting for the breath to ease, and to let the optics grow accustomed to ye olde Stygian darkness.

Remembering the location of the bedroom door was easy, but getting to it was another matter. Advancing across the floor was extremely hazardous—bits of clothing on the floor, a shoe here, a shoe there, low tables for the barking of shins, ferocious chairs that reared up in the dark to frighten even intrepid knights errant like myself. My instincts, however, guided me into the bedroom, and I knew I had arrived because of the sounds of elephantine crepitation emanating from the vaguely outlined bed in the corner.

"So, the swine snores as well," sez I to myself, having no one else to converse with at that moment, "and she will be well out of this dreadful week-old marriage!"

A swift slither to the side of the playpen, and leaning past the snorting carcass of the Capitalist Quisling, I gently shook the shoulder of my newly beloved. The shook bod shot up into a sitting position, a lamp was switched on, and suddenly there was a room filled with light. A swift appraisal of the contents of the bed indicated that what I thought was the damsel in distress was the husband, and that the snore manufacturer was none other than my beloved, and neither one of them had a stitch of clothing on—not a vestige of a pajama, not a hint of a negligée.

By God, sir, this was a fine how-dye-do. I had barely turned my back, and they were clawing each other in the heat of high passion! If ever there was a case of instant infidelity, this was it!

"What the bloody hell do you want," sez the diminutive Brit, frantically trying to cover himself.

The former beloved now bolted upright and, in a querulous, nasty tone, began berating me, to wit: "A thief in the night," sez she, "a pervert, a peeping Mick, a savage Paddy, a robber."

Due to their state of undress, neither one would emerge from under the hastily thrown up covers, so I was in a position of clothed, upstanding power. Looking at this perfidious female, I was glad my mission had failed. She was a snorer, an abuser of the gallant rescuer, and unfaithful—I would never be able to trust her again. On top of that, she was siding with her captor against me!

Sez I, simply and brilliantly, "I came to return your key, which I mistook for my own."

"Wha?" sez the counter-jumping cockney.

I repeated the lie.

"Put the bloody thing on the table and leave here before I ring for the police."

Houdini would have envied my disappearing act, performed in one seamless motion. The key with brass plate was dropped, egress was achieved, and I was up the stairs in a bound, into my room, not even sure whether I had opened the door or gone directly through it. Once ensconced in the bed's embrace, I exhaled a long breath of relief at my narrow escape from (a) a dreary life with an English wife, and (b) an encounter with the not-so-Civil Guard.

Then, of course, the dark, diamond-eyed demons arrived for their nightly gnawing at my soul, humming the tune of deep despair and of longing for the family life, which, of course, never existed, a product of stupidly sentimental nostalgia. Once more, the salty tears of self-pity flowed o'er me, without managing to wash anything away.

In the warmish light of the day, when a cogent thought or two managed to insert themselves between the waves of brain pain, memory asserted itself and the events of the night flushed the visage with embarrassment. Of course, I couldn't face the honeymooners, much less call them to apologize, so for about a week I managed to avoid them—no mean feat in the small community on that little island.

When I was inclined to show my face again, I discreetly inquired about the whereabouts of my treacherous new love and her captor. I was informed they had departed home to the nation of shopkeepers and I could again roam the island untrammeled by embarrassment. I amused myself by summing up the whole affair with "Absinthe makes the heart grow fonder."

Having failed to liberate a new bride, another plot began the germinating process in the booze-damaged brain. If I were to rent one of these villas here and then nip back to the U.S.A., abduct Siobhan and Malachy, and bring 'em back to the island, I could then through devious routes communicate with Linda and extract from her a promise to try the reconciliation under the threat that she would otherwise never be allowed to see the children again.

Into action! There was a handy place on the ocean, which rented for forty dollars a month; spacious, with three bedrooms and a couple of baths, a bit of land, and fully furnished. A chat that combined fractured English and my dreadful Spanish secured the prospective services of child-care personnel. Of course, there was the nagging question of what was to be done about making a living, but I decided I could just continue the gold-smuggling routine.

Everything now in place for my plan, I moved into the new hacienda and plunked the corpus on the terrace with little interference to Fundador flow.

A couple of days elapsed, and I was approached by a tanned and fit woman in the mid-thirtyish range with the most intense blue eyes and the blondest hair I have ever seen. Her manner had all the compassion but none of the delicacy of a Prussian officer. She addressed me as if I were a tank division about to begin battle.

"I am haffing a coketail party on Thursday night at 6:00 P.M. You vill come, hah? And you must not forget there vill be ozzer peeples. You vill vear a lounge suit, pleeze."

All I could say was, "Ja!"

I was there on the stroke of the Angelus, in extremely close proximity to the bar, and I met pilots, stewardesses, and other world-weary traveling types, plus a sprinkling of German aristocracy. I discovered mein hostess was a Baroness von Sausagelink or something, and she was also a painter.

I had not had any grub that day, as I thought that commodity would be supplied at the hooley, but there was not so much as a macadamia in sight, so once more I was fueled solely by liquor.

The do got louder and rowdier, and as I couldn't seem to find an unattached female, I decided to give in to encroaching sleep. The few yards back to my hacienda seemed impossible to traverse, so I trudged up the stairs of mein host's house and found a simple cot in what appeared to be a small studio. It occurred to me that if I laid me down on the top of the bed, someone would come in, wake me up, and ask if I was all right, as people do that sort of thing, so I would forestall that civilized gesture by getting a pillow and crawling under the bed, where I drifted off to sleep to the labored attempts of sozzled Saxonians trying to sing.

I was awakened sometime later by a light being switched on, and the sounds of two people whispering.

Him: "Mein Liebling, oh, oh, oh . . .?"

Her: "Ich bin dein, oh Liebling!"

Him: "I luff you, oh, oh, please me!"

Her: "Ohne Hast, ohne Rast!"

Him: "Do not torture me, oh, aah, oooh, aaaah..."

During all this palaver, items of clothing came floating down into my limited view from beneath the bed—a jacket, a tie, a blouse, a brassiere, a skirt, trousers, the knickers, the shorts. Shoes were then kicked off, and all of it to the sounds of deep breathing, sucking lips, and hands rubbing on flesh, interspersed with sharp intakes of breath.

The light was extinguished and, concomitantly with the flight of light, it seemed as if several tons of humans had suddenly parked themselves on my chest, expelling all air from the lungs. Little did the two lovers care, as they were too busy in the lust arena to give any consideration to the fact that there could be a human being under the bed. Even conservatives, stupid as they are, always looked under the bed for Communists, and brought their children up to do likewise. But not these two Teutons, hammering away, scarring my chest with the imprint of bedsprings. Just as I was about to expire due to decompression, the door was smashed open, a light switched on, and then a screaming, high-decibel chase took place around the room. First, two pairs of bare feet exited the bed, followed by their bodies, followed by me taking a very deep breath and being restored to life. I then observed the only show I've ever seen starring feet: two pairs bare and one pair shod in pointed heels, one of which was removed to be used as a weapon, as I could hear the heel thunk as it hit body parts.

There was a merry chase around the studio, with things being knocked over, vases smashing, and canvasses being trod on. I surmised the identity of the intruder who had caused such a to-do by bursting into the room. She was the wife of the K.L.M. pilot who was slipping the bratwurst into the Baroness, for that was who "Mein Leibling" was. The pilot hurriedly gathered up his portion of the scattered garments and managed to get the frothing wife out of the room, giving "Mein Leibling" a chance to bolt the door to same. She put out the light and settled back into the bed, all undressed with nowhere to go. She sighed and tossed and turned on the mattress on my chest, but, as the weighty partner was gone, I was able to breathe, though the chest was still sore from the previous hammering.

Eventually, the Baroness von Sausagelink sighed her way to slumber. Time for me to exit, though I had no idea what the time was, but I'd no wish to be caught under the bed if they came searching for Communists in the a.m.

I slid out and stood up and was about to leave quietly, when passing clouds allowed a shaft of moonlight to illuminate her visage, now soft in sleep and haloed by golden hair, making her look desirable. Then, in an instant, all was dark again. I knelt down beside her and woke her up.

"May I join you?" I whispered.

"Yes, of course," she answered.

She moved over, and I moved in, *sans culotte* etc., and, as we embraced, she cupped my beard with her hands and said softly, "Oh, you are not the same man..."

"No, I'm not," sez I.

"It doesn't matter," sez she.

"It doesn't," sez I. And life went on.

The next day, the Baroness von Sausagelink resumed her formal demeanor with me, and we never dallied again after that moonlit night in her studio. We nodded and said "Good morning" or "Good evening"; if I'd had a few jars, I'd venture a "Guten Nacht."

———

AS A PRECAUTION AGAINST ANY future trouble with the local gestapo, I began taking Spanish lessons from the daughter of the local police chief. She was a charming, diffident slip of a lass around the eighteen- or nineteen-year mark. Having packed in the formal education part of my life at the age of fourteen, and having never comprehended the vagaries of any grammar, I found this a strange odyssey. My young teacher would usher me into the living room, close the door, and begin speaking to me in simple everyday Spanish—the "How are you?" "I am fine. How are you?" sort of routine.

I was a bit surprised the chief and his missus would leave us in a room *sin duenna*, but, of course, taking into consideration that we were on an island, he was the top cop, and egress was limited to an infrequent ferry and plane, it would have been ill-advised to try any tricks with the Señorita Professora.

She was lovely to look at, with soft dark eyes, and demure in demeanor, so, of course, I decided there and then to secure the divorce from Linda, drop on one knee, declare my eternal love for my teacher, ask her to wed me, then hove off to El Jefe and formally ask for the daughter's hand in marriage.

However, because my Spanish never permitted our romance to advance beyond ascertaining that she was fine and I was too, I was unable to pursue this course, and anyway, island life began to pall on me. So 'twas time to decamp to try my hand at the fleshpots of Paree. In return for letting them use my villa, a young couple let me have the use of a houseboat on the Seine, so off I went on the ferry to Barcelona, having said good-bye to my teacher and various drinking friends.

On the boat, I got chatting with Carol, a young woman who'd a child of about three years, a little girl. She was going back to the U.S. because her husband had left her for some German tourista wench. I decided there and then that I would save her and her daughter by marrying her when we got to Barcelona. Some send-off Fundador and an absinthe chaser can give rise to such thinking.

We checked into the same hotel in Barcelona, but not the same room. A brief spell of sobriety, accompanied by empathetic sadness, impelled me to take Carol out to dinner with the little one. There, we shared tearful stories of lost love, broken marriages, and the misery of watching the children suffer for the lack of the other parent. That evening, some long-buried chivalrous instinct led me to simply see the lady to her door and give her a chaste kiss on the cheek, and we both went off to our cheerless, separate beds. In the morning, she had departed by the time I woke up, and I never saw her again.

———

POPPING UP TO PARIS WAS easily accomplished, but finding the houseboat was something more. I had expected an elegant, well-kept craft, freshly painted, with scrubbed decks, the cynosure of the envious eyes of the native "Parisites," as one Brit expat I knew termed the residents of that city. But the craft I found lay low in the water, an orphan barge, grey and rotting. The deck was soft, pulpy, and dangerous, and a misplaced foot was apt to go straight through the old planking. Under the deck there were three compartments, lit only by portholes that had never been washed. Each compartment had a large bunk with a soggy mattress, smelly pillows, and despairing blankets. Over it all hung a smell of decay and rat piss.

Humming "There's No Place Like Home," I ensconced myself in the middle compartment, found an oil lamp, lit same, and did some further exploration. There was evidence of a female presence in the first compartment, while the third seemed empty. There was no shower or tub or bathroom as such, except for a hole in a cupboard through which the Seine could be seen.

But had I not grown up in the slums of Limerick? So I was not perturbed once the initial twinge of "Aw, Jasus, 'tis not what I had grandmerized in my noggin" had passed. My boatmate appeared in a few hours, a female in appearance and in garb, with an expression on her gob like the keel of the craft we now inhabited, barnacled and unlit. I never found out her nationality or anything about her, outside of the fact that she spoke to herself a lot. She did lay down the law: She did not like to be spoken to, and did not like to speak to people, particularly people sleeping on the boat. I was warned to stay out of her quarters, as she knew, she said, when people pried and disturbed her personal belongings.

The French were having a bit of a bother then with a covert right-wing insurgent army group, who, like the Brits, didn't take to the idea of the people of Algeria, Morocco, and Libya being free of colonial jackboots and deciding their own nations' destinies. So, these military-trained terrorists took to murdering Algerians and Moroccans and dumping their bodies into the Seine. 'Twas a rare day I didn't see the gendarmes and their grappling hooks hauling out well-ventilated or garroted bodies from the river, done in by officers and gentlemen of the French army. So much for *Egalité, Liberté,* and *Fraternité.*

The tall de Gaulle was still saturninely presiding over a resurgent country, whose care and compassion for French Indochina (Vietnam to you, ma'am) he had gleefully passed to the tender mercies of the U.S.A. As the tourist season was now ended in this month of October 1962, there were no signs of map-toting tourists nattering about the Louvre. The time of year was a bit greyish in the climate arena, but still comfortable. A cursory, perfunctory stop at Notre Dame, then a peek at the Mona Lisa, whose smile is not enigmatic to me. Anyone can see it's not a smile, but a grimace, the cause of which is gas.

I had a go under the Arc de Triomphe, which, of course, brought to mind that sobering photograph of the Nazis' entry into that lovely city. I tried to imagine the lusty Aryan voices roaring out the Horst Wessel Song, and the "whack, whack" of the goose-stepping jack-boots thumping terror into the hearts of the fearful French as the Nazis polluted the Champs-Elysées. As always, the underlying taint of anti-Semitism was present in France, in the Dreyfus case and the betrayal of thousands of Jews by Nazi collaborators. On the other hand, I reminded myself, there were the Maquis and the Communist Party, who fought heroically against Hitler's hordes and whores.

Thus cheered, a ride up the Eiffel Tour was edicted, as were visits to the Les Halles markets, and a pop into the Folies-Bergère, and all the other tourist doings, but the heart wasn't in it. Here was the romantic city of Toulouse-Lautrec, strains of music wafting through the foggy air, and here was I, wandering through the streets, yearning for the company of the woman I loved, only because she didn't love me.

I found the Parisians were very impatient with bods like myself who didn't speak French, and I was too distracted to even pick up a phone book, let alone a French phrase book, so it was a standoff. In restaurants, I took to jabbing at the menu, most times not recognizing or caring what arrived from the kitchen. I already knew that all French cooking was built around sauces and gravies, designed to disguise the stink of rotting and decomposing carcasses of long-dead cattle, pigs, sheep, and fish, but I didn't give a fiddler's fuck what was plunked in front of me. Whiskey was horrendously expensive, so the wine of the country was the drug of choice, be it red or white, or in cognac form.

Even though I was traveling on my own passport, I was still in my smuggler's mindset, so I was wary of seeking out the company of Brits, Irish, or Yanks, or any other English-speaking bods, for that matter. I'd come here looking for the Paris of Joyce, Hemingway, Gertrude S., Alice B., Picasso, the Shakespeare Bookshop, Henry Miller, and good old hedonistic Oscar, who preceded the wallpaper in death, but I spent my time drinking alone, eating who knew what, and most every night I would make my morose way, unaccompanied, to my rotting riparian retreat.

One early a.m., I heard the sounds of footsteps on the deck over my hung-over head, and then a "Halloo!"

"Halloo yourself," sez I, grumpily. "Who is it, and what do you want?"

It was someone saying he wanted to speak to "Meester Makort." Thinking it was the gendarme with an extradition warrant, I hopped smartly out of the bed, donned the outer garb, and nipped up to the deck, to find a smallish, smiling chap, decked out in a neat grey suit, compleat with the polished shoes. He spoke decent English and said he was a movie producer, and he had heard from my boatmate, the surly one, that I was an American actor holidaying in Paris. He was producing and directing a film, which needed an American gangster character.

"How about an Irish gangster?" sez I. He laughed and said there was no such thing. I laughed and said there were thousands of them, just check the roster of the Republican Party.

He laughed again, and said he didn't understand. Anyway, he wanted me to learn many pages of dialogue in phonetic French, and also to deliver the lines with an American accent, and he would like me to have it all learned by the following night. *Chevalier d'industrie* that I was at that time, I did try to have a go at it. I spent the afternoon in a café, with wine flowing into me and out of me, and as I got more sozzled, I became more convinced that the Charles Boyers and Yves Montands, and the Jean Claude this, and the Jean Claude that, were all at the end of their careers, and it was fortunate that I had arrived in Paris when I had, as soon I would be Simone Signoret's only love interest.

The afternoon became night, and my fantasies of French stardom shifted from the mere sky-high to the stratospheric, and I wandered from *boite* to *boite*, trying out my phonetic French. Some waiters were amused, while others were offended at my savaging of this, the most sacred of languages—only French-speaking peoples find it necessary to appoint language police—but, *sans souci*, I laid it on the lads.

When I awakened around noon the following day to the throbbing noggin, the totally dry mouth, and a Vesuvius threatening in the belly, it took a bit of time to bring into focus the events of the previous day, which were, when recalled:

I. A Gallic laddie had offered me a part in a film;

2. The character was an American gangster, who gang-
   stered in French;
3. I'd said I would do it;
4. I couldn't find the script.

Rather than face the man, I made myself scarce at the boat for
a few days, leaving a note that I had been summoned to London,
or some other banal lie, and so died my dream of stardom in France.
I never saw the producer again, and my boatmate denied ever men-
tioning my name to anyone, as she didn't know it. Odd, that.

It wasn't exactly flattering when the Académie Française bestowed
all kinds of honors on Jerry Lewis some years later. Scraping the
bottom of the cauldron for something to take the place of a gold-
smuggling, out-of-work, out-of-marriage, drunken actor, it seems
they came up with someone to fit the bill.

———

I STAYED IN PARIS FOR six weeks, suffering the hangovers that come
only from the juice of rotten grapes trampled into insensibility by
the fungoid feet of unwashed farm laborers. It was not a pleasant
time. I developed a mini-mania about conserving the *sous* and the
francs, walking rather than taking the superb Metro, ordering the
cheapest wine, and being not at all squeamish about gnawing on
the remains of deceased equines and fish that had nourished themselves on the foreign bodies found in the Seine.

Clothes went uncleaned, shirts unwashed, socks unchanged, the
hair and beard oily and bedraggled; indeed, the only time I washed
myself was when I checked into a *pension* every ten days or so for
that very purpose, which was a relief to myself and everyone in sight.

When, despite untold quantities of the cheap wine, my mind
would not cease leaping about like a caged and vicious rodent, it
was time for another geographical relocation to escape it.

Off to London again, and the pubs again, friendly, warm, and predictable, with familiar currency, and a comfortable small hotel, where the bod was scraped, and whence clothing went to cleaners, shirts and the more private stuff to the laundry. A trip to the barber for the trim of the beard and the lank, dead hair, and a bit of cheer returned.

I met up with R. Harris again and took to the usual carousing. One riotous, ribald night ended with me on the Underground at about 8:30 A.M., by myself and heading for I do not know where. Spotting a delectable young thing on one of the platforms in the middle of the rush hour, I announced to the on-the-way-to-work assemblage that this particular carriage was being taken out of service, and would everyone kindly take another carriage. To my astonishment, the obedient Brits did as requested, leaving me with a subway car all to myself. If only they would get out of Ireland as quick!

I then summoned the delectable young thing on the platform to join me in my own private car, which she did. She was a fraction bemused, and a trifle hesitant in demeanor, but I assured her I was merely there to ensure she had a decent and untroubled ride to work, and proceeded to sing to her until we arrived at her destination. My beautiful new friend, who shall be known as Constance, was vastly amused at the antics of this fluthered Irishman, and yielded ye olde phone number and a promised meeting for the evening.

Constance was from a rather proper Brit family, ensconced in a decent part of London, with enough shekels to do the travel and have the odd bite of grub in some of the best bistros in the Big Smoke. She loved the laugh, and I was quite willing to provide it, as there was nothing more likely to provoke outrageous behavior on my part than British propriety.

We whirled about London, pub to pub, club to club, with the occasional mandatory foray to the esteemed British theater. Her parents were amazingly courteous to me, considering the fact I kept her out late every night and, indeed, sometimes all night, as we had all those fleshly desires that could only be satisfied alone and in the nude. The crowning bit of news from Constance was the fact that her uncle was the Archbishop of Canterbury, the number two man in the Church of England, the jolly old C. of E. That bit of info doubled me up with glee, as the thought of me ploughing the flesh of a close relative of the Capo of the C. of E. seemed proper redress for some of the forced-fucking tithing my ancestors had to endure.

> Don't speak of your Protestant ministers
> Or your church without morals or faith
> For the foundation stones of your temple
> Are the balls of King Henry the Eighth!

I explained this to Constance, who, in a spirit of rebelliousness and reparations, redoubled her efforts to please.

'Twas a nice interlude for both of us, knowing full well that it was, no doubt about it, a temporary liaison. Her cool demeanor, her good humor, and willingness to have an adventure brought balm to my heart and soothed the soul so that I could really let sunlight into the dark, despairing arenas of my spirit. The violence and rage subsided for a while, so there was no necessity for me to go about hitting inoffensive, or, indeed, offensive people.

Righto! Having been temporarily fixed, 'twas time to move on.

————

AFTER ONE LAST NIGHT WITH cheerful Constance, and no vows of keeping in touch, I nipped over to Limerick—irresistible Limerick, object of affectionate memory and maniacal hatred.

The mother was gone to America again, living in an apartment we'd gotten her in Brooklyn, so I checked into the Glentworth Hotel, a good spot to be in, with restaurant attached, and went perambulating round the town.

The gnawing disease of nostalgia drove me into pub after pub after pub, as if I had no control. I'd very little to be nostalgic about, but even the most oppressed have some sunny memory of the worst of times. Nazis, Fascists, and Conservatives are all great ones for nostalgia—yapping about returning us to the days of glory, family unity, sunny days, traditional values, and happy peasants, engaged in simple pursuits, gamboling about on the village green, where death, disease, and poverty dare not show their faces. It's a strange disease, nostalgia, obscuring all reality, and an evil manipulation in the hands of right-wing swine.

But I was not wandering about Limerick because of the right wing. In fact, it almost occurred to me that conservatives had little to do with any of my troubles.

At about eight o'clock, I returned to the Glentworth for the evening repast, and, running the peepers down the menu, I found it replete with fish: hake, haddock, trout, prawns, salmon, whitefish, bass, etc. And, at the bottom, in a difficult-to-read print, there was an entry which read "Pork Chops (2)." Summoning the hovering equerry (a lad I knew from days of yore, so I was a trifle embarrassed that he was my waiter), I told him I'd love to get the molars into the Pork Chops (2).

"The PORK CHOPS, sir?"

"Yes, the pork chops, and stop calling me 'sir'! We grew up together. Remember?"

"I know, sir, but I have to call you 'sir' here, or I'll get the sack. Now, the PORK CHOPS, sir?"

"Yes, the fucking pork chops."

"Just a moment, sir."

The maître d'hôtel hove into sight, and bore down on my table. "Mr. McCourt," he addressed me, "did you know that it is Friday?"

"I did," sez I, though I didn't, nor did I give a fiddler's fart.

"Well, sir," sez he, with that *coup de grâce* look in his eye, "did you know you ordered the PORK CHOPS?"

I had forgotten the Catholic no-carne on Friday rule, but I wasn't about to admit it, so I told him, "Yes, I know I ordered the PORK CHOPS. I am not Jewish." I was thinking he would laugh, but instead, he said "I see," and went off to secure the whacked remains of the deceased hog for my repast.

I felt somewhat less than welcome at the Glentworth thereafter, and so spent a lot of time with Sean and Mary Costello, a young couple who lived next door to the mudder's council house on O'Donoghue Avenue in Jamesboro. They had four children—Jack, Maria, Ger, and Margaret—and a more hospitable and open-door policy than in their house you could never find. It was a wonderful, lively place, and everyone of that family either sang or played an instrument or both.

I enjoyed taking the drink with Sean, and accompanied him to his local pub on the Roxboro Road, a bit of a run-down place, owned by an elderly man whose wife did the work, assisted by the daughter part-time. I had no shortage of the pounds, shillings, and pence and, though I couldn't say I'd acquired it by hard work, or any work, really, except to suggest I was doing well in America, I was still wont to display the readies at every opportunity.

'Twas not long 'til the rather crafty owner of the pub approached me with a request, doing a pained performance of the stage Irishman in severe convulsions over a fierce and terrible problem.

"Ah, now, begob, Malachy," sez he. "'Tis the way ould Christmas is almost down upon us, and what with wan thing and another, shure amn't I short the do-re-mi for to get in the supplies for the season, and, as you know—God knows who would know better than yourself—'tis the busiest time of the year, and you with the money rolling in, and if you could see your way to letting me have a few hundred quid, shure you'd be the first on the list to be paid—no bother at tall, at tall."

I'd been warned the big touch was on the way, as indeed, 'twas not a small sum in those days. I couldn't say no, so I dipped into the gold dough cache and forked out the readies as requested. If I was at the top of the list for repayment, nobody was paid, for I haven't seen a pound to this very day, and the pub has changed hands many times over.

D ESPITE THE READY QUIDS AND THE CONSTANT DRINKING, 'twas not long before I was again feeling thoroughly useless and purposeless. I'd worn out my status as a minor celebrity in the city of my childhood and found the enveloping gloom of winter in Limerick suffocating. With Christmas fast approaching, I thought it would be a good time to visit Siobhan and Malachy. So, off to Aer Lingus with me, and to booking the flight to New York. Having no abode in New York, the St. Moritz Hotel on Central Park South had to suffice.

Frank and his War Department were doing the Christmas dinner routine for the family, and the mother would be there, so we were set for the holiday. I wanted to murder every Salvation Army Santa Claus and bomb every radio station that played Christmas carols; I wanted to strangle all those who wished me a Merry Christmas, and do in the jerks who blandly breathed "Happy Holidays" in my direction.

I understood perfectly the reasons for the upsurge in domestic murders with carving knives in the kitchen at Christmas. It is the unending demands that we be "merry," while all of us are furious at the commercialization of what is a holy day for many, the birthday of Jesus Christ, however arbitrarily it might have been chosen.

I had the chance at the holiday family tableaux, but instead I chose to wallow in grief, and made sure that my four-year-old daughter and my three-year-old son knew of my misery. Whether as a direct consequence or not, Siobhan developed one of those horrendous high fevers, in the 105°–106° region, resulting in the three of us spending most of Christmas in the emergency room of Roosevelt Hospital. It got so bad we had to immerse her in a bathtub filled with ice cubes and water. You'd wonder why the little girl did not suffer severe hypothermia from the shock.

Of course, I blamed Linda. If that selfish woman persisted in breaking up the family, who knows what's going to happen?

That night, with the crisis passed, after I'd gotten us all bunked down, the recurring nightmare of my children falling out the window of a high building awakened me with the usual strangled cry. I found them both safe, sound asleep in the next bed, so I went back to sleep and entered another nightmare. This one took place on the subway: When the train doors were about to close, Siobhan ran out onto the platform, and the train pulled out of the station. I pressed my face to the window, trying somehow to reach her, but as the train sped into the dark cloacal depths of the underground, she stood on the platform, looking at me, receding further and further into the distance, and I woke again drenched in sweat.

———

WITH A STRANGE 1962 DYING and an unknown 1963 a-birthing, I was bunking down in my mother's place on Flatbush Avenue in Brooklyn. The couch was my nesting place whenever I made my way back at night. The poor mother was in great agony over my fall from marital and social grace, but was forbidden by me to mention anything about what I was doing, what I was drinking, or my lifestyle. There was an abuse of her hospitality and her concern, and whilst I could see the pain in her eyes, I wouldn't allow any discussion of my plight.

My brother Mike was tending bar at Dick Edward's, the designated saloon for the John Birch Society of New York. One night a week there was a meeting there of said society, and from the closed back room came floating the strains of the Horst Wessel Song. I worked there for a bit, serving the lockjawed, the Nazi, the fool, and the high-priced whore, both male and female.

My tenure at this caravansary was brief, as not alone was I insulting, grumpy, ungracious, sarcastic, and envious of the half- and nitwits enjoying themselves whilst I was fermenting inside, I managed even to outrage my brother Mike, who had recommended me for the job.

What was New York in January but a grey island, anyway, barely breathing, with the air full of fractured New Year's resolutions, streets full of angry, holidayed-out people, schools full of children with broken dreams. Hovering above it all now was the warm thought of suicide.

Time, once again, to flee.

My erstwhile employer in Zurich was a little perturbed at not hearing from me for such a long time, but I charmed him out of his querulousness with the usual avalanche of Paddy talk and fake concern for his welfare, all the while assuring him we were on the way to more fortunes. He got the ticket to me, plus another passport, and off to the Indian Consulate with me for the new six-month visa.

Visa secured, passport in hand, passage to India paid for, I made another Sunday visit to my children, Siobhan and Malachy. It's an unmerciful role, being a Sunday father in New York, especially if you don't have your own digs. Too cold for the park and the zoo, and friends don't want two small kids scampering about their habitations on Sunday, whilst they're recovering from the previous night's excesses, trying to lift the quivering porringer of healing coffee to the parched lips and hoping the day will be serene enough for them to peruse the pages of the *New York Times*.

None of my usual haunts would do, since edicts of the law prevented me from taking them to anything resembling a pub or a saloon. Indeed, that day, thinking it safe enough, I took them to Schrafft's for lunch, this being a place famous for its favor with white-gloved octogenarians of the female sex, who came for cucumber sandwiches without crusts. But safe, not bloody likely, as the old ones liked to sip sherry all day, too.

The diligent and observant daughter spotted the bottles of Bacchus's fluid glowing contentedly on the back shelf, and, in a high-pitched, high-decibel voice, yelled, "The judge said you are not to bring us into places where they have whiskey!"

All eyes swiveled to this diminutive banshee, and then upwards to my flaring red countenance. I tried the parental shushing routine, but the little snipe danced away from me, chanting, "I'll tell! I'll tell! I'll tell Mommy, and she'll tell the judge, and he will put you in jail." I slunk out of Schrafft's with two now-dancing kids, who had wrested control from their father and reveled in it.

Fathers! Forgive them, they know not what they do.

Off with Daddy again to far foreign ports, leaving the little ones behind.

THE FLIGHT BACK TO SWITZERLAND HAD ABOUT IT ALL THE adventure of the commuter's morning train ride. I checked into my usual hotel, and the goldman of Zurich arrived with the metal, and away we went with our hammers, flattening the bank's imprint on each gold bar. We went through the routine of the canvas vest with the pockets for the kilos of gold, and I departed for Rome again, with the familiar injunction to send the ambiguous telegram when the mission was accomplished. My itinerary did not include dipping the wick in the fleshpots of the Holy City at this time, so from there it was straight on to Bombay.

The gold-smuggling caper had grown so routine that when Indian customs asked if I had anything to declare, I almost replied, "Just the same old cargo of gold." Of course, prudence and the fear of Indian prisons capped any such notions of levity.

There was no Krishna's Birthday to inhibit commerce this trip, so the transfer took place in the comfortable confines of the jolly old whorehouse run by the respectable English madam, she of basic black, lace, and the cameo brooch. A swift beddown with one of the Lysol-wielding ladies of India's twilight, and then a swift exit to Delhi and environs for the requisite week of touristing to keep things from looking suspicious.

'Twas odd how the whole venture had become so commonplace as to leave me bored and satiated with the exotica, the color, the strangeness of all these places I'd so desperately wanted to visit when I was reading and dreaming about them in the slums of Limerick.

Delhi was all right at that time of year, outside of the little storms of red dust invading the eyeballs. I drank, ate, whored, slept, and drank again for about a week, and then hopped on the jet back to the Eternal City. I took one more trip after that, and then something, it was explained to me, happened to the gold market in India that made it less profitable for Western gangsters and money manipulators to continue the smuggling.

I took another trip to Ibiza, to ensure my villa was still intact, as I had paid a year's rent in advance—almost five hundred dollars, a princely sum in those days. I was once again able to indulge my fantasies of having my children with me. The plot to abduct the children and force the recalcitrant spouse to come to the negotiating table with a view to the reconciliation had been lurking in the rear compartment of my foggy cranium, and now it came to the fore again.

I had refined the plan, as follows: I would pick up the young ones, ostensibly for a weekend stay with me, then I would take a train to Montreal, and from there, a plane to Dublin. Then, onto the overnight steamer going to Holyhead in Wales, and from thence a train to London. A rest-up for a day or so, and then to Dover, and across the English Channel to Calais, and another train to Paris, followed by a plane to Barcelona, and again the boat to Ibiza.

I thought all the zigzagging, on a route that didn't require visas, would throw the international police off the scent, as there would be no record of our travels. But when I sat down on the terrace of the villa, and gazed over the Mediterranean sea, and searched the mind for the flaw in this kidnapping and hostage caper, it came down on me that it wouldn't work. It gradually seeped through the Fundador fumes that the spouse wouldn't be too eager to leap into my arms after I had nearly stopped her heart with the fear of never seeing her children again.

I considered the possibility of leaving the kids with the nanny and meeting Linda elsewhere, perhaps Paris, and afterward she would pledge her troth again. I would take her to the reunion in Ibiza, where we would once more be a happy, All-American family, Mom, Dad, Sis, and Junior. But the scorpion in the balm was that Linda could nominally acquiesce to anything, but as soon as she set the peepers on the fruit of her womb, she would screech for the local gestapo, and I would join Bruno Hauptmann in the annals of infamy.

I highly recommend extended contemplation of the Mediterranean to provide enlightenment, especially when meditating on future criminal activity. Not that I considered my plans criminal—I was just setting right a great injustice. Of course, I didn't consider my gold smuggling criminal either, I was merely a customs evader, and, besides, how else was I going to explore the world with my limited resources?

The projected failure of my plans served to intensify the drinking. Then an irresistible thought would pop into the head. Go to Tripoli, the home of the Barbary pirates, and I'd be off for the little jaunt. More passing thoughts and drunken impulses took me on side trips to Rabat, Casablanca, Algiers, Tunis. There'd be few days and nights of drinking in new places, and mornings waking up wondering what language it was I was being asked to leave in.

These were all the neighborhoods and places I'd read about and had always wanted to see. Some day I shall return sober and do so.

My goldman in Zurich rang to ask me if I could go to Ireland

and buy up some Irish passports for future use, against the day when the gold market would stabilize itself and we were in business again. He sent the readies for purchase of same, plus some expense money, and I left one island, Ibiza—making sure to take with me my traveling companions, self-pity and insanity—and headed off for another.

Of course, I had to stop in London to have a few jorums there. I arrived one evening, and woke the next morning to discover I'd been there for three weeks, and not a passport purchased or a child in the house washed.

There was a bit of wonderment at my reappearance in Limerick, as 'tis not the place to go to in the middle of a dreary winter, especially if you have the necessary funding to be in a balmier clime. Was said to me by all, "Oh! There you are. Are you home again?" Translated from the Irish, this means, "What kind of feckin' eejit are you to come in the bleak winter?" I deflected all inquiries with the deft verbal sidestep, and went about my business.

The buying of passports was a bit complicated there. The applicant had to first go to the local police station. There they were required to apply for a character rating and receive approval after stating why the passport was desired, what the destination was, and when the person proposed leaving—all of which is nobody's business but the traveler's, but that's the way things were. I did manage to snaffle a half dozen of the documents for money, after explaining, in the lying fashion I'd adopted, that they were to be used in some currency transactions. The folks who got passports and sold them to me pretended to understand, nodding sagely as I poured forth a line of gibberish and lies.

One lad I enlisted got nabbed by the wife when she found out from a neighbor that her husband had applied to the police for a passport. She figured he was going to run off with some other lady, and there was a hell of a bloody row. Discreet lad that he was, he didn't say that I was involved in any way, and I must admit that was some misplaced loyalty.

The mission accomplished, I set about lowering the available stocks of whiskey and stout on hand in Ireland. At one point, I set myself the goal of having a drink in every pub in Limerick and environs. I should have gotten on the plane and hied the bod back to New York, but the ease of life in a comfortable hotel, the availability of companionship all hours of the day and night, with never a comment on my drinking, were enough to keep me there.

Soon the money began petering out, so a visit to the chap to whom I'd lent the quids was in order. I went by his pub and his wife said he wasn't in. "Right," sez I. "I'll drop in again."

Some more visits, and he wasn't in, which was strange for a man who it was hard to find out. It dawned on me that the blighter was avoiding me, so the next time I popped in, I said I'd wait, and after a bit I leaned over the bar. There he was, crouching down, as if repairing a pipe that wasn't there. "What time will you be in?" sez I to him.

"Ah, bedad," sez he, "'tis the way now that times is hard and Christmas is not what it used to be, with people not drinking and spending their money on food and clothes and other useless things." And he went on to decry the rise of materialism and the dreadful draw of outside activities that took men away from the pleasures of the pub. He was as loquacious in explaining why he couldn't repay the loan as he was in requesting it. This avalanche of horseshite engulfed me to the point where I forgot my mission, i.e., to retrieve the readies I'd advanced this maunderer.

A call from my goldman, who was now in New York: (a) "Where are you?"; (b) "Do you have the passports?"; (c) When are you coming back?" Answers: (a) "I'm here"; (b) "Yes"; (c) "In a day or so."

———

A MONUMENTAL PISSUP ENDED MY stay in Limerick. Not much can be remembered, except for the absurdity of an Irishman nicknamed Barrow Boy, who drunkenly and weepingly proclaimed his undying love for the Queen of England and his sorrow and distress at the disintegration of the British Empire.

The sight of a curly-headed, ma-faced mick, standing in the sacred precincts of a Limerick pub, tearfully and in an affected Cockney accent singing Rule Brittania, penetrated the whiskey mists wafting around my brain. Not a soul objected, as all politely listened 'til he warbled to the end: "Britons never, never shall be slaves."

It was that same Irish politeness allowed the fuckers to stay for eight hundred years. No one could figure out how to tell 'em they'd o'erstayed ye olde welcome and 'twas time to fuck off, except, sadly enough, for a few of the lads who took up the gun.

As nobody else felt called upon to explain the situation to this traitorous Gaelic Gunga Din, I took him outside and did so myself.

———

THE NEXT DAY IT WAS off to Shannon Airport again, stumbling, bumbling, mumbling, and maudlin, as if I were taking a coffin-ship to America, with small chance of survival. Things looked up though, as the hostesses served me more than my share of the amber liquids, due to my part in quieting a bald-pated, obstreperous arsehole in the seat in front of me. As we were roaring toward take-off, when no one can be allowed to stand, he insistently banged the call button to summon a hostess.

When we were airborne, he began shouting and abusing the uniformed women and, remembering my own bad behavior on previous occasions, I decided that this would be a good time to make the amends. So I leaned over the seat, tapping him on the shining head, and informed him that if his finger went in the direction of the call button once more, I would break it off, plus he would have his cranium stoven, and his body taking an unscheduled solo flight into the icy waters of the Atlantic. Not a word did he speak for the rest of the trip, and those green-clad lassies plied me with a sufficiency of fuel to get me across the briny.

The formalities were completed at Idlewild Airport, and a stroll to retrieve the trusty portmanteau gave me time to conduct an audit of the finances and an inventory of the assets. Assets consisted of three shoes (apparently one had taken a walk by itself), some tattered drawers, some defeated shirts, a woebegone suit, a drove of dead socks, a balding toothbrush, a well-worn passport, and a tie that, if immersed in water, would have made a thick, nourishing soup for to feed most of Calcutta.

The finances, a careful assembly of coinage and notes, included rupees, naye paise, pesetas, centimos, some half pennies, a half crown or two, some crumpled, pathetic lira notes, a brave franc, a one-pound note, and an Irish shilling, but no sign of anything resembling American currency. "Where did it all go?" I wondered briefly, but the answer was too painful and obvious to dwell upon.

I explained to a kindly-looking chap that I had no American money and needed a dime to make an urgent telephone call, and he obliged. Rang the brother Frank in Brooklyn, he was home and told me to belt right over. "Small problem," sez I, "I'm not in possession of the coin of the realm." Decent man that he was, he said he saw no problem: Just get a taxi and bang on his bell and all would be taken care of.

An advance from the kindly brother kept me from the penury regions and he asked me no questions, passed no judgments, gave no advice, just "How much do you need," and off I was to the fleshpots of New York.

Not much after that, I reluctantly signed the divorce agreement with Linda, on the theory that if I let her go free, she would fly back to me. To my astonishment, she hoved off to Mexico and got her liberation papers, and was now the ex–Mrs. McCourt.

And that was how those travels ended, with me as broke and bereft as when they began.

FIVE

FATHER TO THE MAN

Now I'm resolved to try it,
I'll live on a moderate diet,
I'll not drink and will deny it,
And shun each alehouse door,
For that's the place they tell us,
We meet with all jovial good fellows,
But I swear by the poker and bellows,
I'll never get drunk anymore.

A man that's fond of boozing,
His cash goes daily oozing,
His character he's losing,
And its loss he will deplore.
His wife is unprotected,
His business is neglected,
Himself is disrespected,
So I'll not get drunk anymore.

OLD TEMPERANCE SONG

I WAS STAYING IN AN APARTMENT I'D FOUND IN QUEENS, when my mother informed me that she'd had the letter from my father in which he stated that he had not been drinking for several years and was working as a cook in a monastery (Frank said the main activity there was fasting), and he was desirous of a reconciliation, for, as he put it, "What God hath put together, let no man put asunder." He had passport, ticket, and visa, and was all set to begin this happy voyage into the future.

"What do you think?" sez the mother and, without waiting for my answer, proceeds to give all the reasons they should reconcile. He hasn't touched a drop of drink in years ("not since they invented the funnel," sez I), he was healthy, and she still had the old *gradh* for him, and she was getting older, and he was always good company, and they were sure they could make a success of it, and what do you think?

"You've answered all your questions," sez I, "and it's you that's going to have to live with him."

"I'll try it, so," sez she.

After making up her mind that the father, Malachy Sr., could come and share her abode, a quarter of a century after having deserted us, she wrote to him inviting him to get on the swift ship he had prattled about in his letter, and get over here.

She didn't know how to sign it. "Your loving wife" was too intimate, she thought; "your wife" was too cold; "Sincerely yours," too impersonal, as were "Warm regards," and "Yours truly." The ending salutation delayed sending the letter for two days. She finally settled for

> "Yours, etc.
>
> Angela"

and off the bloody missive went to Belfast.

A few weeks later, the telegram arrived saying that he was on the high seas on one of the Cunard ships, and on the 10th of August, 1963, the mother, myself, and Siobhan and Malachy went to the pier to meet the "new" man, the reconstructed saint, the to-be-loving husband, the diligent father, and the doting grandpa.

My arse! Malachy McCourt Sr. came down that gangplank like Toulouse-Lautrec, a legless drunk he was, being carried by two sturdy crewmen. I saw the chief purser at the head of the gangplank and asked about the dad's condition. In the studied tones of the Brit when speaking of outrageous Paddy behavior, he announced in supercilious, upper-class shorthand, "He's not too bad today, ectch-ewly. Had the blighter in leg irons for most of the voyage. Not sorry to see him off this vessel."

That tone and attitude always had the same effect on me—as if a wire brush were employed in scrubbing my spine. There was only the comfort of knowing they had been a syphilized race since Henry VIII infected so many people, carrying all the way to Lord Randolph Churchill, Winnie's papa, who died of the syphilis at the age of forty-four, so who were they to turn up their snoots at my loony pater?

We retrieved his bag at customs and got him out to Flatbush Avenue in Brooklyn, where the mother was domiciled. He questioned my children on the catechism and on Irish history and sang the old patriotic songs again. The man hadn't moved an inch in the inside of his head, going round and round on love for Ireland and love for the Holy Mother Church to two small kids who wouldn't know the Virgin Mary from Typhoid Mary, or Ireland from Coney Island. Bonkers as ever the man was, but hope springs eternal: Perhaps, when he sobered up, all would change and he might be normal.

He tried to explain that sailing the Atlantic on a British ship was such a torment to him, knowing that under the keel were hundreds of thousands of Irish people, asleep in the deep, who met their fate while fleeing Brit oppression. And seeing the Union Jack flying on the mast every morning drove him to the bar, where everything was duty-free anyway.

We put him to bed, where he fell into the deep sleep of the overindulged and slept through the night, but that was the last night of peace for the poor mother. Sober by day, he rampaged Brooklyn by night, urging stray Puerto Ricans, Blacks, Jews, and Arabs to go and fight and die for Ireland. How he wasn't hammered to death or knifed or robbed or beaten into insensibility is a mystery to us all.

Night after night, the mother would telephone: "Would you come over here and get him off me," and I'd go, and he'd preach that she had a sacred obligation to submit to her husband and perform the marital duty, or he'd report her to the church authorities. She wasn't having any of that carryin' on, sez she, and him langers drunk all the time.

I'd arrive to find him standing at the window of her second-floor walkup, exhorting passersby on Flatbush Avenue to go to mass to learn Irish history, honor their fathers and mothers, say their prayers, and be sure to die for Ireland. The puzzled people standing on the street would cheer him on and give him encouragement when he seemed to falter, cheering and clapping, especially when he sang about Roddy McCorley going to die on the bridge of the Toome today. I'd be embarrassed to enter the little building, lest they connect me with him, so I'd have to wait 'til he was either finished or pulled in by my mother.

After two weeks of these whacko goings-on, and after he'd discovered the two elderly ladies next door (whom my mother had tried to conceal from him because of their propensity for the sauce), I got him to go to a meeting of Alcoholics Anonymous. The speaker, in a very moving story, related a horrible descent into hell, which ended with him drinking kerosene.

"Well," said I to the man who had seeded me, "how did that strike you?"

"Ah, I'm not an alcoholic," he responded. "I don't drink kerosene."

The old ones next door hadn't a tooth between them, except the false ones for the daytime, and if there was a screed of hair on their respective heads, it could only be found with an intense microscopic inspection, but they were ecstatic at the arrival of my berserk father, as there hadn't been a man in their apartment in years, outside of the utilities man who read the meters. They had pensions from the telephone company, so there was no shortage of money for the Four Roses and ginger ale, which they were delighted to share with the Da. According to my mother, they were diligent in learning the patriotic Irish songs my father taught them, especially,

> We drink the memory of the brave,
> The faithful and the few.
> Some lie far off beyond the wave,
> Some sleep in Ireland too.
> All, all are gone, but still lives on,

The fame of those who died,
All true men like you men.
Remember them with pride.

And they couldn't wait to die for Ireland, it seemed, but in the meantime, they would drink for America.

About eleven o'clock one pleasant September eve, the call come from the mater. She hadn't seen the old man since the day before, when he went out, ostensibly seeking employment. He hadn't come home last night, and no word of him at all this day, and she was nervous of going into the new patriots' apartment for fear of what she might find.

"What means that?" sez I.

"Well, I think there's been a bit of carrying on there," sez she. "It's something I don't want to know any more about, so would you come over, in the name of God, and see what's going on?"

Once more I trekked over to Brooklyn, and once more comforted the disturbed mother. She had keys to the old ones' flat, as she used in better times to bring in the odd cup of tea and a biscuit or two. I cautiously opened the door and immediately kicked a bottle lying there in the dark. There were several more of those lying about, causing hazardous conditions for any pedestrian.

I made my groping way to what appeared to be the bedroom, opened the door, and stepped inside. There came wafting through the darkness a small symphony of snorts, snores, wheezings, and soft whistlings. I managed to locate a light switch on the wall, which produced the bing-bing-flicker of one of those circular fluorescent lights so beloved by cheap landlords.

In the large bed, I observed three bald heads on the pillows, and about seven miles of gums. I had difficulty in figuring out which one was my father, but of course he was in the middle, the meat in a geriatric sandwich. Leaning over, I shook him, which startled him into a sudden sit-up and, first looking to the left at the old one, and next looking to the right at the other old one, he then looked at me with all the innocence of an ambushed rodent, and saith: "Who are these guys?"

The scene was so absurd, so farcical, so ludicrous, that I almost became helpless with a surge of laughter from deep inside. But that was quelled by a gasp from behind me. The mother had decided to screw up her courage and face the force of this den of iniquity. In a savage second, my laughter changed to rage at the sight of this madman, my father, sordidly snug 'twixt two smelly old wanton remnants of womanhood, and, grabbing him by the shirt, which was all he was clad in, I lifted him into the air and gave him a fist in the gut, which landed him crumpled in a corner.

The old ones slept. He muttered something about the Fourth Commandment, and Honor thy father, and I screamed, loosing all the tamped down rage I'd held within me since he had left us. And I started bawling, and with the tears streaming down my face, I let forth a rope of invective:

"You scrawny old whore's melt! Who in the name of Christ are you to invoke the Commandments, when you've just pulled your puny cock out of an old cunt, and what gives you the right to call yourself a father, and what would you know about honor and decency, when desertion and abandonment were your strategies for dealing with life and death, and you would give up anything for a drink, and you drink anything given to you, you sodden old craw-thumping, statue-kissing hypocrite, with your rosary beads, prayer books, and exhortations to attend to our religious duties. Fuck your rosaries and your missals and your religion and fuck your God and your church and fuck you, above all, fuck you."

He just lay on the floor, with his old cock and balls collapsed on his thigh, whimpering, "Ah, now, don't say things like that, Ah now, don't say things like that."

And I wanted suddenly to pick him up and hug him to make it all right, to comfort him, soothe him, and rock him. But I couldn't.

I had to act the tough guardian of morality and mother's feelings, and so I ordered him out of the house, this small, grey wisp of a man, whose absence had loomed so large in Frank's life, my life, Mike's life, and Alphie's life, and out the door walked this insignificant man with a nondescript bag, murmuring, "Ah now, ah now, there's no need for all this. Ah, now."

I closed the door, we heard him descending the stairs, and he was gone again. Even when he was here, he was gone again. We sat, the mother and myself, in silence, sunk in our own morass of doubts, memories flooding back.

The mother and myself came out of the reveries at about the same time, and she smiled at me, and I smiled at her. Here she was, isolated in a dingy little apartment on Flatbush Avenue, having been abused by brother and sister and mother, her father dead before she was born. Married to an alcoholic, who saddled her with seven children, three of whom died. She had taken up with another abusive drunk in Limerick, and for that, none of us ever really forgave her. Now once more victimized by her own yearning.

"He's gone," sez I.

"Again," sez she.

We laughed ruefully, as the novelist would say.

"What kind of eejit was I to think that he had changed?" sez she.

"No more an eejit than the rest of us trotting after you," sez I, who had thought the same. It was just a hope, and no blame to anyone, except maybe his family in Northern Ireland, who wanted to be rid of him.

"I should have known better," she said.

That should be on her gravestone.

The mother went to her once-more-manless bed, thinking the Irish proverb, "It's all better than a bad marriage." I stretched out on the lumpy dark couch and went to sleep, dreaming dreams that are not in my memory.

The day, the early summer day, when he took me by the hand to go for the walk, I was eager, because he rarely held our hand or carried anything in his own, as he believed it was unseemly for a man to care for a child or carry a parcel in his hands. "Woman's work," sez he!

We walked out by the way of Rosbrien, past the White Gates of the Railway, past the small houses the English built for railway workers. He told me we were going to a place where there is a well that has the sweetest, coolest magical spring waters, which are there to make you happy. I just couldn't get over how much I loved my daddy then, for bringing me to this sacred, secret place. We clambered over one stile, and crossed a field that had cows who looked at me and frightened me, but big, brave father chased them off with a wave of his hand. Over a ditch we went with him, me carried above the clumps of stinging nettles, which he said were good for you when brewed as tea.

We walked to the middle of the field, and there, midst a clump of rushes, was the well. It didn't look to me like it was too magical, as it was just water, surrounded by some built-up stones. "Kneel down and drink it," he said, and I did. I tried to remember something I'd read in a Bible about soldiers being selected for battle by Moses, and whether they cupped their hands and drank the water, or was it that they put their mouths in the water and sucked it up?

I thought it was braver to put my mouth in the water and suck it up. It was the loveliest water I'd ever tasted, and the more I drank of it, the lovelier it became. And then we lay under a big shady tree, which was the home of dozens of birds, and my father made up stories of bravery and dying for Ireland, and he sang many songs, and recited poetry, and manufactured tales of the doings of the shapes in the clouds. The bees hummed, the birds sang, and the insects cricketed all around us as he talked, crooned, and made great use of the language to fill a child's mind with joy and wonder.

The marvelous sun began its descent in the sky, and all around us the natives of nature began the rustling and settling for the evening's rest. My dad told me that all creatures had one thing in common: They all knew how to pray. That's what they were doing now—thanking God for another blessed and wonderful day, and we should go now and leave them to their devotions.

The darkness was falling, as we walked back along the road to the fetid lane, and there were scary moos and caws, and screeches from the fields on either side of us, but my dad picked me up and held me close, and I wasn't afraid anymore, and I fell asleep and didn't wake 'til the next morning.

When my father left us and went to England, I went to find the well again. Over the same stile I went, over the same ditch, where the stinging nettles threatened, past the big sheltering tree, to where the well had been. It wasn't there: no rushes, no well.

I tramped all over that field, and the field to the south of it, and to the north of it, and every other field, but never again did I find that well, and never again did I find the father who brought me there.